BRIAN MURDOCH is Senior Lecturer and Head of the Department of German at the University of Stirling. He has written a number of books and articles on medieval German (and also Celtic) literature, particularly on the legends of Adam and Eve in the Middle Ages. His other works include articles and monographs on twentieth-century German, English and comparative literature, and editions of texts by E.M. Remarque and Stefan Zweig.

EVERYMAN ● CLASSICS

Kudrun

Translated with an
introduction and notes by
Brian Murdoch
*Senior Lecturer and Head of the
Department of German,
University of Stirling*

Dent: London and Melbourne
EVERYMAN'S LIBRARY

© J.M. Dent & Sons Ltd, 1987
All rights reserved
Typeset by Inforum Ltd, Portsmouth
Made in Great Britain by
Cox & Wyman Ltd, Reading for
J.M. Dent & Sons Ltd
Aldine House, 33 Welbeck Street, London W1M 8LX

First published as an Everyman Classic, 1987

British Library Cataloguing in Publication Data

Kudrun.
  I. Murdoch, Brian O.
  831'.2   PT1528.A4

  ISBN 0–460–01430–7

No 1430 Paperback ISBN 0 460 01430 7

CONTENTS

INTRODUCTION

Women and Power: the Story of Kudrun

'This book is about Kudrun.' The descriptive statement found in the sole manuscript in which the thirteenth-century narrative poem of *Kudrun* has survived is quite unequivocal. The work centres upon the princess whose name it bears. Nevertheless, it was for a very long time a standard assumption, in literary histories in particular, that the work fell into three quite distinct sections, something which — rightly or wrongly — cast doubts upon the unity of the text. The division of the work into sections went hand-in-hand, too, with a sometimes excessive emphasis on the ancestry of the thirteenth-century text, and the various discrete elements that were combined and adapted to make up the story as we have it. Much effort went into trying to establish a kind of proto-*Kudrun*, in which the eponymous princess played no part at all. More recently, however, literary critics have come to stress the unity of the work, and this emphasis is to be welcomed. *Kudrun* is an important and, outside medieval German studies, a neglected work, even though it is one of relatively few surviving medieval German heroic epics. Its intrinsic interest is increased, however, in that although it has to do with the deeds of warriors in battle, with defence and with revenge, it is a work in which women are in the forefront of the narrative. The work was described in 1956 by the German medieval scholar, Hugo Kuhn, as a *Frauenroman*, a 'women's novel', with a special emphasis on their political role. This view has been endorsed and expanded in several subsequent studies.

These two points: that the poem of *Kudrun* has a clear narrative unity, and that the actions of the women are in the foreground, are interrelated. In spite of a few contradictions in the work – which probably do derive from earlier versions of parts of the story – there is a unity which depends upon the dynastic development from a fierce and forceful king, through his equally strong-minded daughter to his granddaughter, Kudrun herself, who emerges triumphant from a game of love and power in which she is mistaken for a pawn, but proves herself to be a queen.

The dynastic progress covers a long period of time. The epic tale of *Kudrun*, which is divided up as a whole into thirty-two chapters, opens with the death of Ger, a king in Ireland, and the wooing by his son, Sigebant, of the Norse princess Uote, from Scotland. Sigebant is advised to marry by his mother, the chosen princess is of suitable rank, and the embassy sent by Sigebant is accepted. The marriage takes place and the line of succession is secured when a son is born. As soon as the son is named – Hagen – the narrator indicates that he is to be a central figure, and even though he does not appear again after the first few chapters, his name and reputation recur throughout the story.

Sigebant's wife, Uote, now queen, is the first woman in the story to make a political move (unless the advice given to Sigebant by his mother that he should take a wife is counted as such). Uote points out to Sigebant that he is making insufficient display of his wealth and power, and suggests that he hold a great festival; he agrees. Uote's comments are quite specific and are in fact perfectly justified. Power is expressed through wealth, and the large numbers of invited friends and allies are shown just what Sigebant can command. It is during this festival, however, that tragedy strikes – or appears to strike – the family. Hagen, their son, is carried off by a griffin, apparently to his death. Whether the charge of neglect can be laid at the door of his parents is extremely dubious, however. The narrator blames in the first instance the neglect of the lady-in-waiting who has charge of the boy, and the fact that the whole company is captivated by a minstrel and does not see the danger until too late (a nice foreshadowing of the later abduction of Hagen's daughter). The griffin is also seen as an agent of the devil. At all events, it is Sigebant who is distraught, Uote who is firm, refers to God's will and manages to keep up appearances for the conclusion of the now dampened festivities. She appeals to the guests to stay a little longer, and gives them as they leave the great gifts which continue to underline the riches and power of Sigebant.

Brought to the griffin's eyrie on an island, Hagen, who has been characterised as a child interested at a very early stage in the warrior life, escapes from the beast, and finds there three princesses who have also been carried away. He joins them, acquires weapons after a shipwreck, and kills the griffins. He then kills a kind of dragon and drinks its blood, which endows him with wisdom and strength. The episode is rather like one in the boyhood of another Germanic hero, Siegfried, but in this case the magic element is very much modified. Hagen is not made invincible – the strength he acquires is expressed in terms used for other heroes. Nor is his new-found wisdom of the same kind as Siegfried's. He cannot understand the speech of the birds. He simply manages to cope with increasing ease with life in the wilderness. He learns to survive. The three princesses and the boy are eventually rescued by the Earl of Garadie, who has, however, been at war with Hagen's father, and who now tries to take Hagen as a hostage, and the three girls for his own court. Sudden changes of fortune – the cliffhanger effect – are frequent in the work. Here, Hagen overcomes the Earl, and forces him to take them to Sigebant, but he promises that he will arrange a reconciliation, thus striking for the first time another note that will persist through the work. The reconciliation is effected, and the circle of alliances which Sigebant already has is increased still further. Hagen succeeds his father as king, marries Hilde of India (one of the princesses), and acquires not only a reputation for fierceness in his pursuit of law and order, but also the nickname of 'Devil-King', presumably in grudging admiration. The epithet applied to him regularly by the narrator after Hagen has drunk the dragon's blood is *wild*, 'wild, fierce, savage'.

Hagen and Hilde have a daughter, also named Hilde, and once again a narrative signal is given that she will be an important figure. She grows up to be very beautiful, but Hagen sets up what is in effect a pragmatic test for would-be suitors: succeed or die. It is at this point that the first 'break' in the story is usually perceived, and there is, indeed, a change of scene and a new set of characters. However, we have so far been presented with a background for the birth of Hilde of Ireland, and she dominates the rest of the work, even when the action is directly concerned with her daughter, Kudrun. She is there at the end of the whole work, a central figure, a queen from whose court the other major characters take their leave.

We concentrate now, however, on the successful suitor, Hetel, who is King of the Hegelings, the central people of a network of alliances covering much of what is now Northern Germany, Denmark and the Low Countries. He has no wife, and decides to pay court to Hilde, sending as ambassadors his most trusted men: his uncle, Wate, who brought him up and who is characterised as a fierce fighter of great experience; Fruote, whose very name means 'wise'; and Horant, who is a skilled singer. These travel to Ireland, ostensibly as merchants, but pretending that they are actually escaping from Hetel. Hagen welcomes them, and is impressed in particular by Wate, who pretends to be a novice swordsman and fights a fierce duel with Hagen. Horant's singing, however, is equally impressive, and it gains him entry into the princess's private rooms. He presses the cause of Hetel and obtains the acquiescence of the girl for the planned abduction: this scene is an important demonstration of Hilde's self-will. She is fearful of her father, but aware that a successful courtship must be concealed. The plot is nearly ruined by a chamberlain who proves, however, to be a genuine exile from Hetel. There is a small element of the deliberate cliffhanger here, but the chamberlain does provide a foil for the supposed exiles.

The Hegelings manage to get away with Hilde, and she is welcomed in Hetel's country in fine courtly style and with a tournament, but Hagen is not far behind. He pursues them with an army, and a battle is fought between Hagen's men and those of Hetel, which Hilde and the ladies abducted with her have to watch – just as they watched the jousting with which they were welcomed. This time, however, the fighting is in earnest. Eventually the battle focuses upon a combat between Wate and Hagen, a serious version of their earlier mock-combat. Here Hilde intervenes. She asks Hetel to stop the battle before her father is killed, and, after the fighting has stopped, she pleads with Wate, who is skilled in healing, to tend the wounds of her father. She and her father are reconciled, and Hagen accepts, having learned the hard way, that Hetel and his forces are more powerful than his own; he now agrees to the match. The marriage and an alliance are sealed, and the positive role of Hilde in all this is clear.

Hilde and Hetel have two children: a son, sent like his father to be brought up by Wate, and a daughter more beautiful than Hilde herself, and indeed a more desirable match, as she is the daughter of a very powerful ruler of a large area. The girl is Kudrun, and as soon as she is of marriageable age many men woo her. The author shows us three of these suitors, and indicates that she herself is quite favourably disposed to each of them, although she falls in with her parents' wishes. The first suitor is Sifrit, King of the Moors, who is rejected although Kudrun is impressed with him; he leaves, swearing vengeance for what he takes to be an insult. Another, Hartmuot of the Normans, is rejected by Hilde as being of too low a status – his father had been a vassal of Hagen – although Kudrun is plainly attracted to him. The third suitor, Herwic of Zeeland, is also rejected initially, but seizes the initiative of battle and takes Hetel by surprise. Hetel realises that he has been out-manoeuvred, and agrees to the match. Here, however, Hilde intervenes once again, and her decision this time is a slightly problematic one. She demands that the marriage be put off for one year, to give her time to school Kudrun in the role of being a queen.

The political interventions of the women in the work are frequently positive. Sometimes, however, they lead to problems in the development, though they are not, as decisions, in any way reprehensible. Uote's demand for a festival, which led to Hagen's capture by the griffin, is such a case. The two events are not causally connected in any firm manner. Here there is no real problem in taking Hilde's argument at face value. Kudrun is young and needs to learn. Just as Hilde's counsel to reject Hartmuot was followed, so too her request for a delay is also accepted.

A sequence of events now follows that could not have been

foreseen. Sifrit attacks the successful suitor, Herwic, and on the request of Kudrun, Hetel and the Hegelings go to assist him. A deadlock is reached, with Sifrit's army under siege, when the news arrives that a Norman army led by Hartmuot and his father, Ludewic, have attacked Hetel's lands and carried off Kudrun and a retinue of ladies. This time an abduction has been carried out without acquiescence.

The Hegelings rapidly reach an agreement with Sifrit, allowing his army to go free if they will ally themselves with the Hegelings against Hartmuot, and go with them in pursuit of the Normans to their own kingdom (I have followed in the translation a suggestion that the reference is to the Norman Kingdom of Sicily, not the Duchy in present-day France). To pursue the Normans, however, Wate has to commandeer ships from a group of pilgrims, and the point is made that this brings guilt upon the Hegelings: God will protect his own. Hilde is left to atone for the deed.

The Hegelings catch up with the Normans on a sandy island in the mouth of the Scheldt called the Wülpensand, but in this battle Ludewic, Hartmuot's father, kills Hetel, and the Normans escape with Kudrun. Wate and the others return home to Hilde. Kudrun's brother Ortwin, incidentally, is said to be at this battle, but this is one of the narrative inconsistencies; later on he is said still to be very young, and therefore one may assume that he is in fact a small child at this time, and not yet a warrior.

Reference must be made here to another woman in the work. Much of Hartmuot's action stems not from his own desires as such – though he has seen Kudrun and is clearly in love with her – but rather from the encouragement of his mother, Gerlint. The most negatively characterised of the women in the work, Queen Gerlint is referred to by the narrator (not by others) as a 'she-devil'. Very ambitious for her son, though presumably aware that he is trying to marry above himself, she encourages the abduction even though Ludewic, the king, speaks against it.

Now that her husband is dead, Queen Hilde has no choice but to bide her time. Still assured of the support of her allies, she has no army of her own, and must wait for fourteen years until the sons of the men killed at the Wülpensand are grown and ready for revenge for their fathers' deaths. Only then can she hope to avenge Hetel and recover Kudrun. The concept of revenge is kept alive in the young men as they grow up, and the Normans, being at a distance, can do nothing to prevent this.

What Hilde cannot control, though, is what will happen to Kudrun. She can, on the other hand, make amends to the pilgrims whose ships were taken, and indeed to God, by erecting a cathedral on the Wülpensand. What happens to Kudrun may be seen as the third part of the story, in that the scene now changes to the Norman kingdom, but Hilde is still very much in the background.

Kudrun remains completely constant to Herwic. Abducted against her will, she resists marriage to Hartmuot, who is noble enough not to take her as a concubine – or at least, sensitive enough to what might be said of him if he does. Given into the hands of Queen Gerlint, Kudrun is deliberately mistreated in an attempt to break her will. This proves impossible, and only one of her ladies gives way to the situation, and marries a Norman lord. At the end of the fourteen years that Hilde has to wait, Kudrun has been made a washerwoman, washing clothes in the snow on the seashore, together with her faithful lady-in-waiting, Hildeburc. It is here that the two women are told by an angel that a rescue expedition has been sent to free them, and soon Herwic and Kudrun's brother Ortwin arrive, and let them know that they will be free the next day. Kudrun defies Gerlint, but when threatened, agrees to marry Hartmuot. Gerlint remains suspicious because Kudrun has laughed for the first time, and indeed, the Normans find their fortress surrounded on the following morning. In the ensuing battle, Ludewic is killed – and Hetel is thus avenged – and Hartmuot taken captive. It is significant that Gerlint, who has tried to give advice to Hartmuot, is now cast aside by him as he realises at last the trouble that her counsels have caused. So, too, Kudrun manages to prevent Wate from killing Hartmuot in battle by calling upon Herwic to separate them, just as Hilde had Hetel separate Wate and Hagen. Wate is again angry, but the deed is done. He does, however, kill Gerlint, and also kills the children in the castle, thus preventing the same kind of delayed feud that the Hegelings themselves have just gone through. His act is distasteful to the other warriors, but is let pass in the name of *Realpolitik*. In the same sense, the Hegelings take the other castles in the Norman lands, and Hartmuot and his sister Ortrun – who has been kind to Kudrun – are made prisoners.

The army returns to Hilde, bringing back Kudrun and the news that Hetel has been avenged. Now, however, Kudrun herself comes into her own as a skilful diplomat, and several alliances are made or sealed. Her marriage to Herwic can now take place, and his position as a powerful ally is set – indeed, he has a major voice in other decisions from now on. The Norman kingdom has, it is true, been conquered, but Kudrun organises things so that it becomes an ally, first by arranging the marriage between her brother Ortwin and Hartmuot's sister Ortrun, and then by suggesting a marriage between Hartmuot himself and Hildeburc. Kudrun expresses her confidence that her close friend will be able to smooth over any problems. The sensible decision not to defeat an enemy so completely that revenge is the only option is carried out. Finally – and it is just a little *ad hoc* in this case – the faithful ally Sifrit, who was really persuaded to join the Hegeling alliance under duress in the first instance, is given the unnamed sister of Herwic as a wife.

Two forces dominate the work: first, the role of women as political motivators and reconcilers; and second, the power of arms, seen most clearly in Wate, the archetypal hero, uncomfortable in women's society, grim in battle, sometimes cruelly pragmatic, as in his killing of the children. But the power to stop Wate before he goes too far – either in the killing of Hagen or of Hartmuot – lies with the women. Indeed, Hilde has to pay for Wate's crime against the pilgrims before God.

The women adapt to the system, and do not rule alone unless they have to. Their real roles are those of the consort or the queen mother. But they have for the most part minds of their own, and they take decisions, be it to arrange a festival or to run away with an acceptable suitor.

The family line is of great importance throughout. Kudrun is referred to for a long time, and especially when she is showing great determination, as Hagen's granddaughter; and indeed, the family characteristics can be traced from Uote, properly urging her husband to act as a king should, to the survivor Hagen, and thence to the strong-willed Hilde and her determined daughter. Hilde's mother, Hilde of India, is also in the strictest sense a survivor, a fit match for Hagen. This contrasts interestingly with the Norman line, in which Hartmuot is dominated by his mother, or at least permits her to play on his infatuation for Kudrun to the extent that he believes he can win her by force. Only at the end, when it is virtually too late, does he tear himself from her and join his father on the battlefield. Overall, though, the pattern of the work is political in essence, showing the evolution of powerful alliances. In spite of the actual setting, the fact that the work was written in Austria justifies the quotation here of the celebrated tag from a later age: *Bella gerant alii, tu felix Austria nube*; *nam quod Mars aliis, dat tibi Venus*. Mars plays his part, it is true, but marriages seal the alliances.

Kudrun is often compared, sometimes unfavourably, with the other great German epic, the *Nibelungenlied*, which deals with the hero Siegfried and eventually with the destruction of the Germanic Burgundians. The work divides into two: first the marriage of Siegfried to Kriemhilt, and secondly the revenge of Kriemhilt after her husband has been murdered by her brothers and their man, Hagen.

Kriemhilt marries again, and waits for many years before she can exact revenge for the murder at the court of her new husband, the Hun king Attila, called Etzel in German. Kriemhilt links the two halves of the *Nibelungenlied,* and provides, too, for the comparison of *Kudrun* with this slightly earlier poem. The days are gone when the two works were referred to as the German *Odyssee* and *Iliad, Kudrun* representing the former because of its connections with the sea. However, both revolve around women to an extent, even if the *Nibelungenlied* lays a great emphasis on Siegfried, Gunther (Kriemhilt's brother) and Hagen. Yet it is interesting that the manuscript which preserves *Kudrun* also has a version of the other poem which carries the title 'This Book is about Kriemhilt'. Indeed it is. Siegfried is murdered by the chief ally of Kriemhilt's brother Gunther, by Hagen of Tronege (who in spite of his name is closest perhaps to Wate). The murder is unjustified, and requires revenge, and Kriemhilt has been left with Siegfried's treasure, the treasure of the Nibelungs. When she begins to use it too ostentatiously, Hagen seizes it and sinks it in the Rhine.

Kriemhilt now has no choice but to remarry and to wait, just like Hilde. Many years later she invites Gunther, Hagen and their men to her new husband's court, where they are surrounded, and fight a last-ditch battle. Gunther and Hagen are brought to her, and Kriemhilt demands of Hagen the treasure of the Nibelungs – all that can really be restored to her. Hagen refuses, and she kills him herself, only to be killed in return by a horrified retainer of her husband, Etzel. Siegfried has been avenged, but an entire dynasty has fallen.

Hilde has some features in common with Kriemhilt, even though the latter shares (but only at the end) the designation 'she-devil' with Gerlint. Both wait patiently, both want revenge and restoral. Hilde, however, can be told that Ludewic is dead, and she gets her daughter back. She, therefore, can afford to be magnanimous towards Ortrun and Hartmuot, although she is reluctant at first. The scene in which she is persuaded to kiss Ortrun is a memorable one. Overall, though, the role played by women in *Kudrun* is far more dominant than is the case in the earlier work. Kriemhilt and Brünhilt, the wife of Gunther, play (eventually, at least) a subordinate role to their husbands, and Siegfried even announces at one point that he will be giving Kriemhilt a thrashing.

Above all, however, *Kudrun* does not end in the downfall of a nation. There are, it is true, two bloodthirsty and tragic battles, tragic in their outcome for Hetel and Ludewic, that is; there are other battles, as well, where the outcome is less tragic. Nevertheless, the end of *Kudrun* is the satisfactory sealing of alliances, and the work as a whole ends on a treaty of mutual non-aggression and assistance. The epic of *Kudrun* is not necessarily a deliberate rejoinder to the *Nibelungenlied*, but with similar premises it reaches rather different results.

Kudrun, then, is about government by a royal house in a warrior society. There are very few glimpses of ordinary people, who function only as extras or as battle-fodder. There is, in fact, a kind of parallel in the modern world with the debased novel or perhaps better the television series about big business, which are usually dynastic and often matriarchal. Of course, the analogy must not be pursued too far, but there are other parallels too, such as the great and deliberate display of wealth to indicate power.

In *Kudrun*, the pattern is one of rule by an autocratic king, who will maintain law and order by force, and, if he is very powerful, will manifest the fact by showing how much money or gifts he can give away (or, of course, buy ships and soldiers with); he will hold lavish tournaments in which he will himself fight. He will fight campaigns, but is aware that the securing of alliances – provided honour can be satisfied – is preferable. When a king dies, the situation is threatened, and this is the problem shown to us in various permutations. There is no internecine conflict, of course, and it is assumed that Ortwin will rule after Hilde's death, while Kudrun and Herwic found a dynasty in Zeeland. A king needs a wife, a queen a husband, adviser or son-in-law. Ideally, of course, a son should succeed, and sometimes a son is named king before his father's death, so that the father sees the continuation of the dynasty. Almost the only loose end in the work is the unanswered question of who succeeds Hagen in Ireland.

Marriages in the work must be suitable in terms of rank, although Herwic is actually aware of his slightly lower status. Nevertheless, we are shown a variety of methods of wooing. These range from the successful embassy (Sigebant and Uote) to abduction with consent (Hilde to Hetel), to the forcing of the father's hand (Herwic and Kudrun), to the political arrangement (Hartmuot and Hildeburc). Only abduction without consent and against a legal betrothal (Hartmuot and Kudrun) is not possible.

Characterisation in the work depends to an extent on the formulaic style, but this does not make the main figures into puppets. Wate is indeed fierce but the attribute 'old' means experienced and pragmatic, and he is able to heal or to kill, yet he still needs to be kept in control to an extent. The psychology of the characters can be complex even by modern standards: thus Hartmuot is one of the most interesting figures in the work, encouraged by his mother, who presumably also dominates his father. Finally there is Kudrun herself, aware of her responsibilities – how could she not be, given her mother and grandfather – and tested for many years against the evil of

Gerlint; taking triumphant revenge, but learning through all the years that reconciliation is better than humiliation; emerging from her trials to be a queen beside her mother, a queen who will make war when necessary, and take revenge when it would go against her honour or that of her husband not to do so; but beside all that to value friendship.

The Medieval Text

Kudrun is preserved in only one manuscript, and that is a late one. It is found on sheets 140 to 166 of the so-called *Ambraser Heldenbuch*, a collective codex copied in Austria in the early sixteenth century, which has saved for us this and other texts that would otherwise be lost completely.

We know that the manuscript was copied out between 1504 and 1515 by a scribe called Hans Ried, formerly an excise official in the town of Bozen (now Bolzano), in what is now the Italian Tyrol, on the River Isarco – Eisack in German. The great undertaking of preparing a collective codex with approaching 240 sheets of parchment and containing some twenty-five works was ordered and paid for by the Holy Roman Emperor Maximilian I (1493–1519), a man interested, in an antiquarian spirit, in older literature, and concerned at the decay in older values at a time of political uncertainty. A number of letters are extant detailing arrangements and payments to Ried, who died in 1516, not long after the work had been completed.

It was copied from another collective manuscript, which we know as the *Heldenbuch an der Etsch*, the 'Adige collection' of warrior tales, named for the river into which the Eisack flows. The date of the copy-text has been variously estimated, since it is lost, and recent scholarship puts it in the fifteenth century, though it has been thought of as being earlier.

The *Ambraser Heldenbuch* remained in the Tyrol for over two centuries. It was taken sometime before 1596 to the castle of Ambras, which is not far from Innsbruck, and this is where it gained its name. It stayed there until 1806, when it was taken to Vienna, and it is part now of the Austrian National Library, with the reference *Codex Vindobonensis ser. nov.* 2663. It is of enormous interest to German scholars. The twenty-five texts include a selection of courtly-chivalric works, tales of ideal knights, and a series of later stories. Sandwiched in between is a group of heroic poems, poems of warriors in battle, and the first three of these, between folios 99 and 166, fall together. The first is described as the book of Kriemhilt – an interesting description for the *Nibelungenlied*; then comes the *Klage*, the 'Complaint', which is a sequel to the first work; and finally, with a parallel title, the book of *Kudrun*.

The manuscript, which measures about 48 cm by 36 cm, has every page divided into three columns, and the texts are written out continuously, 66 to 68 lines per column. The language is adapted more or less to Ried's own time and place of work, and the original from which it was copied may not have been much different. The texts, though, *Kudrun* included, are far older, and our epic appears to have been composed between about 1240 and 1250, somewhere in the Bavarian or Austrian linguistic area, possibly in Regensburg. Any number of copies might lie between this version and Ried's text, which shows many of the problems one would expect in a text recopied over a period of some 250 years. We can see where strophes are corrupt, or where they are clearly in the wrong order, but other changes might not even be recognisable. Words have sometimes changed, with results that can be startling, as when a Middle High German verb *hāhen* 'to hang' appears as *haben* 'to have'. Much editorial work has been devoted to the reconstruction of the text in a plausible thirteenth-century form. Possibly a later adapter inserted caesura rhymes or made other changes, but we cannot be sure, so long as we have only the Ambras text. Here is a sample of what the text actually looks like. The hand is not difficult to decipher and the words are clearly divided. This extract is from the verso of sheet 141, lines 2 to 8 of the first column, according to the transcription by Franz Bäuml. It covers strophe 103:

> Das Tier daz Er
> hett ze tode erſlagen. des gedacht Er
> haim ze hawſe mit jm tragen.
> die frawen ze aller zeite genuſſn
> ſeiner guete. Von der frombden
> ſpeyſe hỏchste ſich jr hertze vnd jr
> gemủete.   (141ᵛ a, 2-8)

Many of the features are quite normal in a medieval manuscript: the different types of initials – the D in line 2 is heavier and larger, indicating a strophe beginning; the dots, which are in fact rhyme points; the long forms of *i* and *s*; the erratic superscripts. In Bartsch/Stackmann's edition, however, the text has been normalised – recast into a readable but idealised thirteenth-century form:

> Daz tier daz er hēte (dā) ze tōde erslagen,
> des gedāhte er *ze hūse* *heim* mit im tragen.

die frouwen zaller zīte   genuzzen sīner güete.
von der fremeden spīse   hōhte sich ir herze und ir gemüete.

Most editors make the same decision with this strophe, though others are less homogeneously treated. Punctuation and spelling differ a little, but all editors add *dā* and all reverse the order of *heim ze hūse* for the sake of metre.

Special problems arise with the names. The central figure of Kudrun appears as *Chautrūn* and other forms, Herwic as *Herwigk*, and places might appear as *Hortlannd*, *Ortlannt* or *Nortlannd*, to say nothing of actual confusions, such as that between (*Nor*)*manie* and (*Nor*)*tland*.

Kudrun, then, is far older than the Ambras collection, and although we can date it to the thirteenth century and find an approximate area in which it was composed, we know nothing about the poet – not even his name. What we can say, of course, is that the work was not original to the Bavarian-Austrian area. The princess's name is wrong for that dialect, and she is a North German Gudrun in southern guise. The places, too, are mostly in the north, though there may be some influence from southern place-names. The date, too, is a problem to pin down precisely. The work is later than the *Nibelungenlied*, and there are some possible historical allusions which point to a time after 1230 or so. Beyond that we cannot go.

After it had been transcribed by Hans Ried, the text remained effectively unknown in the castle at Ambras for some centuries. It came to light again, however, by now in Vienna, in 1816, and was edited in 1820, the first time it saw print. Several editions followed in the next decades, and in 1865 Karl Bartsch produced the ancestor of one of the modern editions, one revised in 1965 and then again later by Karl Stackmann. The editions by Ernst Martin in 1872 and that by Barend Symons in 1883 (revised by Bruno Boesch in 1954 and 1964) are also important. It is in the nature of the text and its transmission that editorial work is likely to continue.

Ancestors and Analogues

The Island of Rügen is separated only by a narrow sound from the coast of what is now the German Democratic Republic, jutting out into the Baltic, south-east of Danish Laaland, above the city of Greifswald. On the west coast of that island is another long thin island called Hiddensee, which means the island of Hedin, Hetin or Hetel. The island preserves a very early character-name from the saga that gives rise eventually to *Kudrun*, and perhaps it was here that the battle took place in which Hetel was killed. This battle has been placed in other islands, passing gradually westwards to Orkney, and then to the sandy island in the Scheldt, the Wülpensand.

The thirteenth-century poet of *Kudrun* did not make up the story of Hagen, Hilde and Kudrun, but he seems to have drawn on existing stories or poetic versions of a developing saga. We do not have any of the sources in an identifiable form, but there is quite a lot of evidence of the way in which the component parts of the story once existed, and the history of the saga can be traced back perhaps even to the fourth century. There are brief narratives or allusions, sometimes mere configurations of names, in a range of Germanic works, which give an idea of how elements of the present *Kudrun*-story might have looked at an earlier stage. There are also some full-scale versions of part of the story that are later than our poem, and which do not always derive from it, giving in such cases further evidence for the existence of different versions.

The tale of Hilde is central to the epic of *Kudrun*, even if Kudrun herself is a separate individual arising at a later stage. In its earliest form, what we may guess to have been the Hilde-saga must have related how the daughter of Hagen is wooed by Hetel or his equivalent, who fights with Hagen and kills him. He may himself be killed as well. The battle, tragic in any case, seems to have become a ghostly battle, as the warriors are revived, sometimes by Hilde herself, to fight again.

That brief outline contains the germ of several parts of our epic: of the fight between Hagen and Hetel over Hilde; and also of the fight later on over a princess whose father is killed, even though in the second part the names have either been added or have been shifted. There is even a small foreshadowing of the role of the women in affecting the battle, though Hilde in the early versions appears to be some kind of valkyrie, and in one version incites the men to fight, rather than stopping them.

The earliest references are simply juxtapositions of names, and they come in Anglo-Saxon documents. The poem *Widsith*, which consists effectively of lists of names, refers in the eighth century to Hagen as king of the Rugians – the island of Rügen – and links him with Wada, who is Wate, and Heoden, which is a form for Hetel. The ending in *-en* is actually more usual, and only the German text has the *-el* form of his name. The other rulers named in *Widsith* come from the fourth to the sixth centuries, and some are identifiable historically. A second Anglo-Saxon poem, *Deor*, also of the eighth century, refers to Heorrenda, our Horant, as a man skilled in song, who becomes the chief minstrel of the Heodenings, the men of Heoden, and the equivalent of our Hegelings.

Northern analogues are fuller, and from them we can start to build up a picture of the Hilde-saga in literary terms. A twelfth-century Danish chronicler known to us as Saxo Grammaticus records late in that century the tale of a battle between Hithinus and Höginus, fighting over Hilda on the island of Hithinsö – Hiddensee, off Rügen. Both kings die, and Hilda wakes the dead so they can start to fight again. There is no abduction, however. Hithinus is betrothed to Hilda, but her father, Höginus accuses Hithinus of being too eager in his pre-marital advances.

The tale appears, too, in the late thirteenth-century prose *Edda*, a collection of stories written by Snorri Sturluson; part of this work is a poetic manual, in which Snorri has preserved many older poetic tales, and one of these older poems tells how Högni fights with Hedin after the latter has abducted Hildr, daughter of the former. The battle is on the island of Hoy, in the Orkneys, and Hildr incites the men. Snorri's battle is the *Hjathningavig*, the battle of the Hegelings, as it were, which in this case will go on forever, as Hildr awakens the dead. The Orkney location is preserved in a ballad version from Shetland in the remnants of the Norse language once spoken there. There are other parallels in Old Norse and Icelandic, and in many texts, Hedin – our Hetel – is the son of Hjarrandi/Horant, often described as a singer. The fact that Horant can win a woman by his singing echoes the Orpheus/Eurydice myth, and seems to have been grafted on to the story of Hilda.

Coming closer to our text, there is in a twelfth-century poem about Alexander the Great a reference in Middle High German to a battle on the Wolfenwerde – in *Kudrun* the Wülpensand – at which Hilde's father is killed, and where Wate fights with Hagen. The tale seems to have moved, then, to the Scheldt, and the conflict between Wate and Hagen is there, of course, when they fight in Waleis, having had a mock-battle in Ireland. Other medieval German texts refer to Horant the singer, and Wate is independently known, even in Chaucer.

One major medieval German text has a fairly full version of Hilde's wooing, and the work is later than *Kudrun*. This is the fascinating *Dukus Horant*, written down possibly in Regensburg, but in Hebrew characters, medieval German for Jewish readers, or a kind of proto-Yiddish. The manuscript was discovered in Cairo, and is now in Cambridge. Here King Etene (the text preserves the *-en* form) rules much of Western Europe, and sends Horant to win Hilde, daughter of the king of Greece. He does so – once again the abduction is with consent – aided by his brother, Morunc, and three giants, one of whom is called Wate.

Kudrun's own story derives in part from the Hilde saga. The original Hilde figure embraces Hilde and Kudrun in our text, just as

Herwic and Hetel, and also Hetel and Hagen overlap. Just as some characters are expanded or divided, and so need new names – Kudrun is a case in point – others are, perhaps unfortunately, *not* split. This is why Wate and Hildeburc live for such a long time. A more meticulous modern writer might perhaps have demanded that the Hildeburc who accompanies Kudrun through her sufferings should be the daughter or granddaughter of Hagen's companion on the island! Kudrun has derived in part from Hilde, but Hildeburc has remained herself.

Other evidence points to independent Kudrun-material. Much of this is in the form of ballads, copied down in the seventeenth and eighteenth centuries in large numbers from all over southern Europe, versions existing in Bulgarian, Serbian and Spanish, as well as in German, where two variations are known, referred to as the *Meererin*-ballad and as the *Südeli*-ballad, and both concerned with the motif of Kudrun as washerwoman. From here we can move to tales like *Cinderella*, where the princess forced to drudgery is rescued by a prince.

Specific ancestors of the Kudrun part of the tale have been sought, too, in Low Franconian – since the place-names belong largely to the Low Countries. Although Hilde is usually abducted willingly, there are several examples of heroic tales in which a woman is carried off unwillingly, most notably in the Finn story in the Anglo-Saxon *Beowulf*. There is an interesting *Kudrun*-analogue, however, in an Italian work, the *Orlando Furioso* of Ariosto, in 1532. Here, a princess called Olimpia is wooed by the Duke of Selandia. But while the Duke is fighting the Saracens, the King of Frisia attacks Olimpia's home in Holland, in order to abduct her, so that she can marry his son. In the ensuing battle in Holland, Olimpia's father and brother die, and she is indeed carried off. She agrees to marry the son of the Frisian king, but kills him and escapes. The King of Frisia captures the Duke of Selandia, who is rescued by Ariosto's hero, Orlando, and marries Olimpia. In the end, however, the duke deserts Olimpia for the King of Frisia's daughter, and after her husband's death, Olimpia marries the King of Ireland. The cast, and many of the places seem to be present here, but the parallels seem only to point to a common ancestor.

Other influences throughout the work are smaller or more remote. Hagen's youth may owe details to the youth of Siegfried, notably in the blood-drinking episode; the obscure incident with the lion might echo the romance of *Iwein* (Yvain, Owein), the griffins the epic German tale of *Herzog Ernst* (with echoes back to Sindbad the Sailor and the roc); the speaking bird that tells Kudrun of her rescuers has some parallels elsewhere in German, and so do elements of the

Hegelings' rescue journey across the sea. Names have clearly been borrowed to augment the original cast: Kudrun herself is presumably one of the northern Gudruns; Hildeburc may link with the tale in *Beowulf* of the Frisian king Finn and his wife; Wigaleis is clearly from the romance. The names Hērewich and Wolfwīn occur together in a German source, and this might refer to a tale linking the figures that become Kudrun's husband and brother, the Ort- element of her brother's name coming from his kingdom of (N)Ortland.

There must have been literary sources used by our poet. He refers regularly to the authority of 'the story', points out that Hagen and Hilde are well known, and mentions a literary source in strophe 505, 1. He also expresses his annoyance at others who have told the story incorrectly, as in his curious outburst (in strophe 288) against those who have referred to Hagen as King of Poland. We do not, however, have any comparable version, not even a wrong one, and it is a matter of chance that we have the text at all.

Critics have, of course, drawn up whole sequences of how the story may have been passed on and developed until it reached our poet. They refer to a fifth-century saga, a Low German adaptation, a Rhineland version and then our text. But it is all speculative. What this does not mean, of course, is that it is impossible to read *Kudrun* as a coherent whole. There may be a few inconsistencies, but the thirteenth-century achievement is a real one. A knowledge of the ancestry of the work is interesting, but it is not usually relevant. It may help us to elucidate minor points, but the poem must stand or fall on its own merits, and it is in fact more likely to be harmful if we try to interpret 'our' Wate or 'our' Hagen in the light of their supposed prototypes.

Efforts have also been made to find historical events behind the story. These include the Viking attacks on Flanders after their defeat at the battle of Saucourt in 881, attacks that were coordinated by a leader called Sigifrid, who may have turned into our King of the Moors. If this is so, he is not the first Viking to undergo this curious metamorphosis in literature, as a French *chanson de geste* based on the very battle of Saucourt turns a Viking leader Guthorm (who was not present, in fact) into a Saracen.

The geographical shifts – Hagen rules in Rügen, Ireland and Greece, for example – make real historical parallels difficult to pin down. Nevertheless, wherever the story moves to, the Viking presence is still felt. This is certainly clear in the medieval German poem, for all that it was composed in southern areas. The typical methods of attack from well-stocked raiding ships, the fighting on the shore, all these are Viking methods, even if the places where the battles are fought have been extended to embrace the Mediterranean as well as

Flanders. There is, of course, scholarly disagreement about the identification of the places, too, and a translator is forced to come down on one side or the other. But it is well to remember that the Norman Kingdom of Sicily, however vaguely it is understood in the poem, if indeed it is there at all, is still a country that belongs to a group who were once Vikings themselves, who were Norse-men, Northmen or Normans. It would not be correct to refer to *Kudrun* as a Viking epic, of course, but the Vikings of history have left their mark on the story.

Style

There are clear differences between the medieval German heroic epic and the romance. The former deals usually with native material – the deeds of Germanic peoples; it is usually set in a real world; and it is composed usually in strophic verse. The romance, concerned often with the borrowed world of King Arthur, in an unidentifiable Camelot, tends to be composed in rhymed couplets. Further, the romance deals with the actions of an individual knight, the heroic epic with the fates of whole nations.

Associated with the heroic mode is a dominant stylistic feature, that of the formula. Harking back to an originally oral composition, the formula in the later written heroic epic takes the form of a set phrase or stock epithet, ready-made and invariable, fitting for the metrical pattern. It is visible in the English ballad, in lines like 'Come saddle me my milk-white horse', for example. 'Brown horse' would not scan, but the precise means of transport is not relevant to the story, and it need not be varied.

The use of stock epithets or phrases can be disturbing for the modern reader – who is used to follow texts in large portions with the eye, rather than the ear, and is less likely to accept the stock description of 'fair France' from a Saracen, or 'holy Russia' from a pagan. But the adjective goes with the name, and suits the metre. Sometimes set phrases are impressive – Homer's 'wine-dark sea' is a classic illustration: but it *is* once again a set phrase, filling part of a Homeric line. It is true, of course, that writers of heroic epics could employ set phrases in an ironic fashion. It has been argued that this is the case in the *Nibelungenlied*, where warriors are noble and maidens are beautiful even when they are behaving in ignoble or un-maidenly fashions. For the most part in *Kudrun*, however, formulaic epithets are simply objective characterisations. Wate is invariably old and frequently angry or fierce as well; Fruote is wise, which is what his name means; kings are mighty or powerful, ladies always beautiful. Only rarely do these standard adjectives require comment – the prime example being Hagen, who is termed 'wild' once he has drunk the blood of the creature he kills (before that the adjective was 'young'). Whole phrases recur as well, and again the modern reader may be irritated by being told yet again that 'no richer clothing had ever been seen anywhere'.

The formulaic elements are only a part of the style. The repeated descriptive adjectives serve only to identify the characters. Their words and deeds characterise them in fact. The heroic epic makes much of direct speech, and it is a literature of action. The vocabulary is relatively limited, but it is important that the work be taken as a whole. Indeed, the modern reader's view of what constitutes interesting action may also conflict with that of the medieval writer. Here passages of clear movement, action or debate, at court or on the battlefield, alternate with descriptions of apparently interminable jousts, festivals or the preparation of clothing. The elements do, however, belong together. Power and kingship can be expressed in two ways: in the assertion of battle, or in the display of wealth. They are equally necessary.

The contrast between the world of the warrior – the battle-field, the campaign and the single combat – and that of the court can lead to humour. Wate, for example, the archetypal fighter, is shown to be splendidly embarrassed when he is placed amongst the ladies at Hagen's court.

Kudrun has some inconsistencies, and this is not unusual with heroic epics. They are presumably due to the fact that various elements have come together to make up the story as we have it. The variation in the age of Ortwin is one case, and the extreme ages of Wate and Hildeburc have been noted already. Not that the last phenomenon is quite unknown in the modern world, as characters in radio or television serials – works watched or listened to over a longish period, of course – can also age somewhat inconsistently. There are some confusions over court positions and indeed over family relationships in the work, and Sifrit does have to change colour at the end to make for the fourfold wedding, in which he marries Herwic's somewhat *ad hoc* sister. But instances like this are rare.

The plot moves fast, and there is considerable suspense, as when Horant and Morunc are surprised by the chamberlain in Hilde's rooms. Suddenness in attack is a constant feature – be it Hagen's arrival in Waleis, Herwic's on Hetel's fortress, or the Hegelings in the land of the Normans. But there are also many lyrical and pathetic incidents, as well as some of high drama: Hagen and Wate in mock battle; Horant's song (which causes the very birds to stop singing); Hagen waving his great war-spear; Wate returning after the death of

Hetel and seen at a distance by a wondering Hilde; Kudrun and Hildeburc in the snow; Kudrun's sudden laughter which so unnerves Gerlint – all these incidents remain in the mind.

There is little that is supernatural here. Hagen's strength is increased when he drinks the blood of the dragon, but he is not invincible. The magic mountain which attracts the ships is a stock tale, and was probably believed. Only the angel disguised as a sea-bird is unusual. For the most part, however, the work is realistic, just as its message is clear, a message underlined by motif-variation and repetition. The theme is marriage and alliance, with rule that can assert itself by force when necessary, but which emphasises reconciliation with honour.

Form

Kudrun is in verse, specifically in 1,705 four-line strophes, each a coherent unit. The work as a whole is in thirty-two chapters of irregular length, each (with a few exceptions) headed in the manuscript with a brief title referring to what happens in the chapter as a whole, or at least at the beginning of the chapter. In its thirteenth-century form, *Kudrun* will have been read in sections to an audience, and the perception is likely, then, to have been aural. Translating such a text for the eye-reader is already a large step.

With any prose translation of a text that was originally in verse, something will be lost. It has to be accepted that the metrical regularity of the strophic form and some of the specifically poetic effects will be missing. We may, however, consider here just what that strophic form was like, and before looking at the *Kudrun*-strophe proper it is worth examining its probable progenitor, the strophe used in the *Nibelungenlied*. There are, in fact, a number of *Nibelung*-strophes used in *Kudrun* itself.

The *Nibelung*-strophe (for which various sources have been suggested, most notably that it was originally a lyric form) consists of four lines, each one divided into two parts by a strong caesura. The first half of each line has three stresses and a feminine ending. The second half of the first three lines also has three stresses, but the ending is masculine, ending, that is, on a full beat. After each of these masculine endings a pause is 'felt', and this is usually interpreted as a kind of silent beat, so that the designations of the metre used by German critics can be confusing. The last half-line of the whole strophe is longer: it has four stresses, but once again there is a masculine ending. The lines rhyme AABB, and sometimes there is an additional rhyme at the caesura, giving a pattern ABABCDCD across the half-lines.

This is best illustrated, of course, by example, and I have attempted a translation of one of the *Nibelung*-strophes in *Kudrun*. It is a free translation, and is designed only to show the metre:

'Whén I wás a máidèn // in Scótland fár awáy, ^
(Lísten tó me kíndlỳ, // my lórd and kíng, I práy!)^
Thére I nóticed dáilỳ // mén of my fáther déar ^
For fáme and glóry jóustìng, // but have néver séen it
                                                        háppen hére.'(30)

It will be noted that there is a certain freedom in the number of unstressed syllables (even at the beginning of a line), although the metre is usually fairly regular. It is clear too that the style is based on the line, and thoughts rarely run over into another line.

The *Kudrun*-strophe varies this. There are again four long lines, and like the *Nibelung*-strophe, the end-rhymes are AABB, although rhymes at the caesura are frequent. The lines are metrically somewhat different, however. The first half-lines have, like the *Nibelung*-strophes, three beats with a feminine ending providing an extra weak beat. The latter part of the first two long lines also mirror the older text, in that they have three beats and a masculine ending (with the so-called 'silent beat'). The final half of the third line, however, is another with three beats and a feminine, not a masculine, ending, and the final half-line of the entire strophe has five full beats as well as a feminine ending, a very long and somewhat leisurely line. Once again I have tried to indicate the effect with a translation:

Ít was ín the séasòn // when wínter díes awáy^
And spríng provídes the réasòn // for bírds to síng all dáy,^
Trýing to bést each óthèr // with sóngs for Márch chósèn.
In snów and ícy wéathèr // they fóund the twó maídens
                                                        shívering and frózèn. (1217)

I have tried to imitate the caesura rhyme, but again the verse is for demonstration purposes only! There is again freedom in the un-stressed syllables, and the form is a flexible one.

It is in the nature of verse for emphases to fall on ideas depending upon their position, and this is not always imitable in prose. Fre-quently there is no enjambement, which can lead to a somewhat hacked effect. The long last line often incorporates a separate idea. Once the reader or listener has become accustomed to the metrical form, a cumulative effect can be surmised. The *Kudrun*-strophe is not an easy one, however, especially in the long last line, and the frequent need for rhyme leads to a certain sameness in vocabulary. It is not clear why the poet used a number of *Nibelung*-strophes in addition. There are either 100 or 101 of these (depending upon how strophe 1143 is emended), but they have no clear structural principle. Most of them are found in the earlier part of the text.

The Translation and Its Predecessors

There have been two full-length English translations of *Kudrun*, both with the title *Gudrun* and both made, appropriately enough, by women. One was published nearly a century ago, the other some sixty years ago, and neither is acceptable to the modern reader, though for different reasons.

The first was that by Mary Pickering Nichols, which appeared in Boston in 1889. Her English is closer to the original than the present version in that she took the decision to present the work in verse. In doing so, she demonstrates the dangers of verse translation very clearly indeed. These dangers are always present, but are acute when the verse-form being imitated is unfamiliar to English ears. Her translation (based on the 1874 third edition of the text by Bartsch) is accurate in the main, but if her verse does sometimes succeed, more usually the unnaturally long-looking last line causes the whole structure to fall. Indeed, she adheres to the strict *Kudrun*-strophe even in those places where the text has the manageable *Nibelung*-strophe. A desultory sampling of her version makes it clear that the decision to translate into prose is at least a safer one. Her ingenuity can be stretched to the limit, and what remains in the mind is an overwhelming preponderance of present continuous forms. Here, for example, is Hilde's answer to the envoys from Hartmuot (strophes 612–613), rejecting him as a suitor. The passage is typical:

'Say you now to Hartmut   she ne'er his wife shall be.
Your lord is not so worthy   that he to boast is free,
That he doth love my daughter,   and she doth not disdain him;
Bid elsewhere him be looking,   if he be fain a queen
                            for his land to gain him.'

The herald's hearts were heavy;   twas not for their good name
That they, for miles full many,   in sorrow and in shame,
Back to their home in Normandy   this news must carry sadly.
Hartmut, as well as Ludwig,   was vexed that they herein
                            were foiled so badly.

However much the translator may have hoped to establish the metrical pattern by repetition, the verse – unfairly but unfailingly – recalls the efforts of McGonagall.

It might be noted that German translations into verse, of which there were many in the nineteenth century, are more successful. Even though Friedrich Neumann, the most recent reviser of Karl Simrock's nineteenth-century version comments on the need to retain archaic words and forms for the sake of rhyme and metre, the syntax can survive so much better. Nevertheless, the most recent modern German version is a prose re-telling appended to a Middle High German edition.

The nineteenth century also saw several prose adaptations into English, though no real translations beyond that by Nichols. Emma Letherbrow's version – as early as 1863 – expands the story in a commendably creative manner, and John Gibb in 1881 presented the story for children, starting rather oddly with Kudrun and working back to Hagen, making an implicit comment on the unity of the text. The main English version, however, has long been that by Margaret Armour, whose husband, William B. Macdougall provided the illustrations for her first edition ('done into English') in 1928, the text of which became part of Everyman's Library in 1932, a companion to her version of the *Nibelungenlied*, published first in 1897, and then in Everyman's Library not long before the First World War. Both works, translated with some degree of accuracy into prose, are couched, however, in a deliberately archaic pseudo-medieval English, the English that the nineteenth century thought that the Middle Ages would have used had it used modern forms. Armour's characters are never unhappy; they are almost invariably 'right doleful of their cheer'. They do not hold festivals or feasts, but 'hightides', a literal version of Middle High German *hōchzīte* difficult to justify in any language. The first chapter (they are called 'adventures') is called 'The King of Ireland Holds a Hightide', which makes him sound like a rather more successful King Canute. As a brief but again typical illustration, here once more is the dismissal of the envoys from Hartmuot:

> 'Tell Hartmut she will never be his wife. That the knight should dare to deck out his body to win the love of my daughter! He shall go elsewhere to win a queen for his lands.' Whereat the envoys were heavy of their cheer, and sore misliked to ride back so many miles in sorrow and in shame to Normandy.
>
> Ludwig and King Hartmut were wroth at what they had endured . . .

This is, of course, preferable to a verse translation, nor did Margaret Armour permit herself to be too greatly restricted by the strophes, but wrote in natural paragraphs wherever she could. However, although the work is lively enough, it contains too many damsels in sumptuous raiment and too many 'doth's and 'hath's for the modern reader to find it acceptable.

Prose is the familiar form for the epic in modern English, designed for reading rather than listening to. This fact, coupled with the obvious pitfalls of verse, make the translator's first decision an easy one. The aim is to make *Kudrun* accessible to a reader quite unfamiliar with Middle High (or even modern) German, or with the stylistic features of medieval epic narrative. The sometimes overly paratactic sequence of ideas in a single strophe can be run together, but it is often more difficult to avoid the dictation of paragraphs by the strophic form. The modern reader demands longer stretches, and where possible the strophes have been run together into paragraphs here. If the balance of strophes is structurally important, of course – as in dialogue – they have been left. Page-head references to strophe numbers (those of the manuscript) are to those found in whole or in part on the page concerned.

The basic text is that published by Bartsch in 1865 and revised fully a century later by Karl Stackmann, with an updated version in 1980, but the other major editions have been taken into account for this translation, however, specifically those by Martin and Symons, the latter re-edited by Bruno Boesch. The order of strophes is basically that of Bartsch/Stackmann, but some changes have been made, and recourse has also been had throughout to the exact transcript of the manuscript published so usefully by Franz Bäuml in 1969.

Individual Middle High German words can cause problems, and the pitfalls are well known: *arebeit*, *āventiure*, *gast*, *guot*, *helt*, *rīche*, all of them classic cases, for which a satisfactory rendering may not always have been found, although variations or expansions have often proved necessary. There are special difficulties in presenting for the modern reader a work in formulaic style. The formulas can be varied to relieve the monotony, but probably only in cases where they *are* just formulas. If they have been used carefully (rather than just functionally), then they must be translated carefully. Thus I have tried to vary *scoene* 'beautiful' – although there are not too many suitable synonyms – given that the use is not ironic in *Kudrun*; but I have made Hagen's epithet of *wild* into a sort of regal designation.

The relatively limited vocabulary can also lead to problems. Although variations for *helt* may be found – as 'warrior', 'fighter' and (less comfortably, because of the overtones of shining armour) 'knight', the ladies prove more problematic. 'Damsel' is no longer really possible, still less 'damozel', while 'maiden' is becoming old-fashioned and 'girl' is less suitable. Even 'lady' has problems, and the designations of nobility are invariably difficult, especially in speech. Hollywood-medieval is not unlike nineteenth-century pseudo-English ('Good my liege . . .') and modern Court Circular has the wrong connotations, too ('Her Majesty the Queen . . .').

A certain licence has to be taken. Expansion is needed from time to time, and reminders and qualifiers, to say nothing of names of speakers, have to be inserted to avoid a welter of footnotes. Of course, the text is sometimes vague itself, and here the translator has to make an almost editorial decision.

The translator as editor is clearest in the solution to problems arising from the geographical names in the text. *Kudrun* mixes real places with genuine names in the wrong geographical position, with quite unidentifiable names. I have identified as many as possible, and have taken in disputed cases the interpretation that best fits with a more or less consistent geography. A real Denmark, however, has to be placed near a less clear Northland. Although the decision may well be disputed, I have interpreted the Norman lands consistently as Sicily rather than as the Duchy.

Personal names are also a problem, and a list of characters' names is appended. In the text I have this time used the Middle High German form in the nominative, since many of the names are unfamiliar anyway (unlike the geographical names). It has to be noted, though, that the final -*e* is sounded in names like Hilde-è or Wat-è. In 1889 Nichols actually printed the names as 'Ut-e' and so on, but the effect is like a primary school reader. Armour gives the feminine names a final -*a*, as in Hilda, but not the men. Even so, her version of Fruote as a quasi-modernised Frute looks rather strange. I have kept the epony-mous princess as Kudrun quite deliberately, in spite of the philolog-ical problems. There are plenty of Gudruns in Germanic medieval literature. There is only one Kudrun.

The notes to the text offer explanations of points of historical detail, or comment on textual problems. The translation is, however, in no way designed as a crib for the Middle High German version. A specialist will use the original, and students of Middle High German are better served with a fairly literal modern German verse adapta-tion. The aim of this translation is quite simply to introduce or reintroduce to an English-speaking audience an unusual and unjustly neglected text in which women play a dominant role, in an acceptable modern form that does not, it is hoped, do too much violence to the spirit of the original narrative.

THE NAMES OF THE CHARACTERS

Personal names are used in the text as consistently as possible in their Middle High German forms. Some of the names can, it is true, be modernised, such as Ute for Uote, or given modern equivalents, such as Siegfried for Sifrit. Even so, a number of unfamiliar names would be left, and of the familiar ones, some might be familiar for the wrong reasons. It is probably more helpful than harmful to keep Sifrit, King of the Moors, quite separate from the Siegfried of the *Nibelungenlied*, even if we can do nothing about Hagen. With some names there is no alternative: Fruote cannot reasonably become Frodo without interference from a more modern work, and Frute is impossible for the Anglo-Saxon eye, especially with the attribute 'old'. I have used the names in their base form, such as Ludewic: if Ludewig is closer to Ludwig, the version adopted has a parallel in Ludovic, and Lewis or Louis might have served as well. Marks of length added to the Middle High German form have been omitted in the text, but it must be noted that the final -*e* is sounded, so that Uotè, Hildè, Fruotè, Watè and so on are disyllables. Length-marks are given in this glossary of names, vowels being short if they are not marked long. The name of the central figure of Kudrun is retained, too, even though it represents a mixture of North and South German forms. A 'proper' northern form would be Gudrun, a 'proper' southern one Kundrun. What we have is a North German name with a South German accent, something not inappropriate to a text put together in the south, but based in the north. There are, too, very many Gudruns in medieval Germanic literature, whereas the name Kudrun can refer only to our titular heroine. The vowels in her name, however, are both long, *Kūdrūn*, both sounds being as in English 'whose' rather than southern 'but.' For further details of the characters and their analogues in other Germanic literature, see the immensely informative *Catalogue of Persons Named in German Heroic Literature 700–1600* by George T. Gillespie (Oxford, 1973).

FRUOTE of Denmark: relative and ally of Hetel, apparently the same age as Wate, with whom he is often associated. The name means 'wise, old'.

GARADĪE, Earl of: unnamed lord of territory adjacent to Sigebant's in Ireland, originally an enemy; he rescues Hagen from the griffins, and is eventually reconciled with Sigebant.

GĒR(E), King of Ireland: grandfather of Hagen and great-great-grandfather of Kūdrūn.

GĒRLINT, Queen of the Normans: wife of Ludewīc, mother of Hartmuot and tormentor of Kūdrūn. She is referred to as 'she-wolf' and 'she-devil'. Killed by Wate.

HAGEN(E), King of Ireland: grandfather of Kūdrūn and central figure of the first part of the work; given the title 'devil king' and known as 'Hagen the Wild'.

HARTMUOT, Prince (King) of the Normans: unsuccessful suitor and abductor of Kūdrūn, son of Gērlint and Ludewīc. Married eventually to Hildeburc.

HĒREGART, Princess: one of the ladies abducted with Kūdrūn to the kingdom of the Normans, who proves disloyal by marrying a Norman noble, and is eventually killed by Wate.

HERWĪC, Lord (Prince, King) of Zeeland: betrothed and eventually married to Kūdrūn. His SISTER is not named, but plays a brief role in the story at its conclusion, when she is married to Sīfrit.

HETEL(E), King of the Hegelings: High King, of whom Hōrant, Fruote, Wate, Mōrunc and Īrolt (and later Herwīc and Sīfrit) are the major allies. Abducts and marries Hilde II, daughter of Hagen and Hilde I. Father of Ortwīn and Kūdrūn. Killed by Ludewīc.

HILDE I, Princess of India: with Hagen on the griffins' island, she later marries him, becoming Queen of Ireland, mother of Hilde II and grandmother of Kūdrūn.

HILDE II, Queen of the Hegelings: daughter of Hagen and Hilde I, abducted from Ireland by Hetel's men, married to Hetel and mother of Ortwīn and Kūdrūn

HILDEBURC, Princess of Portugal (Galicia): companion of Hilde I and Hagen on the griffins' island, next in age to Hilde. She goes with Hilde II to the land of the Hegelings, and is abducted with Kūdrūn to the Norman kingdom, sharing the princess's hardships. Now termed 'of Ireland', she is married at the close to Hartmuot, and becomes Queen of the Normans.

HŌRANT, Lord of Denmark: major ally of Hetel, and referred to both as Hetel's sister's son, and as Wate's sister's son. His capital is at Jever in North Germany. Famed as a singer, his skills in that area help in the abduction of Hilde II, aided by Hagen's unnamed CHAMBERLAIN, who is Horant's first cousin.

ĪROLT, Lord: vassal of Hetel, linked with Mōrunc, and associated with Northland, Frisia or Holstein.

ISERLAND, Princess of: unnamed third and youngest companion of Hilde II and Hildeburc on the griffins' island with Hagen. Married to an ally of Hagen, the unnamed PRINCE OF NORWAY.

Kūdrūn, Princess of the Hegelings: daughter of Hetel and Hilde II, brought up in Denmark, betrothed to Herwīc and abducted by Hartmuot. Eventually marries Herwīc and becomes Queen of Zeeland. Sometimes referred to as Hagen's granddaughter as a reminder of her ancestry.

Ludewīc, King of the Normans: father of Hartmuot, husband of Gērlint, he kills Hetel in battle and is himself later killed by Herwīc. Technically-historically we are told that he is a vassal of Hagen.

Mōrunc, Lord: friend of Īrolt and like him a vassal of Hetel, associated with Waleis, Nifland and Frisia.

Ortrūn, Princess of the Normans: daughter of Ludewīc and Gērlint and sister of Hartmuot, she befriends Kūdrūn and is eventually married to Ortwīn and becomes Queen of Northland.

Ortwīn, Lord (Prince, King) of Northland: son of Hetel and Hilde II and brother of Kūdrūn, he is brought up by Wate and is married at the end to Ortrūn.

Otte, King: mentioned briefly and *perhaps* to be linked with the real Otto IV (though this is unlikely), his brother is said to have held lands in fief from Hagen and to have quarrelled with Ludewīc, another vassal.

Sīfrit, King of Karadie (of the Moors, of Moorland): suitor to Kūdrūn, he first attacks Herwīc, her betrothed, and then allies himself with him and Hetel to rescue her. He is variously described as dark (as a Moor or Saracen) and (later) as fair, since he has a Christian mother. He is married at the end to Herwīc's unnamed sister, who becomes Queen of Karadie.

Sigebant, King of Ireland: son of Gēr and Uote I, father of Hagen and great-grandfather of Kūdrūn.

Uote I, Queen of Ireland: mother of Sigebant, wife of Gēr and great-great-grandmother of Kūdrūn.

Uote II, Queen of Ireland: Norwegian princess married to Sigebant. Mother of Hagen and great-grandmother of Kūdrūn.

Wate, Lord of Stormarn: most powerful ally and possibly brother or half-brother of Hetel, brings up Ortwīn and acts as chief ally to Hilde and to Kūdrūn. He is skilled in healing, but generally savagely pragmatic in his actions. Always referred to as Wate the Old.

Wīgāleis, Lord: vassal and counsellor of Hetel.

ACKNOWLEDGMENTS

I should like to acknowledge the help received in the preparation of this work from various sources, and wish in particular to thank the following: Miss Hilda Swinburne of Exeter University, who introduced me to the text as a student; my own students at Stirling University with whom I have read the work; my colleague Dr Lewis Jillings; my wife, son and daughter for valuable comments; and Miss Linda Archibald of Stirling University for reading and commenting upon the whole translation in draft. Remaining errors and infelicities are my own responsibility. Thanks are also due to the Verlag F.A. Brockhaus of Mannheim and to Professor Karl Stackmann, whose edition has been used as the basis for this translation.

October 1986

BM

THE STORY OF KUDRUN

CHAPTER 1

The Birth of Hagen[1]

There grew up in Ireland[2] a prince who was to become a great and famous king. His name was Sigebant, and his father was called Ger. His mother's name was Uote, and she was a queen whose high nobility made her worthy of the love of a powerful ruler.

As is well known, Ger was a mighty king, to whom a great number of cities owed allegiance. Seven kingdoms were subject to him, and from them he could raise more than four thousand armed men. Both his wealth and his standing increased daily.

Sigebant was brought as a young boy to his father's court,[3] and there he was set to learn all the skills that he would require – fighting on foot with a spear, how to take cover and how to thrust – so that when he was faced with an enemy he would be able to acquit himself well. And so he grew up, until he reached the age at which he was entitled to bear arms. As befits a warrior, he was skilled in all the things that would gain for him the respect of those who were subject to his father, either by ties of blood or as vassals. The well-born warrior never wasted a moment in idleness.

But it was not long before death divided them, something which still brings great suffering to noble families. Reports of such events can be heard everywhere, and we ourselves must, to our great sorrow, always be prepared for them.

Sigebant's mother was now a widow. However, the brave and noble warrior was not yet inclined to look for a suitable wife,[4] and many a royal princess pined for his love.

His mother advised the powerful young king that he ought, after the great sorrow that his family had suffered, to take a wife, both to enhance his own position and for the sake of his country. The sadness caused by his father's death, she said, would then give way to great joy and delight. His mother's advice pleased him, and he decided to follow it, as is proper with the advice of a close relative. He sent his men to seek on his behalf the hand of one of the finest of noble ladies, a Norwegian princess named Uote.[5] His kinsmen readily gave him the help he asked for, and we hear that she was, indeed, duly betrothed to him. She was given as her retinue a large number of beautiful ladies-in-waiting, and also seven hundred warriors from Scotland,[6] every one of them willing to accompany her because they knew the fine reputation of young King Sigebant.

With all the ceremony due to a princess, her travelling-companions brought her to his lands, in accordance with the custom of great kings. Those who had been eagerly awaiting her arrival hurried to receive her, and the procession which filled the streets stretched back for more than three miles. All along the roadside the grass and flowers were trampled flat by the crowds of people. It was springtime, and the trees were coming into bud, while the birds in the trees were singing their sweetest melodies.

A large group of lively young people rode with the princess, and very many pack-mules were required to carry all the fine clothing that her retinue brought with them from their own country. A thousand mules came with her, in fact, all laden with treasure and with rich garments.

A westerly wind brought the lovely girl across the sea, and she was received on the borders of Sigebant's own country[7] with great pomp, and brought to the lodgings which had been placed at her disposal by the young king. A full tournament had been arranged as a welcome for the noble maiden, and when this was over, with its great shows of strength, she was taken on into the lands once ruled by King Ger, lands over which she herself was later to become a famous and mighty queen. Every service that could be rendered to her was performed willingly. The fine horses provided for her had saddle-cloths and livery that hung down to the ground, right to their hooves. And in what fine spirits was the young Lord of Ireland!

When the time came for him to receive the lovely girl with a formal kiss, his men all thronged closely round him, and their richly decorated shield-bosses clashed against one another in the crush of men, as they jostled for a place.

The next day, envoys were sent out with news of her arrival in the young lord's lands, where she was to rule as queen beside the warrior Sigebant. Later she did indeed receive that crown, and gave him cause to praise her greatly.

It was not thought fitting for him to take her as his wife at once, since she was a princess, and he had not yet been made a knight. He had first to assume the crown as overlord of many powerful princes, and indeed, with the help of his kinsmen, he went on to win fame and high esteem.

Five hundred young warriors were made knights with him. All their wishes were granted at that time, and they were given horses, garments, and armour of all kinds. The noble young king was careful to maintain the dignity of his rank. Afterwards he ruled in Ireland for a long time, and did so with great and unblemished honour. He issued judgments where they were needed, and he avenged wrongs done to the poor. The revenues from his lands made him rich, and his wife, the queen, was also of such a generous turn of mind that if she had had at her disposal the lands of thirty kings, she would still have given away all their riches as gifts.

Three years later, we are told, she bore the king a fine son. The child was baptised, and was given the name Hagen – and Hagen's story is a famous one. Orders were issued that he should be brought up with great care and looked after well. If he grew up true to his family line, then he would become a mighty warrior. Wise old women and beautiful ladies-in-waiting had charge of the young boy, and his father and mother doted on him.

By the time he reached the age of seven, he was often given into the care of warriors. He was no longer content to be with the women, and preferred now to be with the men. But he was destined to be taken from them, too, and carried far away from everyone.

Whenever the child saw weapons there at court – and he soon knew all about them – he would often demand to put on a mail-coat and a helmet. Soon, however, he was to be snatched away from all this, and his hopes of training as a warrior at that court were to be dashed.

One day, Sigebant was sitting on the terrace in front of his great hall, and his wife, the queen, was under the shade of a cedar tree, when she said to him: 'We are held in high esteem, but there is one thing that surprises me, and I cannot hide it from you.' He asked what this was, and the royal lady replied: 'I am very much saddened by the fact that I so rarely see you in the company of your brave fighting men, something that would give me great joy to see. This makes me very unhappy.'

'How do you wish to see me at the head of all my warriors?' asked the noble king. 'Tell me, my queen, and I shall gladly make every effort for your sake.'

'There is no man living who is as powerful as you,' she replied, 'and no-one has so many castles and such extensive lands, with silver, precious stones and heavy gold. We are not using these riches properly, and that is what saddens me. My lord king, please do not take this amiss, but when I was a girl in the land of the Scots I used to watch daily as my father's vassals fought in tournaments for rich prizes. I have never seen anything like that here. A king', she continued, 'as powerful as everyone knows you to be, should let himself be seen more often. He should fight in tournaments with his warriors, and so bring honour to the lands that he has inherited, and indeed, bring honour upon himself! Mighty princes with almost unlimited riches cannot fail to appear weak if they do not share that wealth with their warriors. How else can they make recompense that will heal the deep wounds their vassals suffer for them in battle?'

'My lady, you are making me blush with shame!' answered the

noble king. 'May I never lose the desire to be instructed in the way a royal prince should behave.'

'You should send word to all your lords,' she said, 'and offer them gifts of treasure and fine garments. I shall send messengers to my own people inviting them here in love and friendship – and the result will be the banishment of any dullness from our court!'

'I shall be happy to do as you suggest,' said the King of Ireland to his wife. 'Indeed, many a man has, in the past, arranged for a festival of this sort on the good advice of a woman. I shall have my people and yours come to our court.'

'I am delighted,' replied the queen. 'I shall myself make a gift of five hundred gowns to ladies of the court, and I shall provide rich clothing, too, for sixty-four unmarried maidens.' When he heard this idea, the king readily agreed.

And thus he promised a great feast. Eighteen days later he arranged that their friends and kinsmen be sent word that if they wished to visit them in Ireland, they should wait until the winter was over, and summer had come. Then – so the story goes – he arranged for the building of great stands, for which wood had to be cut from virgin forests. Sixty thousand warriors were detailed to make these benches, and the king's stewards and chamberlains were well able to organise the work.

The guests began to ride in from all the points of the compass, and when they came to Sigebant's court they were given the best of attention. Eighty-six thousand noble guests came to the king's court from all the different realms. Fine garments were taken from the king's storerooms and were given out generously to everyone who desired them, together with shields and Irish horses. The queen, too, gave gifts of rich clothing, which enhanced the beauty of many of the women. She presented gowns of the finest quality to about a thousand of the noble ladies, and also to very many of the unmarried girls, always giving them clothing which suited them especially well, decorated with gold embroidery and with jewels. These lovely maidens were an adornment in their new garments.

Anyone who desired to have fine clothing duly received it. Young squires led out high-stepping horses, and they brought with them bright shields and valuable spears. Queen Uote sat in royal state in an upper window-recess.

The host gave the command for his guests to begin the tournament, and the many bright helmets soon lost their shine in the battle! The ladies sat as close as was proper, and were able to watch all the brave deeds of the warriors. The tournament lasted for a very long time, as is often the case. The king then wished to join the guests in their sport, and his wife, the queen, applauded this greatly as she sat with the women, enjoying a good view from high up in the castle.

Once he had participated in the tournament – as his rank demanded that he should – the king called for the jousting to stop. It was both honourable and appropriate for him to do so now, after such strenuous activities, and he conducted his worthy guests into the presence of the ladies.

The lovely Uote welcomed both strangers and old friends, and her courteous behaviour endeared her to the multitude of guests. Nor would anyone ever have refused to accept the fine gifts that the queen offered them. The knights and the ladies now enjoyed some time in each other's company, and all of them knew that the king was well disposed towards them. Then, towards evening, the king gave the signal for the noble guests to begin the jousts once again.

The celebrations went on for nine days. However much the king and his guests indulged in chivalric pastimes, the minstrels had no cause for complaint. They were kept busy too, and they also wanted to get the most out of the great festival. The trombones and the trumpets played loudly. Flutes, harps, stringed instruments, singing, piping and fiddling – the entertainers set to with a will, and earned a great amount of finery as their reward.

But then came a shock.[8] On the tenth day, after all these delights, many had cause for sadness. After all the pleasures of the festival, the news was now of heartbreak and of sorrow.

As the king was sitting contentedly amongst his guests, a minstrel came up, and so well did he play, that – unbelievable as it may seem – he far outshone all the others. Mighty princes were compelled to stop what they were doing and listen to him.

A beautiful maid-in-waiting held the young son of the King of Ireland by the hand. With her were other ladies of the court to whose care he had been entrusted, and also some of the king's men, charged by Sigebant with the child's upbringing.

A great noise came from the king's hall, and everyone was laughing. Those who were looking after young Hagen moved in closer, and lost sight of the girl and the child. But disaster was approaching, and great misery for the king and for his lady, Uote. The devil himself had sent his agent right into Sigebant's kingdom, and the outcome was to be tragic for them all.

A wild griffin came flying down. King Sigebant had brought up his son with love, and now he had to suffer the greatest of misfortunes, for he lost his son to the fierce griffin. Wherever it flew, its huge wings plunged the whole land into darkness, as if a cloud had covered the sun, so massive was the beast. But the people were so absorbed in their amusement that they hardly took any notice. The young girl and the child were left alone in front of the hall.

The griffin was so strong that the beat of its wings could bring down trees. When the well-born girl saw the great bird flying towards her, she made her own escape, and left the child behind. The story of these dreadful events is a truly remarkable one!

The griffin flew down and seized the child in its talons. It was plainly both evil and angry, and the assembled warriors and nobles had good cause for sorrow. The child began to scream with terror, but the beast carried him upwards with massive strength, turned against the wind and flew off into the clouds. The King of Ireland could do nothing but weep.

Sigebant's friends were all overcome by this tragic event, and bewailed the death of the child. The king and his wife were cast into gloom, and everyone mourned for the life of the noble boy. With this tragedy, the worthy gathering had to break up – the griffin's strength had destroyed it, and the guests would have to depart in sorrow and in pain.

The king wept and wept, and the tears fell on to his breast. But the noble queen – with great self-control – said that he should stop mourning. All men, she said, had to die. 'The end has come according to the will of God.'

The guests wanted to take their leave, but the queen said: 'Noble warriors, spend a little more time here, and accept gifts from us of silver and of gold. We are much indebted to you all.'

The guests acquiesced, and began to express their thanks in fine words. Many of them had come from far away to this festival. The king ordered whole bales of silk to be brought out, and he also gave them horses, palfreys for the ladies, battle-chargers and great strong Irish stallions. He made gifts of red gold, and of silver by the handful.[9] King Sigebant ordered the very best for his visitors.

The queen, too, bade farewell to the many ladies, married and unmarried. Her parting gifts were an adornment to them, and they now wore the finest of garments. The festival was over. They left the kingdom of Sigebant.

CHAPTER 2

Hagen Is Carried off by the Griffin

We must turn now from the leave-taking at Sigebant's court, and take up the story of the child's headlong journey in the claws of the wild griffin, the event which caused his family such heartbreak. By God's grace the child was still alive, but he was in very great peril indeed, because the griffin was carrying him to its young. When Hagen was faced with these, then he was really in danger! When it reached its nest, the old griffin dropped the child from its claws in front of its young, and one of them seized hold of him. It is clear proof of the goodness of God that it did not devour him immediately. The young griffins were just about to tear him to pieces with their talons when the story of Hagen's misfortunes took, as we shall hear, an amazing turn, and the young Lord of Ireland survived.

One of the young griffins had him firmly in its claws. It flew off with the child, from one tree to the next, but the griffin was not sure enough of its own strength. It landed on a branch, was too heavy for it, and fell to the ground, unable to get back to the nest. The child broke away from the griffin when it fell, and, small as he was, ran off and hid in the undergrowth. He was suffering badly from hunger – and yet he was destined to provide help for several maidens who were castaways like himself.

It may truly be said that the ways of the Almighty are wonderful. Just before this, three princesses had been carried to that place by the strong griffins, and they were now not far away from Hagen. It is impossible to tell how they had managed to survive so long, except to say that God himself provided for them in His great mercy. Hagen, then, was not to remain there alone for long. He found the three lovely girls in a cave.

When the maidens first saw him creeping round the side of the mountain, their first thoughts were that he was some kind of savage dwarf, or some fantastic creature that had come up out of the sea. Later, when he came closer to them, they welcomed him with open arms.

Hagen became aware of them, and they retreated fearfully into the cave, unaware that this was a Christian child. Indeed, it was to be by his hand that they were to be rescued from their many tribulations.

The eldest of the three said to him: 'Do not dare to come closer to us! God has given us this hiding-place. Go back to your fellow-monsters in the wild sea! We are in great danger, and we have suffered much.'

7

'Let me join you,' said the noble child, 'and please believe that I am a good Christian. One of the wild griffins carried me to these rocks. I should like to be with you. I do not want to stay here alone.'

Hearing that, they welcomed the small child in a loving fashion. Later they were to discover how useful he would be to them. They asked him where he came from, but the pangs of hunger made him disinclined to answer them. The high-born child said: 'I must have something to eat. Please share your food and drink with me – I have had nothing for three whole days, because the griffin carried me a good hundred miles.'

'Our state is such', replied one of the girls, 'that we have not seen our steward, nor our chamberlain, the people who used to bring us food, for a long time.' Young as they were, they had had to be resourceful. Quickly they began to search for roots and plants for food, and with that they hoped to satisfy the hunger of Sigebant's beloved son. They brought him plenty of the food that they them-selves lived on, although for him it was a very unfamiliar kind of food that the girls brought. Hunger, however, forced him to eat the plants they brought, for it would have been bitter to suffer death. Hagen lived with the princesses for a long time, and did them great service.

They, in their turn, took care of him, and so he passed his early childhood growing up in these extreme circumstances, until a day came when the young people, who were living such a perilous existence, saw something new and strange from the mouth of their cave.

Across the sea there came from some unknown shore a large company of pilgrims, who sailed close to the cliffs where the cave was. The great breakers were causing them many difficulties, and the castaway maidens were in fear for the pilgrims' lives. The keel broke up, and the people were lost. The old griffins flew down when this happened, and carried many of the dead off to their nest. These events were soon to lead Hagen into danger.[1]

Once they had fed the young griffins, the parent birds flew away from their eyrie – I have no idea where – out over the open sea. But they had left a fierce neighbour behind them at the cliffs.

Hagen could see that people still lay on the shore, members of the group of drowned pilgrims. He had it in mind to salvage some of their provisions, and crept very quietly down to the shore, past the griffins. He found just one man in armour lying there, and this was to cause him problems with the griffins. He forced himself to strip the dead man of his mail-coat, and close by he found his bow and his other weapons. The small child put the armour on, but suddenly he heard a rushing of wind above him. The child-warrior had delayed too long.

The old griffin had returned, and Hagen was too far away from the cave.

It swooped down angrily to the sand, and wanted to devour on the spot that fierce neighbour whom it had left behind when it had flown away. But brave Hagen behaved like a warrior hero. With his small strength he drew the bow and loosed a strong stream of arrows, but he could not break the skin of the griffin. How was he to escape? He drew the sword, and he heard the maidens weeping and crying.

Inexperienced as he was, Hagen fought very fiercely. He hacked a wing from the great bird, and cut deeply and strongly into one of its legs, so that it was no longer able to take off and carry itself away.

Hagen had won a victory. One of the griffins was dead, but its mate soon came down, putting him in great danger. With God's help, however (for his own strength would not have been sufficient), he killed all of them, young and old.

When he had accomplished this amazing deed he called to the ladies to come out of the cave. 'Come and enjoy the sun and the fresh air,' he said. 'God has granted us some benefits.'

They came up to him with great affection, and the ladies kissed him again and again. Their tyrant overlord, the griffin, lay dead. Nothing now prevented them from exploring the craggy lands.

Now that their greatest peril had gone, thanks to the boy, that homeless child became such a good archer that no bird could escape him. As he grew used to their situation, he quickly acquired skills that would be useful. He was brave, quite without fear, but disciplined. He learned by oberving the wild beasts how to jump and pounce, and would run across the rocks like a wild panther. He had to be his own tutor, for none of his kinsmen was there. And how often did he spend time down at the shore! He watched the fish swimming there, and he would have caught some, had he been able to do anything with them. But there was no fire smoking in his kitchen, something which was a source of constant irritation to him.

One day he left his shelter and went into the woods, where he saw a large number of fierce and wild beasts. One of them wanted to devour him, but he killed it with his sword. It felt the full force of his fury.

The beast was like a monstrous lizard.[2] Hagen set to and skinned it, and from it he gained great powers. Something made him drink its blood, and when he had drunk his fill he acquired great strength and also wisdom.

The young warrior wrapped the beast's skin around himself. Close by he came across a lion, which did not run away from him, but came up to him, without wanting to do him any harm. This pleased the warrior.[3]

He had the idea of taking back to the shelter with him the beast he had killed. The women now benefited at all times from his thoughtfulness. However unusual the food may have been, it put new heart and spirit into them. They needed to make a fire. There was plenty of wood, and Hagen struck sparks from a hard stone. Now they were provided with things that they had lacked up to now. As there was no-one to do it for them, they roasted the meat themselves.

Once they had eaten the food, they gained in strength. By God's grace, too, their minds grew sharper. They grew up to be beautiful and most admirable, almost as if they were each still at home in their fathers' lands.

Hagen the Wild[4] now had the strength of twelve men, and eventually he would win great admiration for this. He and the maidens were much oppressed by the fact that it seemed as if they would have to stay in the wilderness for ever. The girls asked Hagen to lead them down to the sea-shore, although they were very embarrassed, because their clothes were extremely poor. They had had to make them themselves, in the place where Hagen had first discovered them.

For twenty-four days they walked through the forests. Early one morning, however, the young man spotted a ship full of travellers from the land of Garadie.[5] By this time the three homeless girls were exhausted.

Hagen shouted out, and shouted again and again, no matter how strongly the wind was whipping up the waves on the sea. The ship began to crack, and its crew started to steer it over towards the shore, but they saw the maidens standing on the sands, and were frightened that they were some kind of fearsome water-sprites.

The ship's master was from Salmé.[6] Hagen and his family had been known to him for a long time, as their lands were close to his, but not one of the pilgrims recognised Sigebant of Ireland's son.

The Earl of Garadie would not allow his helmsman to take the ship into the shore. The warrior castaway shouted out to them to rescue them, in God's name, from this wild coast, and their fears were allayed when they heard him call boldly on the name of Christ. Twelve men, the earl amongst them, jumped into a small skiff. It seemed a long time to the earl before he established whether these were wood-demons or sea-monsters of some kind. He had never seen unknown creatures of such beauty, however.

Before they pulled into the shore he called out and asked: 'If you are Christian children, what are you doing here?' He saw their fine bodies, clad in garments made of leaves, and they all begged the newcomers to let them sail away with them.

CHAPTER 3
Hagen Is Taken on Board

Before they were taken on board the ship, they were given clothes from those that the pilgrims had brought with them. In spite of their modesty, the girls had to put on these men's clothes, although they did so with great embarrassment. However, their tears soon stopped. When the beautiful princesses were brought out to the ship, they were received and greeted courteously by the fine and noble knights, even though these had previously imagined that those girls were strange and monstrous.

They spent the night there on the sea, but were rather unhappy in the strangeness of their new surroundings, although they should really have accepted that they were being treated with due respect. The Earl of Garadie arranged for them to be given a good meal. Once they had eaten, the earl joined them, and asked them how such beautiful girls came to be there on that shore. His questionings, and the sufferings that they had undergone, brought tears to their eyes.

The eldest of the three girls said, however: 'My lord, my own country is a long way from here, the good land of India, where my father, while he lived, was king, but where I, to my sorrow, shall never wear the crown.' The middle girl spoke next, and said: 'I have come from a far country, too, from Portugal. A wild griffin carried me off. The man that called me his child was the ruler of that land, and he was known far and wide as a powerful lord.' Then the youngest of the girls sitting there with the earl said, modestly and politely: 'My lord, I come from Iserland,[1] where my father ruled. I have been carried far away from those who should have had me in their care.'

The well-born warrior then said: 'God's work is good. He did not permit you to stay with your relatives, but by His grace you have been saved from great peril, now that I have found such lovely maidens on this desolate coast.'

His next questions – how it came that they had escaped death when the griffins had taken them to their nest – were asked in vain. They had suffered so much that they could no longer even speak about it. The mighty earl turned, then, to address the young man. 'My good friend,' he said, 'now that the maidens have given their stories, tell me about your country and your people. I should very much like to know about them.'

'I will tell you,' replied Hagen the Wild. 'I, too, was carried here by one of the griffins. My father is Sigebant, and I am from Ireland. I have shared the sufferings of these ladies for a long time.'

Everyone wanted to know: 'How can it be that you survived for so long with the griffins?' Young Hagen replied: 'Through God's grace. I tested my courage and strength against the griffins.'

'So tell me,' said the Earl of Garadie, 'how you escaped from their fatal clutches?' – 'I killed them all, young and old. Not a single one of them survived. I was in mortal danger while they lived.'

'You are so strong', exclaimed the whole company, 'that no-one, man or woman, could fail to praise you. A thousand of us could not have managed to kill the griffins. It was truly a miracle that you were able to do so.'

By now, the earl and his companions were fearful of the young man and his great strength, and this led them into trouble. They tried to take his weapons away from him with a trick, but he stopped them angrily. Soon they would have cause to regret his arrival!

The earl said: 'Things have turned out well for me after the string of misfortunes that I have had to suffer. If you are the heir of Lord Sigebant of Ireland, then I shall claim you as a hostage for ransom. Your arrival is most opportune, I may tell you. Your kinsmen have done much damage in Garadie, in my country, which lies so close to theirs. My warriors have been killed or taken prisoner in the fierce attacks that they have been ordering.'

'I am completely innocent of all that they have done to you,' said young Hagen. 'Bring me to them, and I am sure that I can arrange a reconciliation of this enmity and quarrel. I hope that in mercy you will return me to my own people.'

'You are my hostage,' replied the earl to the young man. 'These beautiful maidens, too, shall serve at my court. I want them in my own country, where they will be an ornament for me.' Hagen considered this speech to be shameful and despicable.

'I will not be your hostage,' said the young warrior angrily. 'No-one demands that and escapes with his life! Sailors! Bring me to land, and I shall gladly reward you for it with gifts of treasure and of fine clothing. This man[2] seems to think that my ladies are to become part of your company. They will survive very well without him! If any of you has any sense, he will follow my advice: trim the sails and let us make for Ireland.'

The earl gave the command to seize him, and the men tried to do so, but he was standing too close to them, and they were the ones in danger. He hurled about thirty of them into the sea by the hair. The pilgrims soon discovered just how strong he was. He made no distinction between high and low born, and would have killed the Earl of Garadie, too, had the lovely maidens not prevented him from doing so. The sailors had no option but to set course for Ireland. In great fear of young Hagen's anger they made the best speed they could, or they would have been lost. For seventeen days they did not dare to be idle, such was the terror that they all felt when they saw him in an angry mood.

And then he came in sight of his father's land. He had known its great castles as a small child, and he picked out from the sea the massive keep. He could make out three hundred firm and strong towers. This was the home of Lord Sigebant and his royal wife. The pilgrims were now in fear of their lives, that the Irish king would kill them all when he found out who they were. But Hagen, to his great credit, did not allow this to happen.

The impressive young man addressed the travellers: 'I want to effect a reconciliation, although I have no power in this land. I shall send envoys, and try to bring to an end the old hostility between you and the king. If anyone wishes to earn riches from me, let him go to the king and carry the message I shall give them. I shall present gifts of gold to anyone who is prepared to do that, and he will be richly rewarded, too, by my father and my mother.'

He commanded that twelve of the pilgrims should ride to Sigebant. 'Ask the king', said the young man, 'if he would like to see his son Hagen, who caused him great sorrow when he was carried off by a griffin. I am sure that the king will not believe the story. You are then to ask my mother if she will admit that I am her child if there is a birthmark in the shape of a golden cross on my chest.'

The messengers set off to ride inland. Sigebant and Uote were in their hall, and they recognised the men of Garadie when they came towards them. These were his enemies, and Sigebant and his men were very angry. He asked how they dared to set foot in his lands. Then one of them said: 'Your son, Hagen, sent us. If you or anyone else wishes to see him, he is so close at hand that this could be arranged very quickly indeed.'

'This is a foolish deception,' replied Lord Sigebant. 'He was carried off, and my child's death has often brought sadness to my heart.' — 'If you do not believe us, ask the queen, your wife. She often held him close to her. If there is a birthmark like a golden cross on his chest, and if this serves to prove the truth about the young warrior, then you may after all be prepared to admit that this is your child.'

When Queen Uote, who had suffered so much, heard this, she was delighted by the news and said: 'Let us ride and find out for ourselves.' The king had horses saddled for himself and for his immediate circle.

Then one of the pilgrims said to the lovely Uote: 'My lady, if I may give you some advice, you should bring with you clothing for the lovely maidens that have come with us, and who will bring honour to

13

you all. We call them "the young ladies of Hagen's court". '

And so fine garments were brought along by the ladies, and many bold retainers followed the queen when she rode out. Lord Hagen had jumped on to the shore, and that is where they found the returned exile, surrounded by the men of Garadie.

CHAPTER 4
Hagen Is Welcomed by His Father and Mother

Hagen saw the men and women riding towards him and went to meet them, keen to see who was coming to greet him. His friends and relatives thronged forward. The king welcomed him to his country with the words: 'Are you the warrior who sent envoys to us, and who claims that the noble queen is your mother? If all you say is true, then I shall be happy beyond all my dreams.'

The beautiful Uote spoke out with quiet dignity: 'Make way for us in the throng. I shall certainly be able to recognise whether he has a right to the crown.' She found the distinguishing marks, and then embraced the young warrior. With tears in her eyes she kissed him on the lips. 'Until now, I was a sick woman, but now I am well again. Welcome, Hagen, my only child. Those who came here with Sigebant may now trust in your identity.'

The king approached them and his joy was great. So full of emotion was his heart that he wept with the natural love he felt towards the young man.

The three homeless girls were now presented to the Lady Uote. She gave them gifts of different ermines and of silks lined with fur, garments which suited them well. King Sigebant's wife made their sorrows easier to bear. The lovely young ladies were now dressed in an appropriate manner – they had had to be patient for a long time and suffer great embarrassment until they could once again wear gowns of richly embroidered material. The king and his men welcomed the young maidens with great courtesy.

Hagen asked the king and his warriors to show mercy to the men from Garadie, requesting that the king should forgive them any damage or debts of honour. The young Hagen earned thereby the admiration of the pilgrims. Once the king had made a formal reconciliation with a kiss, they were given recompense for all that they had lost. This was a great advantage for them, and much to the honour of Hagen. They never took up arms against Ireland again from that day on.

Now that Hagen had made peace between them, orders were given for the provisions and belongings of the guests from Garadie to be brought on shore, so that they could rest for fourteen days. The bold pilgrims expressed their thanks to him for this. Singing joyfully, they all rode away from the sea-shore. A great many men came to the castle at Ballynaree,[1] when they heard the strange news that the mighty king's son was still alive – no-one could believe the story.

After fourteen days, the travel-weary warriors who had been their guests took their leave. For the sake of his son, the king gave them gifts of bright gold. He wanted to have them as firm friends.[2]

Hagen did not ignore his three ladies. He gave orders that they should bathe whenever they wished, and he was unobtrusively attentive to the needs of the lovely girls. He was wise beyond his years, and he had presents of rich garments made to them.

Now Hagen grew to full manhood. With the king's warriors he took part in all the activities most fitting for a knight, with or without weapons. Later he was to become powerful in the lands of his father, Sigebant.

Young Hagen learned all the skills a warrior would need, so that he could bear himself without shame, and he did so better than most. He was the idol of beautiful women. Furthermore his generosity was so great that it could hardly be believed. It is reported of him, too, that he was so brave that he avenged any wrongs done to his friends. He was jealous of his honour in all things, and songs and tales were made up about him throughout the land. These told how the young prince had grown up in a wilderness surrounded by wild beasts, so that he could catch anything he wanted with one leap, and how nothing could escape him. He and his ladies had seen many marvels there on that sea-coast.

His real name was Hagen, but he was later to be called the Devil-King,[3] a name given him because of his great strength, and by which he was known in all lands. Hagen the brave warrior lived up to the name that he came to be known by.

His relatives advised him to marry, and a suitable wife, in fact, was very near at hand, a lady more beautiful than anyone in the whole world. She had herself looked after him when he was young, and with her he had grown up in perilous circumstances. Her name was Hilde of India. She had often shown him her love in times of great trouble, from the day when he had first found her in the cave. There was no-one in any country that he desired more strongly than her.

His father advised him to be made a knight as soon as possible, together with a hundred of his fellow-warriors. For every four of these companions, he would allow a thousand marks worth of silver to buy them horses and clothing. The young warrior readily agreed to all this.

The king sent word to the lands of his allies telling them when the ceremonies would take place. They would soon realise just how great his generosity was. The great festival was set for one year and three days ahead.[4] All the warriors who intended to come now began to equip themselves. They had shields made, either of bright metal or colourfully painted, and they prepared richly fashioned saddles, as well as halters and bridles covered with pure gold.

Orders were given that the camp for the mighty king's guests should be set up in a great field. Everything they could possibly wish for was provided. The tents covered an enormous area, and the guests began to ride in from all directions.

Those who were to be knighted at the same time as Hagen were given, at his request, clothing of the most suitable kind. A thousand warriors came from foreign lands to Ireland at that time, and they, too, were provided with fine horses and clothing.

Hagen said to his friends and relatives: 'You have advised me to take the title of king.[5] It would be more fitting if she whom I love with all my heart should take the crown beside me. I shall not rest until I have repaid her for all she has done for me.'

His followers asked whom he meant, which lady was to be given pride of place at the head of his warriors. 'Lady Hilde of India,' he replied, 'and she will be a great credit to me and to my followers.'

When they heard this, his mother and his father readily agreed that Hilde should be crowned with him. She could not fail to bring honour to their country. About six hundred or more young warriors were knighted at the same time as Hagen.

According to Christian custom, the young couple were both anointed at their coronation. Then right away Lord Hagen and Lady Hilde rode out at the head of their men. A great number of excellent jousts then took place between their warriors. Lord Sigebant also took part in these. He was in the best of spirits, and he gave no thought to cost. As was usual at court, as soon as the jousting was over it was the turn of the many servants in the king's household to busy themselves. They brought out benches that were both broad and long, together with chairs and tables. After Mass had been sung, Queen Uote, too, rode to join the court, with a great number of her ladies (whom the young warriors were very eager to see!)

Then King Sigebant took his place beside Queen Uote, and Hagen next to Hilde, and everyone said that the king was fortunate in having such a fine son. As they sat at high table, their followers went on jousting and broke many a spear, with great gusto.

After the King of Ireland had dined, the flowers and grass of the ground before him were soon trampled flat as men rode in noisy jousts. All who were fit and strong enough to do so took part in the tournament in front of the ladies of the court.[6]

Twenty-four knights rode on to the tilting-ground together, shields at the ready, and this made for good sport as they fought a great number of exciting combats. The beautiful ladies watched with interest, and it would have been a serious omission if such a combat had not been arranged.

Sigebant's son, Hagen, joined in the jousting as well, and his bride watched this with great pleasure. If she had given him any support during their exile he repaid her for it now. He was a very gallant warrior.

Fifteen other kings rode in the dust of the tournament beside Sigebant, all of whom held their lands in fief from him, both Christian and non-Christian.[7] But they gave honourable service both to Sigebant and to Hagen.

The festival lasted for a very long time, and people took great pleasure in the jousts, with much noise and shouting. Then the king gave the order for the guests to take their ease, and they were given permission to sit with the ladies. Lord Sigebant now addressed his followers. 'I transmit into the hands of my son Hagen', he said, 'my country, its people and its fortresses, be they near or far. Let all my warriors now take my son to be their lawful lord.'

Now that King Sigebant had abdicated, Hagen began with a good will to grant fiefs of land and castles. The men that received them were those that he considered especially valuable to him, and they received their fiefs from him gladly. Many men took the oath of fealty to the young king at once, in accordance with feudal law. Whether they came from near or far he gave his guests handsome gifts. A feast held by such a generous lord would be most welcome to the poorer of us even today!

At the court there were still two ladies who had been brought back to Ireland with Hagen. He now sent for one of them, and the Princess of Iserland, a lady of quite perfect beauty, was brought before the king. A young prince who had seen her with Queen Hilde had fallen in love with her. He told her with all justification that she had every right to share a crown, and so the lady who had been Queen Hilde's companion was rewarded in her turn with a powerful land to rule.

Now the guests took their leave, and the king said farewell to his vassals. The noble lady of Iserland was taken to her prince's lands in Norway. She had suffered much in the past, but now God had been good to her.

Thus began the rule of Hagen in Ireland. When he found that crimes had been committed, the wrongdoers were punished very severely indeed. Within a single year he had eighty or more criminals beheaded. Then he led a campaign against the lands of his enemies. For the sake of the ordinary people there he did not, however, lay waste to the country with fire. But if he found some lord to be arrogant, then Hagen razed his castle and took the grimmest of deadly vengeance. In battle he always behaved in a chivalrous manner, but he broke the pride of the most arrogant warriors, just as he had always done.[8] He was known far and wide as the Devil-King, something that his enemies had cause to fear.

Life was good for the great warrior, and he was content. Hilde of India, his wife, bore the king a fine daughter, who was named Hilde after her mother. Her story, too, is a very famous one.

Hagen the Wild gave orders that his daughter should be brought up so that the sun would not burn her, nor the wind chill her. Noble-women from the court and those relatives that he trusted the most had charge of her.

By the time she was twelve, this lovely maiden had grown up to be extraordinarily beautiful. Powerful and well-born princes gave thought to how they might seek the hand and the love of the daughter of Hagen the Wild. One of these princes lived in the country of Waleis,[9] near Denmark. When he heard of the great beauty of the girl, he desired her very much, but Hagen was scornful of him, and deprived him of his honour and his life.

Whenever envoys were sent in suit of the maiden's hand, the over-proud Hagen had them killed. He had no intention of giving her in marriage to anyone weaker than himself, and news of this was soon widely known. He must have had twenty or more of these envoys hanged[10] (to the sorrow of those who were unable to avenge them) – all those, in fact, who were sent to woo his daughter. Many a man, hearing of this, decided that he no longer wanted her as a wife.

But for all that, brave warriors continued to woo her. There is a saying that if a man is too proud, then someone is bound to come along who will be his match. The wooing of the maiden, however, was still to lead to great anguish.

CHAPTER 5
Wate's Expedition to Ireland

Everyone knows that the warrior king Hetel grew up in the land of the
Danes, in the border province of Stormarn, where he was brought up
with great care by his kinsmen. He was Lord of Northland, too, and a
very powerful ruler indeed.

One of his kinsmen was a man called Wate. He held lands and
castles in fief from Hetel, and because of their blood-relationship it
was Wate who had brought him up. He instructed Hetel in all the
virtues, and kept him well in control at all times.

The ruler of Denmark itself was Wate's sister's son, the lively
Horant, who was later to earn his crown and the full tenure of these
lands in freehold from King Hetel as a reward to the warrior.

It must be explained that King Hetel himself ruled in the land of the
Hegelings, not far from Northland.[1] In that territory alone he
commanded more than eighty fortresses, and these contributed daily
to the great esteem in which he was held. He was overlord of the
Frisians on the mainland and on the islands, and both Dithmarschen
and Waleis were his as well. Hetel was extremely powerful, with a
wide network of allies. Furthermore he was both fierce and bold, and
frequently trapped his enemies into defeat.

Hetel was an orphan, and it was highly expedient for him to take a
wife. Both his father and his mother, from whom he had inherited his
lands, were dead, and although he had many other relatives, he was
not inclined to live with them. His principal counsellors advised him
to marry someone of equal status to himself, but the young lord said:
'I know of no lady worthy of being Queen of the Hegelings or who
might fittingly be brought to me.'

Morunc, however, the young vassal-lord of Nifland,[2] said: 'I know
of one lady who is, so I have heard, more beautiful than any woman
on earth. We should make every effort to bring her to be your bride.'

Hetel asked who this was, and what her name was, and was told:
'Hilde of Ireland. Her father is called Hagen, from the line of King
Ger. If she were to come to this country, she would bring you joy and
delight for ever.'

'I do remember hearing', said Lord Hetel, 'that her father regards
any suitor of hers as an enemy, and that a great many men have died
for that reason. I do not intend to send any of *my* men to their death.'

But Morunc persisted: 'Send to Denmark and have Horant
brought here.[3] He knows all about Hagen's ways, and has even seen
him. Without his help it will indeed not be possible.'

'I shall take your advice,' replied Hetel, 'since she is so beautiful. But if she is to be won at all, you must take part as well, for I have good grounds to trust your judgment in all things. You will earn honour and respect if she becomes my wife here in the land of the Hegelings.'

He sent envoys to ride to his cousin Horant in Denmark, with the request that that warrior should come to him within the week if he was prepared to do him a great service. When the envoys reached Horant, and he had heard the request, he agreed at once that he would carry out whatever task was asked of him. He was to meet with great peril and hardship because of it!

Horant rode immediately to the land of the Hegelings, taking sixty of his men with him. As soon as he had taken leave of those at home, he made all speed to find out in what way he could be of service to the warrior King Hetel. He and his companions arrived on the seventh morning, all dressed in fine clothing. The king welcomed the noble warriors, and saw that they had Fruote of Denmark, a brave knight, with them. The king was more than pleased that they had come. He was delighted to see them, and their presence raised his low spirits a little. He smiled and said: 'Welcome to you, cousin Fruote!'

Fruote and Horant came to the king. He asked first about Danish affairs, and they told him: 'We inflicted a great number of deadly wounds in battle just a short while ago.' Hetel asked where they had fought this battle, and they replied: 'In Portigale.[4] The great and powerful king of that country was for ever attacking our border lands, and would not cease from doing so.'

'Do not concern yourselves with that any more,' replied young Hetel. 'I am sure that Wate the Old will be quite able to defend the marches of Stormarn, since his own fortress is there. You would have to be a very bold warrior indeed to capture one of *his* castles!'

The three warriors then went and sat in the great hall. As young men will, Horant and Fruote began to talk about love and noble women. The king was greatly entertained, and rewarded them well. And then Hetel asked Horant: 'What is the story concerning the Lady Hilde, the young princess? If you know anything, please tell me. It is to her that I want to send envoys with my proposal of marriage.'

'I know a great deal about the situation,' replied the other brave warrior. 'I have never seen a more beautiful girl anywhere than noble Hilde of Ireland, the daughter of Hagen the Wild. She would indeed be worthy of a crown.'

'Is there a chance that her father would grant me his lovely daughter's hand?' asked Hetel. 'If I thought that he might be well disposed, I should try and win the maiden. Anyone who helped me to do so would be rewarded very greatly indeed.'

'Impossible,' said Horant. 'No-one travels as an envoy to Hagen's country, nor am I in any hurry to do so myself. Anyone sent there is sure to be slaughtered or hanged.'

But Hetel replied: 'My desire for her is very great indeed. If he were to hang one of *my* envoys, then King Hagen of Ireland would be a dead man! However fearsome he might be, this fierceness of his may one day prove his own undoing.'

'If Wate were to go to Ireland as your envoy,' said the warrior Fruote, 'then we could probably succeed in the mission to bring the maiden back. Any other way, and we should be hacked down and our wounds would be fatal ones!'

'Well then,' replied Hetel, 'I shall send word to Stormarn. I am quite sure that Wate will not refuse to go anywhere I ask him to. Have Irolt of Frisia and his men come to me as well.'

The messengers rode at great speed to Stormarn, where they found bold Wate with his warriors. He was given word that he was to come to the king, and he wondered what the lord of the Hegelings wanted of him. He asked whether he was supposed to bring arms and armour, or any of his soldiers, but one of the messengers said: 'As far as we know he needs no troops. It is you alone that he wants to see.'

Wate set out. He left his land and castles in the care of his lieutenants, and when he rode away he was accompanied by no more than twelve of his men. Wate, who was a very brave warrior, rode as fast as he could to the king's court.

He arrived in the land of the Hegelings, and when he reached Hetel's residence at Campatille, Hetel was delighted, and ran to greet him, wondering how he should best welcome his old comrade Wate. He received him joyfully, and shouted out: 'My Lord Wate, you are welcome here! It has been a long time since we saw each other and sat together – it was the time when we joined in that attack on our enemies.'

'Friends and allies should stick together,' replied Wate to the king. 'That way they can preserve themselves so much more easily from strong enemy attack.' He took Hetel's hand in a warm and friendly manner.

They went in and sat down together, apart from the others. Hetel was a powerful king, but Wate was both a noble and a proud man in all his doings, and Hetel was concerned about how to persuade Wate to go to Ireland.

Eventually the young warrior said: 'I sent for you for a reason. I need to send an envoy to the country of King Hagen the Wild, and I know of no-one who could accomplish this task better than you,

Wate my dear friend. You are entirely suitable to act as an envoy.'

'Whatever embassy you have for me,' said Wate the Old, 'I shall be more than pleased to carry it out for your sake, and in your honour. You may trust me to bring any task to a successful completion and to your satisfaction, or I shall perish in the attempt.'

'My friends have advised me', replied Hetel, 'to see whether the mighty King Hagen will give me his beautiful daughter to be queen in my country. I have set my heart upon this.'

At that, Wate became angry. 'The person who gave you that advice would probably not worry if I were to die here and now! I am quite sure that the only person who could have aroused in you the hope that I might be able to bring you the beautiful Hilde was Fruote of Denmark. That lovely girl is so strongly guarded! I shall not rest until Fruote and Horant, who told you about her great beauty, are joined with me in this expedition in your service.'

Hetel decided to send for the two warriors there and then, and other close friends passed the message to them that they should appear at court to see the king. This was the end of his private conversation with Wate.

As soon as bold Wate saw Horant and Fruote he said quickly: 'May God reward you, my two brave warriors, for your great concern that I should come to this court, and about my honour in general. You seem very anxious for me to act as an envoy. Well, you two are going with me! That way we shall *all* be of proper service to the king. Anyone who puts my peaceful existence in jeopardy will have to share with me the results of my honest loyalty to the king.'

'I shall be glad to go with you,' replied Horant at once. 'Even if the king wanted to excuse me, I should not shy away even from the prospects of great hardship, so long as beautiful women are involved who could bring joy to me and to my kin.'

'We shall need to take seven hundred men with us,' said Fruote. 'King Hagen is no respecter of persons, and he thinks that he is all-powerful. If he tries to use force against us, we shall then be able to subdue his arrogance. My lord king, have a seagoing ship built of good solid cypress, one that can carry your men. Let the masts be bound with silver. Make sure, too, that it is fully provisioned, and have helmets and mail-coats made for us to take with us. This will make it easier for us to win for you the daughter of Hagen the Wild. My cousin Horant, who is not without cunning, should be set up as a merchant – I am happy for him to take that role – and should be ready to sell buckles and brooches, gold and jewels to the ladies. The disguise will make us plausible. We should have both clothing and weapons with us for sale. Since the situation is so dangerous with

Hagen's daughter, that no-one can pay court to her without having to fight, Wate must choose for himself who is to accompany him.'

At this point Wate the Old said: 'I cannot act as a merchant! I have never sat and looked at my possessions – I have always shared them out with my brave warriors, and I hope to go on doing so. I am really not the sort of man who can display fancy goods for fine ladies. My kinsman Horant suggested my name, and he knows himself just how things are with Hagen. Hagen has the strength of twenty-six men, and if he finds out that we are there to woo his daughter we shall have a hard enough job to escape with our lives. My lord king, tell your men to hurry. Our ship will have to have a layer of planking, and must be filled up beneath with good soldiers to help us fight if Hagen the Wild will not let us go in peace.

'At least a hundred warriors, armed for battle, will have to go with us to Ireland. Furthermore, my kinsman Horant will need two hundred men with him at the merchant's stall that is to be visited by the fair ladies. You will also need to have three supply-ships built to accompany us, with horses and provisions enough to last for a year. We shall tell Hagen that we have had to flee from Stormarn and that this was on account of the displeasure of King Hetel. We shall visit Hagen and Hilde often at their court, and take rich gifts, and in that way we shall be sure of peace with the king. We shall all maintain that we have been banished. Then Hagen the Wild will take pity on us right away. They will find lodgings for us as exiles in that land, and Hagen will allow us to lack for nothing.'

Hetel asked the three warriors: 'My dear friends, when do you have it in mind to set out?' 'Once the winter is over,' they replied, 'at the beginning of summer. By then our own equipment will be ready and we shall ride to your court again. Meanwhile, have your men make the preparations. Sails and oars will have to be well made, and so will the supply-ships and galleys that we shall need for our journey, if the waves and currents are not to harm us.'

'Ride home to your own lands, then,' said King Hetel, 'and do not spend any of your own money on horses or on clothing. I shall provide everything for you and your followers, so that you will not be ashamed to show yourselves before any noble women.'

Thus Wate took his leave and returned at once to Stormarn, and Horant and Fruote to Denmark, the lands in which they all held royal titles. And as allies, they would always hold themselves ready at the service of King Hetel.

At home, Hetel gave immediate evidence of the seriousness of his intent. His carpenters and shipwrights were not idle for a moment, and made for him the finest ships that they could. The joints by the bulkheads were riveted with silver. The masts were firm and strong, and the helms were plated with gold and shone like fire. The king was very rich, and now that the journey was indeed to take place, the preparations for it were made with great care. The cables, too, were imported from as far away as Arabia, and such firm cables had never been seen before or since. These ships were very well equipped indeed when they sailed from the land of the Hegelings out on to the open sea.

By day and by night work went on to make the sails. The king gave instructions that these were to be made as quickly as possible, and an oriental silk was chosen for them, one from Abalie,[5] the best that could be had anywhere. Those charged with the making of these sails worked every hour of the day.

It is hardly to be believed, but the anchors of these ships were made of solid silver. The king had his mind firmly fixed on the wooing of a noble lady, and his eagerness for the venture kept his men very busy indeed. The ships were timbered and protected against the weather and against enemy attack. And then word was swiftly sent to the men who had agreed to go on the quest for the lovely lady. Only those whom the king was able to trust entirely were to go on this journey.

Wate rode back to Hetel's court from Stormarn, his horses laden with silver and with fine garments. Four hundred of his men came with him, so that the good Hetel had very many bold guests.

After him came Morunc, the bold warrior from Frisia, and with him rode two hundred men-at-arms. News was brought to the king that they had arrived, helmeted and in armour. Hard on their heels came Irolt, too – all these leaders were kinsmen of Hetel.

Horant, the bold warrior from Denmark, arrived then, and Hetel was able to send more than a thousand good men on his quest, a quest that could never have been carried out if he had not been such a powerful ruler.[6]

Irolt of Northland was so well prepared that even if the king had not provided him with all he needed, he and his men were fitted and equipped to go anywhere without having to ask for a thing.

The king welcomed them all in proper fashion, taking Irolt affectionately by the hand. Then he went to seek out Wate the Old, who was sitting apart, before the bold warriors set out on the journey.

Everyone was told to check very carefully that he had all the things he was supposed to take, and the warriors then saw how richly prepared the ships were. Hetel was taking the greatest care in sending this embassy in suit of the lovely Hilde. The force consisted of two new and strongly built galleys and, sailing with them, two supply-ships and the flagship itself, the best that could be seen anywhere on any waters.

They were ready to set out. Horses and equipment had already been put on board. Wate told the king to look after himself well until they returned, and assured him that they were all glad to serve him. The king said with concern, however: 'Take particular care of the young men who travel with you in my service. For the sake of your own honour give these young men your advice and instruction at all times.'

'Whatever may happen now,' replied Wate, 'you may trust us completely. Guard our lands for us. The young warriors will not want for instruction.'

The bold warrior Fruote was given access to the king's store-rooms, which were full of gold and treasure and many other things. The king gave out gladly whatever was required, and whatever Fruote asked him for, the king gave him thirty times as much as he had asked.

A hundred men were now selected to be hidden in the ship when they came to woo the maiden by trickery, in case it should come to a battle. The king willingly gave them a large share of his riches.

All manner of men went on this quest – thirteen hundred of them, knights and squires alike, as if they had really fled from their own country after political troubles. Hetel addressed his warriors with the words: 'May God be with you on this journey!'

Horant told the king: 'Do not worry. When you see us return you will also see women so beautiful that you will be delighted to welcome them.' The king was very pleased to hear these words. However, their return was still a long way in the future.

He clasped many of them in a farewell embrace. When he thought of all the hardships that they would have to face, the king became very sad. He feared for them constantly, and it was not in his character to accept lightly their absence on this quest.

The north wind that the warriors had been waiting for sprang up, the sails filled and the ships sailed smoothly away. Those who had experience of sailing gave instruction to the younger men. It would be quite impossible to say where they spent the nights, because they were thirty-six days at sea. All those who sailed with them, however, took a formal oath to support each other in the venture.

Although their resolve was firm, there were times when the wild seas brought them great discomfort, though at other times it was calm. But anyone who ploughs the ocean has to reckon with some lack of comfort!

They journeyed more than a thousand miles across the sea until they came to Hagen's fortress at Ballynaree (and those tellers of the tale who say that he was a despot who ruled in Poland are completely wrong: they simply do not know the story!).[7]

As soon as the Hegelings got close to Hagen's castle they were sighted. People began to wonder from which king's land the waves had borne these men. They could see that they were wearing rich clothing.

The ships dropped anchor and the sails were quickly furled. Nor did it take long before word was brought to Hagen's hall that strangers had arrived in port.

The Hegelings left their ships and carried all their wares on to the sands, offering for sale all things that men might require. They were in reality very rich, but be that as it may, they had been sent to sell and not to buy. More than sixty of the brave men took up their positions on the beach as merchants, with Fruote of Denmark the master amongst them. He wore better clothes than the others, and was thus set off from them.

The chief magistrate of Ballynaree rode out with his fellow council-lors to meet the supposed merchants, because these strangers seemed to be so rich. The latter behaved as best as they could in their role. The magistrate asked them where across the seas they had come from. 'Our country is a long way from here,' replied the warrior Fruote. 'We are merchants, and we have rich gentlemen with us on board.'

Lord Wate then asked for an agreement to be struck with the overlord of the land. It was easy for the others to see that here was a proud and forceful individual who could behave sharply towards those he had in his charge. The strangers were conducted to Hagen and their request made known to him.

'I grant them safe-conduct and peace,' said Hagen. 'If any man causes hurt to these strangers he will pay for it on the gallows. Let them rest assured: no harm shall come to them in *my* lands!'

With that they gave the king rich gifts, worth well over one thousand marks. He had not asked for a single penny, but simply that they should display whatever they had for sale that might be of interest to noble men and women. Nevertheless, Hagen thanked them greatly, and said: 'Even if I had only three days to live I should try to make fitting recompense to you, my guests, for all that you have given me, for if my guests should want for anything it would shame me for ever.'

The king then began to divide up all the things that had been given to him. There were bracelets that would delight the heart of any woman, richly embroidered cloths, head-dresses and rings, all of which the king gave out generously.

His wife and daughter had watched this, and they were well aware that such rich gifts were not often given by merchants in the king's lands. Horant and Wate were the first to bring their gifts forward at the court. Sixty bales of silk, the best that could be seen anywhere, and forty pieces of cloth-of-gold were brought from the ships. Royal purple and silk from Baghdad would have looked paltry beside these. They also gave a hundred bales of the finest linen that could be found.

To match the silk that they brought to Hagen's court they gave in addition at least forty rolls (and probably more) of the finest lining material. If any men ever won respect by the gifts they gave, then the Hegelings did so with these. They also presented Hagen with twelve Castilian horses, all saddled, and they ordered many fine mail-coats and helmets to be brought out as well, together with twelve shields with gold inlay. The guests of King Hagen were generous indeed!

Horant and the strong warrior Irolt rode to court with their offerings. The king had been told (for by this time more news about the guests had been brought to him) that these two were men of power in their own country, and this was evident from their gifts. Twenty-four of their men rode with them to court, all fine warriors, and all dressed as if they were on their way to be knighted – a spectacle indeed for Hagen's own knights.

One of Hagen's advisers said to him: 'My lord, you should accept the magnificent gifts that have been offered to you, and show your gratitude, too, towards these strangers.' Although he was very rich himself, Hagen offered the guests his most fulsome thanks.

'I am greatly in your debt,' he said, 'and I thank you most sincerely.' Then he sent for his chamberlains and told them to examine all the gifts separately. Once they had done this, they expressed their great amazement at the quality of the gifts. One of the chamberlains said: 'My lord, I may say that there are chests here with gold, silver and jewels, all precious and costly. They have made you gifts of at least twenty thousand marks in value.'

'God's blessing on these guests!' said the king. 'I shall share it all with my warriors.' The king gave them everything that any of them wanted. Every single man received what he desired to have.

The king commanded the two young men, Irolt and Horant, to sit with him, and he asked them where they had come from to reach his country. 'Never before have strangers brought me such magnificent gifts.'

'I will tell you, my lord,' said the warrior Horant, 'and we must throw ourselves on your mercy with our complaints. We have been driven out as exiles from our own lands. A powerful king made us the objects of his anger.'

'Who is this king', demanded Hagen the Wild, 'who made you leave your castles and your lands? You are plainly such fine warriors, and you seem to me to be such excellent men that he would have done better, had he any wits about him at all, to keep you.' He went on to ask the name of the man who had driven them into exile, and who had caused them such problems that they had had to flee from him and seek refuge in foreign lands. 'We shall tell you,' the warrior Horant assured him. 'His name is Hetel, of the land of the Hegelings. His strength and his power, and the force of his hand robbed us of the greater part of our delights, and we have been made wretched by him.'

'Things have now begun to go well for you again,' answered Hagen the Wild. 'All that he has taken from you shall be given back, as long as I have anything to give. You will not need to ask the King of the Hegelings for a thing. And if you warriors', he went on, 'wish to stay here, I shall share my lands with you and do you honour in a way that King Hetel never did. Whatever he took from you I shall make good ten times over.'

'We would willingly stay with you,' said Horant the Dane, 'but we are afraid that if Hetel of the Hegelings finds out that we are here in Ireland—he knows the routes to this land—he will have us killed. I am in constant fear of this.'

King Hagen said to the two comrades: 'Come to an agreement together that you will stay, and do not worry. Lord Hetel will scarcely dare to seek you out or do you any harm in *this* country. It would be to my considerable shame if I allowed him to do that!'

Straight away he had quarters made available for them in the town. Hagen the Wild asked his townspeople to show them all the honour they could, and the warriors, weary after their long sea-voyage, were quickly made comfortable. The townspeople did as they had been asked. They gladly relinquished and left empty for them more than forty of the very best houses, moving out so that the Danes might move in.

All their many belongings were now brought on shore. The soldiers hidden in the ship thought many times that they would rather fight it out with a quick attack than wait for the others to win the beautiful Hilde!

The king asked the noble guests if they would share his table until such times as they had lands to rule for themselves, but Fruote of Denmark replied: 'To do that would be a matter of great embarrassment to all of us. If King Hetel were to act as justly towards us as he should, and even if we ate nothing but gold and silver, we would find so much of that at home that we should always be able to satisfy even the greatest of hungers.'

Fruote gave orders for his merchant's booth to be set up. Such wonderfully rich merchandise had never been seen before in any country, nor that were ever parted with so cheaply. They could have sold everything in a single day. Anyone who wished to could purchase jewels and gold ornaments. The king was particularly generous towards his guests. If, on the other hand, anyone wanted to have some particular item without paying, they often gave things away, as an act of kindness.

However much people talked about these bold men, Wate and Fruote, and about how they behaved there, their liberality was even greater than anyone could ever have believed! They were concerned to win respect. Soon, word reached the lovely ladies of the court about this.

Even the poorest amongst them could be seen wearing garments from the Hegelings' stock. Those who had run into debt very often had their pledges redeemed or written off. The young princess heard a great deal about what was going on from her chamberlain.

'Dear, dear father,' she said to the king, 'ask these noble strangers to come to court. I hear that one of them is such a striking fellow that I should be very glad to see him here, if it is at all possible.'

'Of course it is possible,' replied the king to his daughter. 'I shall let you see how he bears himself and what he is like.' Hagen did not yet know much about him. Nevertheless, the ladies could hardly wait to meet Wate the Old.

The king sent word to his guests and pressed them to see whether they wanted for anything, and asked if they would ride to court and dine with him. Fruote the Dane, who was both brave and wise, advised that they should accept.

The Danes took care that when they went to court no-one would be able to cast aspersions on the way they were dressed. Wate's men from Stormarn did the same. Wate was himself, after all, a skilled swordsman and warrior. Morunc's men wore splendid cloaks and coats made in Campalie.[8] The gold ornaments and jewels that they wore flashed like fire. The noble warrior Irolt, too, did not ride to court unaccompanied. But no man could claim to be better dressed than bold Horant! The brave Danes were an imposing sight in their broad, full and brightly coloured cloaks.

Although he was a powerful and proud man, King Hagen stepped forward to welcome them. The noble queen also rose from her throne when she saw Wate. He had the look of a man with whom one could not trifle lightly.

'Welcome,' she said courteously. 'My lord the king and I have heard that you are warriors who are weary after much fighting. But now the king will be mindful of his duty in showing you every honour.'

They bowed to her in most courtly fashion. The king invited them to

29

be seated, as one should with guests, and they were then served with the best wine that could be found in any king's hall. The company sat, laughing and joking. Later, the noble queen left the hall, having asked Hagen the Wild if he would promise to let these bold warriors come and entertain her with their adventures in her own chambers.

We are told that the king agreed to this without demur. The young princess, too, was not displeased. All the women vied with each other in the clothes and jewellery they wore, and they were all eager to see what the strangers were like.

The elder Hilde, the queen, sat beside her daughter. The lovely ladies-in-waiting took great care not to do anything that might cause people to say that their behaviour dishonoured the queen.

And then Wate the Old was sent for and admitted to the presence of Princess Hilde. His hair was grey, but still the princess behaved in a somewhat coy fashion towards him, although she greeted Wate in a courtly manner. She received him first, but she was not inclined to kiss him in greeting.[9] He had a full beard and his hair was decorated with gold threads wound into it. She invited both Wate and Fruote of Denmark to sit with her.

These impressive warriors, who now stood before the queen and the princess as they sat on their thrones, knew how to behave, and in the past they had done great deeds in many a heated battle. They had won praise and acknowledgment for this.

Queen Hilde and her daughter asked Wate in jest if he would prefer sitting there surrounded by beautiful ladies, or whether he would rather be fighting in the heat of battle.

'I prefer the latter,' said Wate the Old. 'I have never been able to relax with beautiful ladies without thinking that I would rather be with good fellows somewhere else, fighting in the thick of an attack.'

The lovely girl, Hilde, laughed out loud at this reply, and she could see perfectly well that he was ill at ease in the company of beautiful women. There was a lot of laughing and banter about this in the queen's chambers as Hilde and her daughter talked with Morunc's warriors.

They asked questions about Wate the Old. 'What is his name? Has he lands and castles, and has he a wife and children? I am sure he isn't the most affectionate of men towards those he has at home!'

'He has a wife and children,' answered one of the warriors, 'but he risks life and lands in the pursuit of honour and esteem – he is well known for that. He has been a brave and strong warrior all his life.'

Irolt then said of the brave Wate that no king had ever had such a fearless knight in all his lands. 'He may seem well mannered here, but he is an amazingly fierce fighter in battle.'

At this the queen said: 'My lord Wate, since King Hetel has driven you out of Denmark, let me advise you to stay here. There is no-one so powerful as to be able to drive you away.'

'I once had lands of my own,' he replied to the queen, 'and I gave gifts of horses or fine garments to anyone I pleased. I should find it very difficult to serve as a vassal. I do not propose to be away from my own lands for more than one year.'

King Hagen continued to press the offer of great riches upon them, but these noble warriors were not minded to take a single mark's worth from anyone. King Hagen was a very powerful man, however, and he found their attitude a little too arrogant.[10]

They left the queen's chambers. The queen asked that they should be allowed to come at any time to sit and talk to the ladies, without shame, and Irolt said: 'We were granted that same privilege in my own lord's lands.'

When they returned to the king, many of his knights were with him, and all kinds of activities were taking place – chess, fencing and parrying. The Danes did not behave towards Hagen the Wild with such awe as the others did.

According to Irish custom, much of the time was devoted to these enjoyments and to various pastimes, and it was through them that Wate eventually won the king over. Horant of Denmark, for his part, often joined in these sports to please the ladies.

Wate and Fruote, bold and brave warriors both, were roughly the same age as each other. Both had grey hair, which they decorated with gold thread. Where good fighters were needed, these two were always found to be valiant.

The king's men jousted at court with great shields, with maces and with bucklers. There was single combat with the sword, and spear-throwing at shields set up as targets. The young warriors never tired of it.

King Hagen then asked Wate and his men whether such fiercely contested combats as he had seen from these warriors in Ireland were known at all in his own country? Wate smiled slyly. 'I've never seen the like of it,' said the warrior from Stormarn, 'but if anyone is prepared to teach me how, I would be glad to stay a whole year to learn how to do it properly. I should be happy to reward my master for such tuition.'

'I shall have my most skilled man teach you,' said the king to his guest, 'as a favour to a friend. At least you can learn three strokes that will come in useful in close fighting – you may need to use them some time.'

Accordingly an expert was brought along, and he began to give Wate instructions, but very soon he was in peril of his own life. Wate fended every blow just like one who is a fighter by trade, to the great amusement of Fruote the Dane. The only thing that saved the instructor was that he was able to leap aside like a wildcat. The fine sword that Wate had been given rang out noisily as he wielded it, and sparks were struck from the shields.

'Give me the sword,' shouted Hagen the Wild. 'I want to have some fun, fighting with the man from Stormarn. I'll see if I can teach him my four favourite strokes, and he'll thank me for that!' Wate the Old welcomed the suggestion, and said to the king: 'I want a promise from you, my Lord Hagen, that you will not put me in real danger. If you were to inflict wounds upon me, that would shame me in front of the ladies.' In reality Wate could fight, of course, quite unbelievably well.

Hagen was hardly able to hold his own against the supposed beginner, and began to fume like a doused firebrand, although he was the teacher and the other was the pupil! But Wate was very strong. The king and his guest struck blow after blow against one another.

People watched eagerly, because both men were so strong. Hagen soon realised Wate's true skill, and would have lost his temper had he been less mindful of his reputation. They were both powerful, but Hagen was seen to be the stronger at this point.[11]

Wate shouted to the king: 'Let us both fight now without quarter! I've surely learned your four strokes by now, and I want to thank you for them.' And with that he gave him the sort of reward that you might expect from a mad Saxon or a Frank.[12]

Now that they were fighting without quarter the hall resounded with their blows. It would have been better if they had indulged in some other pastime! So swift was the cut-and-thrust that their sword-blades were knocked loose from the hilts.

They stopped, and sat down. The king said to his guest: 'And you are supposed to be a beginner? I have never seen a man from whom I would rather learn this art! Wherever such things are practised, you must be a champion in set combats.'

'It is true, my lord,' said Irolt to the king. 'This was done so that you could test your strength. We *have* seen combats like this in our master's country, and both knights and squires practise it there every day.'

'If I had known that,' replied Hagen, 'I would never have laid hands on a combat-sword! I have never known anyone learn the skills so quickly.' Many of the nobles present laughed at this. Hagen gave the guests permission to take part in any sport they wished, and the travellers from Northland did so. If they were bored, they would have contests hurling heavy stones or throwing the javelin.

CHAPTER 6
Horant the Sweet Singer

It happened by fortunate chance one evening that the brave warrior Horant of Denmark sang with such a fine voice that he delighted the entire company, and even the birds remained silent to hear him sing. The king and all his men listened with great pleasure, and Horant the Dane won many friends. Moreover, Queen Hilde had heard him too, the sound carrying through a window to the upper part of the castle, where she was sitting.

'What is that sound?' said the beautiful Hilde. 'I have just heard the most wonderful melody that has ever come to my ears. Would to God that my own chamberlains knew it!'

She asked that the man who had sung so beautifully should be sent to her. When she saw Horant, she thanked him very much for making her evening pass so pleasantly. The warrior was very well received by Queen Hilde's ladies-in-waiting.

'You must sing for us', said the queen, 'the melody that I heard you sing tonight. Sing for me every evening – as a favour to me – and you shall receive an appropriate reward.'

'My lady, every night I would sing a song so fine that it would banish all sorrow from anyone who heard it – just for a word of thanks from you! My sweet songs can make the cares of anyone who listens and understands so much easier to bear.'

He assured her that he would be glad to be of service, and then he took his leave. Horant was to win greater rewards for his singing there in Ireland than he had ever done at home. It was in this manner that the young nobleman from Denmark served Hetel, his king.

When the night was over, and dawn had broken, Horant began to sing, and in the groves the birds all stopped their own singing because of his sweet song. Those men who had still been asleep quickly woke up. The song rang out with great beauty, clearer and better than ever. Hagen, who was sitting with his wife, heard it too, and it made them leave their rooms and come out on to the battlements. Everything was going according to plan. The princess was listening, too.

The daughter of Hagen the Wild sat with her ladies-in-waiting and listened when the birds that sang near the castle stopped singing. All the knights of Hagen's court listened when the Dane sang so sweetly.

Everyone, men and women alike, thanked him. Only Fruote of Denmark said: 'I wish my kinsman would stop his wretched singing! For whose benefit is this dreadful dawn chorus of his?'

But Hagen's men responded: 'Come, sir! Surely there is no man alive who is so sick at heart that he would not take delight in the sound of that voice?' 'I wish to God that I could sing as well as that,' added the king.

By this time Horant had sung three melodies in full, but those who listened felt that the time had rushed by. If he had gone on singing for as long as it takes to ride a thousand miles they would not have thought that more than a moment had passed.

When he had finished singing, and had risen from his seat, the young princess rose for the new day happier than she had ever been before, and they dressed her in bright clothes. The noble young woman then sent for Hagen, her father. The king hurried to his daughter, and she placed her hand affectionately on his cheek and begged: 'My dearest papa, have that man sing at court more often!'

'My dearest daughter,' he replied, 'if he would sing for you in the evening I would give him a thousand pounds. But these guests of mine are so proud that it would not seem right for me to ask to hear their melodies at our court.'

She begged and begged, but the king left. Nevertheless, Horant *did* sing again, finer courtly melodies than he had sung before. Whether those who listened were sick or well, their whole being was completely taken up by his song. The animals in the woods stopped feeding, the creeping things in the grass and the fish in the waters all became still. Horant made good use of his skill. Whatever he sang, people felt that the time had flown by too quickly. The song of the priests in their choirs seemed less sweet and the sound of the church-bells by comparison less noble than they used to be. A sense of great longing for him overcame everyone who heard Horant sing.

The beautiful princess sent for him, saying that he should come secretly, without the knowledge of her father or her mother – no-one was to tell them that he would be coming to her rooms in such secrecy.

A compliant servant earned his fee for bringing this about. The princess gave him twelve heavy arm-rings, made of red gold, and shining and valuable, for arranging that the master of song should come to her chambers that evening.

Everything was organised in secret, and Horant was very pleased to have found such favour at court. He had, after all, come there from a far country with the task of wooing the lady. Now, because of his skill, she was very kindly disposed towards him.

She ordered her chamberlain to stand watch in front of the house so that no-one would come in after Horant until she had heard his songs to the end. There was no-one with her except Horant and young Morunc. She asked the two warriors to be seated. 'Sing me the melody that I heard before,' said the noble maiden. 'I am very eager indeed to hear it, because your voice is pure gold, far surpassing any other delight or pleasure.'

'If I dare to sing for you, most lovely lady, when your father, King Hagen would have my head for doing so, then I would gladly serve you in all things – if only you were nearer to the lands of my own lord.'

And with that he began to sing a melody from Amalie,[1] which no man in Christendom has ever been able to sing before or since, and which Horant perhaps first heard on some far and mysterious ocean. Thus Horant, bold and good knight that he was, served at her court.

When he had finished singing the sweet melody there at court, the lovely maiden said: 'My friend, you have earned my gratitude for that.' She gave him a ring from her own hand, and no finer gold could be found. 'I am more than happy', she said, 'to be able to reward you.'

She promised him further, and did so very willingly, that if she were to become a queen with lands of her own, he would need to go no further than her castle. There he could stay, and be held for ever in the highest esteem.

But Horant refused all the things the lady offered him, except for a narrow belt, which he took as the lady's favour. 'This, my most lovely lady,' he said, 'is so that men will believe how well I was received here. I shall take it home to my lord, and this will give him the greatest pleasure.'

'Who is your lord,' she asked, 'and what is his name? Has he lands and a crown? I am already beholden to him in my admiration for you.' The warrior from Denmark replied: 'There is not a more powerful king anywhere. If no-one betrays the fact that we are here,' he went on, 'I shall be glad to tell you, my lady, about the parting words my lord said to us when he sent us to your father's castles and lands – my lady, he sent us on your account!'

'Tell me', she replied, 'what message your lord sent from your own country, and if it is in accord with my own wishes, then I shall tell you so, before we part.' Horant was afraid of Hagen, and was beginning to feel uneasy at his court, and so he said to the lady: 'What my lord sends you is the love of his heart, pure and without a blemish. Please look upon him kindly, my lady. For love of you he has forsaken all other women!'

'May God reward him for these feelings towards me,' she said, 'and if he is of equal standing with me, then I shall gladly become his wife, if only you will sing for me morning and evening.' 'I should be happy to do so,' he replied, 'you may be assured of that.'

And then he said to the beautiful Hilde: 'Most noble lady: you may hear any day at my lord's court a dozen men who can sing far better than I can, and however sweet their melodies may be, my lord sings best of all.'

'Since your dear lord is so skilled in courtly behaviour,' she replied, 'I shall forever want to reward him for seeking my love. I should be glad to follow you to his lands – if only I dared to defy my father.'

At this point the warrior Morunc said: 'My lady, we have seven hundred fighting men ready, who will support us for good or ill. Once you are on the sea with us, you need have no fear that we shall leave you to Hagen the Wild! We shall be glad to get away from here,' the warrior continued, 'and what you must do, most noble princess, is to ask Hagen to let you visit our ships, with him and with your mother.'

'Willingly, if my father will permit it. You must also ask permission from my father and his men for me and my ladies-in-waiting to ride to the shore. If my father agrees, you must let me know three days in advance.'

The king's high chamberlain had authority to come into Princess Hilde's apartments, and he did so often. But when this bold knight now entered to talk to the women, he discovered the two warriors there, and they were at once in fear of their lives.

'Who are these men?' he demanded of Lady Hilde. The two warriors had never been in such a precarious situation. 'Who granted you permission to come into the women's quarters?' he said. 'Whoever said that you could do so gave you the worst advice possible!'

But Hilde said: 'Calm your anger! Nothing will happen to *them*, unless *you* wish to find things very difficult for yourself from now on. Take them secretly back to their own quarters. Otherwise this man's beautiful love-songs will not have helped him much.'

'Is this the knight who can sing so well?' asked the chamberlain. 'I once knew a man like him, and no king ever had a better knight than he was. My father and his mother had the same father. He was a very fine warrior indeed.'

'What was his name?' asked the maiden, and the chamberlain answered: 'He was called Horant, and he came from Denmark. He is not a king, but he is worthy of a crown. Although we have not seen each other for many years, we once lived happily together at the court of King Hetel.'

At this, Morunc recognised in him a man who had been exiled from their homeland, and he was very moved, and tears of sadness came to his eyes. But the princess looked with kindness at the knight.

The chamberlain, too, saw how the knight's eyes were full of tears, and he said: 'My dear princess, these are my kinsmen. If you will help them to escape punishment I shall be the protector of these two warriors.'

The hearts of all three knights were troubled with emotion. 'If my lady permitted,' said the chamberlain, 'I would embrace both of these men. It is many years since I had the chance to hear news of King Hetel of the Hegelings.'

'If these are relatives of yours,' said the maiden, 'then the strangers shall be all the more dear to me. You must make the fact known to my father, and he will be all the more eager to keep them here.'

The two brave warriors took the chamberlain aside,[2] and Morunc told him what was in their minds, how they had come to that country to woo Lady Hilde, and how King Hetel had sent them there for that purpose.

To this, the chamberlain said: 'My loyalties are divided – I am concerned about the honour of the king, but also about how to keep you from death at his hands. If he were to find out that you want to take the maiden, you would never escape from here alive.'

'Listen to what I have to say,' said Lord Horant. 'We plan to make a formal leave-taking four days from now, and go away from this country altogether. The king will be bound to want to give us gifts of treasure and fine garments. But we desire nothing more – and this is what you must help us to ask for – except that Lord Hagen should be kind enough to ride down to the harbour and inspect our ships. His wife, the queen, should come with him. If this is done, then our troubles are at an end, and all our great efforts have not been in vain. If the noble maiden, too, rides with them to the sea, then we shall be given great rewards by King Hetel when we reach home.'

The chamberlain brought them out of the apartments with such cunning that the king never heard a word about it, and they quickly reached their own lodgings again. They had good reason to be pleased to have found such useful help at court. They then told Wate in secret that the noble maiden would indeed give all her love to their kinsman, King Hetel of the Hegelings, and they discussed with the warrior how they should bring her home.

'If I could get sight of her just once outside the castle gates,' said Wate, 'then however much we might have to fight with the soldiers of the fortress, they would never bring her back under lock and key in her father's cells again!'[3]

The whole dangerous plan was kept quiet. They prepared themselves in all secrecy for their departure, although they did tell the men-at-arms concealed in the ships. These were glad to hear what was happening – they had been waiting for a long time. They then brought together all the men they needed, to confer in secret. This conspiracy would give cause for sorrow in Ireland, but no matter how much pain it might cause Hagen, the Hegelings were in pursuit of honour.

On the fourth morning they rode to court. The guests wore fine new clothes, cut to perfection. They were ready to set off, and they asked formal leave to depart from the king and all his men.

'Why do you wish to leave my lands?' King Hagen asked his guests. 'I have made every effort to make my country and kingdom pleasant for you. Now you want to leave, and I shall be robbed of your company.'

Wate the Old replied: 'The Lord of the Hegelings has sent word to say that he wants to make his peace with us. Those we left behind at home miss us greatly, too, and for that reason we are all the more eager to hurry.'

'I am sorry to lose you,' replied Hagen the Wild. 'But do me the honour of taking gifts of horses and clothing, of gold and of jewels. I must equal the great gifts that you brought me, so that no-one can reproach me.'

'I am too rich to be able to accept your gold,' replied Wate the Old. 'The mighty King Hetel, whose favour our kinsmen at home have won back for us, would never forgive us if we did so. But there *is* one thing that we can ask of you, my lord king. It would be a great honour for us if you would agree to come and see for yourself how well our ships are provisioned. Our food supplies would keep a strong force of men for three full years. Now that we are leaving, we shall give it to anyone who desires it. May God preserve you, and the esteem in which you are held. We must depart, we can stay no longer – and we should like the very noblest of escorts to ride with us to our ships. Permit your beautiful daughter and my lady the queen, your wife, to come and see our possessions. If we are granted this honour, noble King Hagen, it will be a memory to cherish all our days, and we shall ask for no further gift.'

The king made a courteous reply to the guests: 'If I cannot persuade you to stay, then early tomorrow I shall have a hundred mares saddled up for the maidens and the ladies, and I myself shall ride with them. I shall be glad to inspect your ships.'

They took their leave, and that night they rode down to the shore. There they put on land good wine and much of the food that they had kept in the supply-ships, and that way the ships were made lighter. Fruote of Denmark's plan was a wise one.

CHAPTER 7
The Young Ladies Inspect the Ships and Are Abducted

Next day, immediately after early Mass,[1] the young maidens and the ladies whom Hagen was going to take with him down to the harbour competed with one another in their finery. And beside them rode at least a thousand bold Irish warriors.

The Hegelings had heard Mass in Ballynaree. The king had no inkling of the great troubles that were about to come his way, although the fact that his guests were leaving put him in a bad light. Far worse, he was to lose his noble daughter with them![2]

When they arrived where the ships were moored, Queen Hilde and her ladies-in-waiting were helped down on to the sands, and then the beautiful ladies boarded the ship. The display booths all stood open, so that the queen could marvel at the goods that were on show. King Hagen also inspected the things that were laid out on display there, including very many rich jewels of enormous value. When he and his attendants had seen everything, the young ladies were allowed to come and look, and they were offered the finest bracelets to keep.

The king had gone on to one of the supply-ships to inspect it. But before the display-room door was completely opened, Wate's ship weighed anchor, and in that way they got away with the young ladies without using force – but as fast as they possibly could!

Wate was not concerned with anyone's feelings, nor was he perturbed about what would happen to the goods on display on the supply-ship. The princess had been separated from her mother, the queen. The men who had been hidden on the ship now came out, and Hagen was bitterly angry. Under the very eyes of Hagen's men they unfurled the sails. A good many men got a soaking when the Hegelings threw them overboard, and they had to swim for the shore like birds on the water. The queen was in great anguish over her dear daughter.

When Hagen the Wild saw all the armed men, the grim warrior shouted out in his fury: 'Quickly, fetch me my great war-spear![3] Any man that I lay my hands on shall die!'

Morunc replied calmly: 'Do not be in such a hurry. You may pursue us, ready for a fight, as fast as you like, but even if you have a thousand armed men we shall still throw them all into the sea. We shall give them a home that's cold and wet.'

Hagen's fierce fighters could not let that pass. Weapons and armour were reflected in the sea, and the fighting began. Swords were drawn and spears flew. The Hegelings plunged their oars into the water and the ships moved away from the harbour. Bold Wate jumped from the jetty on to a galley with a great crash of mail. With fifty warriors, his ship now sailed quickly after Hilde. However, the men from the castle were by now eager for war, and now the warrior Hagen was back, fully armed, and wearing a sharp and heavy broadsword. Wate the Old had delayed a little too long. Hagen was in a grim mood, and carried his mighty battle-spear high.

He roared out in a great voice, urging his men to hurry, and forcing them on constantly, so that he could overtake the erstwhile guests who had now done him such a wrong. He wanted to slaughter or hang every one of the Hegelings. He quickly gathered together a body of soldiers, but he found himself unable to follow the Hegelings out on to the open sea. His own ships were not seaworthy, and they were unprepared for swift pursuit. This was reported to Hagen, but there was nothing he could do as he stood there on the shore with his men, except order his workmen to make brand new ships as quickly as possible, ships that could undertake a sea voyage. All the men who were able to do so rallied to him, and he soon gathered together many fine warriors.

Seven days later they were able to set sail from Ireland. The men that King Hetel had sent to woo Lady Hilde did not number more than a thousand, but Hagen brought three thousand men with him in pursuit of her.

The bold Danish warriors had sent a message on to Hetel, telling him that to his great honour they were bringing Hagen's daughter back to his lands. It is certain, however, that they did not guess how much suffering this was still to bring them.

King Hetel was very happy. 'All my sorrows are over, and I am delighted with the efforts of my warriors in Hagen's lands. I have been anxious the whole time about the men who set out from my country. If you are speaking the truth, most welcome messenger, and do not lie when you say that you have seen the maiden with my kinsmen in this country, then I shall reward you handsomely for the news.'

'I can assure you in all truth that I saw the girl, but she said that she was very much afraid that her father would pursue them with his ships, even though they were now many miles away. That was her greatest fear.'

Hetel ordered that the messenger should be given gifts worth a hundred marks of silver. Helmets, swords and fine shields were then brought out for the many brave warriors who wanted to ride from Hetel's palace to greet the new lady of his court. Hetel called together as many men as he could, and he hoped that he would be able to muster and ride out with such a company that no princess would ever have been welcomed so magnificently, nor with such great honour.

Although the men that he had summoned made all speed, it took some time before he assembled the force that he needed. They all felt that the time was passing very slowly. Nevertheless, he brought to greet Hilde more than a thousand of his friends and allies. All of them, high and low, were finely dressed in bright mail – it could hardly be otherwise! – when they went to conduct the lady to her new home in this land. The bold and proud warriors rode confidently out on the journey.

They left Hetel's castle with a great tumult. On their way, in the hills or in the valley, there was always a crowd of people to watch them pass. Hetel was very eager to see his beautiful bride.

By now, Wate the Old, the warrior from Stormarn, had landed at Waleis, in the border country. Weary of their sea-voyage, the warriors went on shore, and here on friendly territory they found lodgings for Lady Hilde.

There on the shores of Waleis, the Danes refused to believe that Hagen's warriors would come after Hilde – until they saw it with their own eyes. They rested beside the sea in a cheerful mood. Wate the Old had his men set up tents in sight of the ocean, and now life seemed good to them all. Then came fresh news: word was brought to the brave warriors that Hetel, King of the Hegelings, was approaching, and was riding with his retinue to meet his bride. The beautiful lady herself was looking forward to being escorted into her lands with due ceremony. She did not suspect that there would be any more fighting.

Everyone had whatever they wanted – both food and wine. Those local people who were to join in the escort brought their guests everything they could, anything the guests might wish for. They lacked for nothing.

Hetel came nearer, with the band of warriors that he had assembled in the lands left him by his father. They duly arrived, richly dressed in shining mail-coats, and the travellers were delighted to see them. The Hegelings rode on to the level ground by the sea, and the bold warriors began jousting, which greatly pleased the young people in the audience, and brought the knights much credit. And then Fruote the Dane rode up, and with him the wise counsellor Wate.

Hetel saw them from far off, and was overjoyed. He galloped his horse towards them, such were his feelings for them. These were two of the best men that he had sent to Ireland with the other worthy adventurers, to sue for the daughter of Hagen the Wild.

The two brave knights were equally pleased to see him. Every day now seemed to bring new delights. Wate and his companions had undergone much suffering whilst abroad, and now Hetel made recompense to them for their hardship. He embraced them both with great emotion, these two grey-bearded men. The king had not been as pleased to see anyone for many a year as he now was to see these two. There had surely never been as many things to delight Lord Hetel in such a short space of time before.

Full of joy at the sight of his friends, King Hetel said: 'My most dear envoys, I had great fears for you, my warriors, fears that all my men might have been taken prisoner in Hagen's lands.'

'No, that did not happen,' replied Wate the Old. 'But I have never come across such great power as that which the mighty Hagen wields in his country. His people are a warlike race, and he himself is a fighter of no mean repute.[4] And yet it was a happy hour in which the idea of the quest first came to your advisers. For we have brought back the most beautiful woman – there is no doubt of it, you may believe me – that I have ever set eyes on. Nevertheless,' continued the noble knight, 'the enemy are brave, and as soon as possible we should see to it that grim Hagen does not surprise us here on our own frontiers. His fierce pride could make things very difficult for us.'

Wate and Fruote then conducted the bold warrior Hetel and his men to the place where they were to meet Lady Hilde. But their bright helmets and shields would receive heavy blows before too long.

The noble maiden stepped forward, wearing a fine head-dress. The Hegelings who had come with the king now dismounted and stood on the grass. The noble company was in the best of spirits.

Irolt of Northland and Morunc of Frisia walked at either side of the beautiful Hilde when she first met the king. She was a lady worthy of great praise, and now she was eager to greet the king. Twenty or more of her maids-in-waiting accompanied her, all dressed, of course, in fine white linen. These noble young ladies wore, too, the very best silks that could be found anywhere, and they felt very well in these garments.

Hetel, a fine figure of a man, gave his greeting in courtly fashion to the lovely maiden who was to share his crown, and whom he loved so much. He embraced her, and kissed her fondly. Then he welcomed the beautiful ladies-in-waiting one by one. Amongst these was a girl who was herself of royal birth, and who came from a very powerful family. She was one of the three ladies who had for so long been held captive by the griffins, and her name was Hildeburc. Queen Hilde, Hagen's wife, had brought her up in honour and virtue. She had been born in Portugal, but she had lived amongst different people in foreign lands, and she greatly missed her own kinsmen.

Hetel had greeted all the maidens in courtly fashion. However, if they all thought that their sorrows were at an end, they were wrong. The very next day brought them great troubles.

Hilde's noble retinue was made welcome by everyone, and they took their seats beside Hagen's daughter under fine silk awnings in a field of flowers. But Hagen was not far off. Great hardship would come from this.

CHAPTER 8
Hagen Gives Chase in Pursuit of His Daughter

At dawn on the following day[1] Horant, the brave warrior from Denmark, saw something that he recognised all too well – a cross and other symbols on a ship's sail. Wate the Old, too, had no love for pilgrims of this sort! Morunc shouted across to Irolt: 'Find out from King Hetel what his orders are! I can see Hagen's war-badge on a great sail. We have slept too long, and our farewells to Hagen were far from affectionate.'

Hetel was given the news that his father-in-law had come from Ireland with a force of ships and galleys, and was not far from their shores. Wate and Fruote now held a war-council with the king.

Princess Hilde, the beautiful maiden, heard the news and said – noble and good-hearted girl that she was – 'If my father has really come to this country then he will give cause for mourning to more ladies than can be imagined!'

'We shall be able to hold him,' said the warrior Irolt. 'And besides, even if you offered me a mountain of gold, I would not want to miss seeing my uncle Wate in the fury of battle with Hagen the Wild.'

Hilde and her ladies wept bitterly. The ships tossed on the sea. A westerly wind had brought a great army of warriors to Waleis, on the frontiers of Hetel's lands. The travellers were to find a bloody resting-place in the fierce heat of battle.

Wate gave instructions that Hilde should remain on one of the ships, and more than a hundred shield-bearers were detailed as protection for the women, to cover the whole of the vessel as guards. Meanwhile, those on shore prepared for battle, both the men who had come to meet Hilde, and those who, to the great anger of King Hagen, had abducted her from Ireland. Many of these hardy warriors were now in peril of their lives.

Hetel shouted to his men: 'To arms, brave fighters! If there is any man amongst you who has never yet earned gold from me, then he can earn it now in full and unstinted measure. Remember! Prepare yourselves to meet the men of Ireland – you have the advantage.'

Weapons at the ready, they ran down on to the sands. All of Waleis was filled with the sounds of war from these valiant warriors. Old friends and enemies now joined together as they all made for the same battle-point.

Hagen's force had by now reached the shore. The spears began to fly, hurled by his experienced fighters. The men on the sands knew how to defend themselves against the Irish, and the number of wounded began to rise. No-one had ever surrendered up a daughter before and received a reward of *this* sort! The sparks flew as swords struck against helmets, and all while the ladies looked on. Hilde was sorry now that she had ever left Ireland with the strangers.

Hetel's men stood firm behind their shields as the fierce spear-thrusts were exchanged, and they returned deep wounds, cutting through the solid hauberks of the enemy. The sea ran red with their blood.

Hagen shouted encouragement to his men. He was a man of enormous strength, and his words echoed against the sea as he told them to inflict deep wounds and help him to take this land. They fought with a will, and the temper of their swords was soon put to the test.

By now, Hagen had almost reached the sands. The clash of swords resounded, and then Hagen found Hetel, who had fought his way magnificently to the fore, standing at the very edge of the sea. In his fury, Hagen jumped into the water. The brave fighter waded to the shore, while the arrows of the Hegeling bowmen fell about him like snow-flurries in the wind.

The ringing of sword against sword grew louder. Many of those who wanted to kill Hagen had to give way before his blows, and so Hetel, the noble king, came face-to-face with his father-in-law. All the while the beautiful Hilde could do nothing but weep.

Hagen's more-than-human strength is legendary, and it was a miracle that the King of the Hegelings was able to stand his ground against him. They began to fight, and the sounds of sword against armoured helmet were very soon heard. The battle, though, was not swiftly decided. The valiant King Hetel was wounded by Hagen, but his relatives and closest allies rallied to him – Wate of Stormarn, Irolt and Morunc, brave fighters to a man!

The warrior Fruote now joined the battle beside Wate and his followers – a thousand men forced their way down with him. Hetel's kinsmen among the Hegelings dealt great wounds, and many of the invaders lay dead on the ground.

Hagen's lieutenants had by now also battled their way on to land, and the men of Ireland joined the brave fighters already on the shore. Helmets were split in two as they fought grimly for their womenfolk.

Hagen became aware that young Hetel was there in front of him. The Danes and the men from Hetel's own country inflicted a great deal of damage in the close fighting, and they made a path for Wate to fight towards Hagen the Wild.[2]

Hagen broke his way with great strength through the thickest of the fighting. His sword cut deep, as he took his revenge for the abduction of his lovely daughter and her ladies. In his sorrow and in his fury he wrought havoc on the mail-coats of his enemies. The sword alone was not enough for Hagen's grim vengeance. He used his great war-spear, and many a bold warrior was laid low by it, and never returned to tell the tale of how he had fared in that battle.

Wate, brave fighter that he was, made his way quickly through the throng until he saw the bright mail-coats of his kinsmen red with blood from the sword-cuts. Five hundred of those who had fought at his side now lay dead.

By now, the battle was at its height, with the invaders and the defenders locked in combat. The noise was immense. Wate and Hagen fought towards one another, and those who managed to keep out of their paths counted themselves fortunate. But at last King Hagen fought his way with great blows up to Wate the Old. He hoped to overcome him with his great strength. That day their swords struck sparks from each other's armour, and both had enough force to cleave right through a man's helmet.

Wate the Old struck such blows that the very shore echoed with them. By now the women were under threat. Hetel's wounds, meanwhile, had been bound up, and he wanted to know where his kinsman Wate was in the fight. He found him – in single combat with Hagen the Devil-King. Wate of Stormarn defended himself so strongly that ballads could have been composed about both men, and about the time when the bold warrior Wate took arms against Hagen the Wild.

Hagen smashed the war-spear that he had been using in the fighting across Wate's shield. There were no warriors in the world who might have fought better. Wate refused to yield to Hagen. But then Hagen struck Hetel's friend and ally, brave Wate, a blow that cut through his helmet and drew blood. The winds blew cooler,[3] evening came on, and still the armies fought.

Wate was able to take his revenge for the deadly and murderous blow that had brought him such bloody tears. He struck Hagen the Wild a blow against the rim of his helmet that sent up sparks which glinted on his sword-blade, and darkness came to Hagen's eyes.

Brave Irolt of Northland had been wounded too, although many men lay dead from his blows. He was unable to separate Wate and Hagen. The women wept as they heard the noise of so many swords clashing. The beautiful Hilde cried out in her anguish to the noble warrior Hetel that he should stop the fighting between her father and Wate the Old, who had him in a position of great danger. Hetel ordered his standard-bearer to urge the men forward.

King Hetel fought valiantly towards Wate the Old, although this made Wate angry. However, the king shouted to Hagen: 'For your own honour, call off the feud, so that no more of our friends have to die!'

Hagen shouted back angrily to find out who was asking for a truce, and the warrior king replied: 'I do, Hetel of the Hegelings, who sent his dearest friends so far across the sea to bring back Hilde.'[4]

Hetel leapt forward, as he had to, to divide the two combatants. Wate's mood was still grim, but both sides fell back, and Hagen stood aside with his men. Lord Hetel removed his helmet, and peace was proclaimed all around. Hilde's father now declared an end to the battle. The ladies had never heard such good news. The men who had been so eager in battle now laid down their arms. Many wanted only rest, but the deep wounds earned by others in the battle gave great trouble. Many were found in this condition, men who had been overlooked when the fighting was still at its height.

King Hetel went to Hagen the Wild and said to that warrior: 'Since I am conferring great honour upon your daughter Hilde, you should allow her with good grace to wear the crown of a country where so many noble knights will serve her.'

The other proud warrior replied: 'I have seen that all the men who came for her are indeed excellent fighters, and your own honour is unimpeached. But you used a fine trick to rob me of my daughter!'[5]

Hetel sent messengers to fetch Wate. It had long been known that Wate had learned the art of healing from a wise-woman of the woods,[6] and the famous warrior had helped many a fighter back to life and health. Once he had taken off his armour and had first of all seen to his own wounds, he took good herbs and a chest with dressings for wounds. And then the beautiful Princess Hilde prostrated herself before him.

'Wate, dearest of friends,' she said, 'heal my father! Whatever you ask of me, I shall do. Help his warriors too, those that lie wounded. Do not begrudge your arts to the men who tried to help my father to victory. Nor can you neglect the Hegelings, Hetel's friends. Their blood has wet the sand like rain. I shall always have reasons for sorrow at this journey of mine.'

'I shall not heal the outsiders,' replied Wate the Old, 'and I shall go on refusing to do so. Until I hear news of a formal reconciliation between the mighty King Hagen and my Lord Hetel I shall not heal their wounds.'

The noble lady then said: 'If only I were able to approach Hagen! But alas, I have done so much against my father that now I cannot even go near the man who is so dear to me. I greatly fear that Hagen and his men would treat any greeting of mine with contempt.'

The request was put to Hagen: 'My lord, grant permission, if you will, for your lovely daughter, the young queen, to see you. She could bring healing for your wounds if you would receive her in friendship.'

'Let me see her. No matter what she has done, I wish to receive her. What grounds could I have for rejecting her, here on foreign soil? King Hetel may well make amends for the sorrows that I and my daughter have had to suffer.'

Horant the Dane took her by the hand, and with the warrior Fruote they went to King Hagen. Only one of the ladies-in-waiting went with her to inspect her father's wounds. She mourned for her friends. Even Hetel allowed that this was quite proper.

When Hagen saw his daughter and Lady Hildeburc coming towards him he jumped up from his seat and said: 'Welcome, Hilde my daughter, most noble child. I shall never be able to do anything other than greet you with my love!'

Hagen did not want the two young women to see his wounds, and the noble ladies were sent away whilst these were bound up. Wate hurried to heal King Hagen, so that the anguish of the women should be ended. When Hagen had been treated with salves and medicinal herbs he was healed of his great pains. After Wate had finished dressing his wounds, his daughter returned and found him restored to health.

Wate, the master of healing, found much to do. If he had accepted money and gifts from these warriors, even a camel-train would not have been able to carry it all away for him. Healing skills like his were miraculous.

Next, Wate quickly healed Hetel, King of the Hegelings, and then all the others that could be found. He was able to heal even those whom it seemed no skills could save, and snatched them from death.

Now it was felt that the women should stay on the battlefield no longer. Hagen said to Hilde: 'Let us meet again in different surroundings, while those who were surprised by death today are carried from the field.'

Hetel invited Hagen to his lands. Hagen was somewhat reluctant until he discovered how rich and extensive the territories were over which the Lord of the Hegelings held sway. He went with his daughter to Hetel's home in peace and honour.

The young warriors sang as they marched home. These were the survivors, but they had left three hundred or more dead, high-ranking men and those of lesser status, cut down by sharp swords. When the weary warriors reached their homeland the people received them with great acclaim. Only for the relatives of those who lay dead was the rejoicing hollow, and their suffering was real.

When Hilde arrived with Hetel at his home, the ladies who had been abducted with her and taken from their families were sad at first, but they came to feel at ease in their new country. Hilde was crowned by the king, and this was an honour to the Hegelings.

Hetel[7] had achieved what he wanted. Old men and young all came to court in full regalia, as did all the guests of the noble prince. Queen Hilde's wedding was surely a great joy to Hagen, her father.

How graciously did the noble and beautiful maiden take the bridal seat! It is reported that a hundred men were knighted that day. Wise Fruote of Denmark acted as chamberlain.

Hagen was delighted when he saw the riches of the house. Hetel's men had already told him that Hetel held the crown of seven separate and prosperous lands. The ordinary people all had comfortable lodgings. To celebrate the occasion, Hetel gave so much silver, rich clothing, gold and horses to the men from Ireland that they were barely able to take everything away. Thus he cemented firmly the alliance between them, and this was an honourable settlement as far as Hilde was concerned.

Twelve days later the men of Ireland took their leave. Danish horses were led out on to the sands, their silky manes falling to their hooves. Now the guests were pleased that they had come to hear the name of Hetel.

Steward, marshall, major-domo and chamberlain all rode as escorts with Hagen. Whatever happened to them later, Hagen and his men were never again treated as magnificently as they were now. Hagen was very satisfied that Hilde now wore the crown of that country.

On the journey home they were provided with food and with lodgings for the night. Hagen and his men were so well cared for that when they arrived home they made known to everyone the great respect they now had for Hetel's kinsmen and allies.

Hagen embraced Hildeburc before he left. 'Look after Hilde,' he said. 'Your loyalty is great. A sea of new faces can be confusing for a woman. Be good to her, and it will reflect with honour upon you.'

'My lord, I shall do so gladly. You know well how I stood by her mother through all her tribulations, and never did anything to forfeit her trust and friendship. I was with her for a long time before she took you as a husband.'

Hagen then called the rest of the women together. They all wept, but he commended them to Hetel and said to him: 'Be good to them all. They are young, and in a country that is not their own.' And then he said to his daughter: 'Bear the crown in such a way that your mother and I hear no evil reports that you have incurred the hatred of any man. You are now in a position of such power that it would discredit you if you were thought to have behaved other than with generosity.'

Hagen kissed Hilde, and made a formal farewell to Hetel. Neither he nor his men ever saw the land of the Hegelings again, for the distance was too great. King Hagen now took ship for Ballynaree.

When Hagen arrived home and was welcomed by the queen, young Hilde's mother, he reported that his daughter could not have found a better match. If he had had more daughters, he said, then they, too, would have been sent to the land of the Hegelings.

Queen Hilde the elder gave thanks to God that things had gone so well for her daughter: 'My heart and mind are at ease. And what of Hilde's retinue, and the good Lady Hildeburc?'

'They, too, are well placed in that land amongst the Hegelings,' replied King Hagen. 'Our daughter's ladies wear richer garments than they ever did here at home. There Hilde shall stay! Many a warrior's coat of mail was hacked to pieces on her account.'

CHAPTER 9
Wate, Morunc and Horant Return Home

The tale moves on. It must be remembered that Hetel's kinsmen held their castles and lands, which were in his territories, in feu from him, and they all came to court whenever King Hetel and Queen Hilde summoned them.

Wate now rode home to Stormarn, Morunc to Nifland, and Horant of Denmark led his warriors back to Jever, the coastal lands which he ruled.[1] Each of these men was well able to defend his own fortresses, and the name of their overlord was known far and wide.

Irolt ruled with great might in Northland as the lord of that country, and because of his position he could serve Hetel very well indeed at

49

home and abroad. He was such a brave prince that no-one could ever find a better ruler.

Whenever Hetel found beautiful and well-born maidens living in his lands he wanted them to come and to enhance his court, and he brought them back to his own hall to join his retinue. All those who were personally chosen by Queen Hilde were glad to serve the daughter of Hagen the Wild.

The king lived very happily with his wife. Everyone knew that their love was such that he would have sacrificed the whole world for her sake. Nor had any of his kindred ever seen a more beautiful woman.

In the course of the next seven years, Hetel went to war three times. There were men who were jealous of Hetel's position of honour, and they plotted against him day and night. However, King Hetel soon made sure that they came to grief.

He fortified his castles, and brought peace to his lands, exactly as a king should. Many of his deeds were reported in far-off countries, and men heard of his firm rule. His name was held in great honour. King Hetel ruled with renown. Wate, who was very wise, came regularly three times a year to talk with his sovereign, and he served him faithfully whether he was near or far away. Horant of Denmark was also a frequent visitor at court, and he brought jewels and fine garments, gold and silks for the ladies. He brought from Denmark things for the ladies to wear, and gave them to all who desired them. King Hetel's reputation was augmented in the eyes of other warriors by all the service done for him by so many vassals. The noble and influential Queen Hilde also played her part in all of this.

Hilde, the daughter of Hagen, bore King Hetel two children. As soon as they were born, arrangements were made to have them brought up in the proper manner. The news was spread that Hetel's lands and castles were no longer without heirs to take them over.

One of the two children was destined to become a warrior, and his name was Ortwin. Hetel entrusted his upbringing to Wate the Old, who brought the child up[2] to strive always after the highest virtues. This was impressed upon him from his earliest days, and he grew up to be a brave warrior.

The other, a most lovely daughter, was called Kudrun the Beautiful, Princess of the Hegelings. She was sent to Denmark to be brought up by her closest relatives. They were never reluctant to serve Hetel in any way they could.

The young maiden grew up to be very beautiful. Men and women praised her loveliness, even in far distant lands, where everyone had heard the name of Kudrun, who was brought up among the Danes. She grew up, and reached the stage at which, if she had been a man, she would have been dubbed a knight.[3] Now many princes began to desire her love, and many paid court to her, but they suffered dire consequences because of this.

However beautiful Queen Hilde, the wife of King Hetel, might have been, Kudrun was more beautiful still, and more lovely, too, than her grandmother, Hilde of Ireland. Kudrun's beauty was praised daily above that of all other women.

Hetel rejected the suit of a king who ruled in Alzabey and who was very hurt when he heard that he had been refused. He considered himself to be so powerful that there was no-one who could match his great prowess. This king was Sifrit, who ruled the land of the Moors,[4] a man whose forceful character was well known everywhere. He was powerful, the overlord of seven client kings, all of them noble. He desired Hilde's daughter because everyone held her in such esteem.

With his companions from Ikaria, he had often won great praise when he and his comrades-in-arms jousted with one another in the sight of the noble ladies in front of Hetel's castle.

When Hilde and her daughter came into the great hall from their rooms in the castle of Lord Wigaleis,[5] they would often hear the great tumult made by those from the land of the Moors as they jousted for their benefit. The clash of shields and spears would ring out.

There could not be a more noble knight than Sifrit, and on several occasions Kudrun's bearing revealed that she was not entirely indifferent to him, even though his skin was dark. He would gladly have made her his love, but she was not given to him as a wife.

Sifrit complained bitterly, and he was very angry that he had come such a long way, only to lose her. He issued a threat to King Hetel that he would fire his lands. The men from Sifrit's country shared his downcast mood. But Hetel was proud, and denied Sifrit his daughter. Thus the bond of friendship between them was dissolved, and Sifrit declared that he would take the first possible opportunity to make Hetel suffer for this.

With that, they left the land of the Hegelings, and because of them, a certain noble knight named Herwic was – long after this – to suffer hardship, for they caused him as much harm as they could.

CHAPTER 10
Hartmuot Woos Kudrun

Word came to the land of the Normans,[1] too, that there was no-one more famed for her beauty than the noble Kudrun, daughter of King Hetel. The prince of that land, whose name was Hartmuot, very much wanted to have her as his love. His mother – whose name was Gerlint – had suggested this to him, and the young lord acted upon her advice. Once they had decided, they sent for the old King of the Normans, Hartmuot's father, whose name was Ludewic.

The old king rode to see Hartmuot, his son. The latter did not conceal what he had in mind, but when his father heard young Hartmuot's plan it worried him. However, the young warrior commended the idea very strongly to him.

'Who says that she is so very beautiful?' asked Ludewic. 'Even if she were the most beautiful woman in the world, her lands are not so close to ours that we can woo her easily. Any envoys that we send might very well perish in the attempt to woo her on your behalf.'[2]

'No distance should be thought too great', replied Hartmuot, 'when a ruling lord is seeking for himself both a love and the lands that she will bring – these are things that last until the end of his life. Agree to my plan! I want envoys sent to her.'

The old Queen of the Normans, Gerlint, said then: 'Have letters written. I shall be glad to provide riches and garments for the envoys to take. Let us find the route that leads to Princess Kudrun.'

Ludewic, however, replied: 'Have you heard the story of how her mother, Hilde, was taken from Ireland? Or what happened to the brave warriors on that journey? These are an arrogant race. Kudrun's kinsmen will treat us with no great respect.'

'Even if I had to lead a great army over land and sea to reach her,' said Hartmuot, 'I would willingly do so. I shall not rest until I have won the daughter of the beautiful Queen Hilde.'

'I shall help you, of course,' said the warrior king, Ludewic, 'but be satisfied if I provide twelve pack-mules laden with silver for you, so that the whole enterprise may perhaps have an honourable outcome after all.'

Hartmuot then chose sixty of his men to be sent as envoys to the lady. They were well provided with clothing and supplies, and they were given a good escort, on the advice of the old king, Ludewic, who was a wise man.

As soon as everything that was needed had been prepared, bold Hartmuot and Queen Gerlint gave the envoys sealed letters, and the gallant company were then quickly sent out on their quest. They rode as hard as they could by day and night until they were able to deliver their messages from the Norman kingdom. Meanwhile, Hartmuot's thoughts were filled sometimes with love and sometimes with foreboding.

They had a punishing journey of at least a hundred days, over land and sea, before they found their way to the land of the Hegelings. Their horses were weary by the time they were able to discharge their embassy. However, they did come to the end of their journey, and travelled across the sea to Denmark. They had suffered great hardships before they found the king. Now they requested an escort, and they were provided with a suitable one. The news was brought to Horant, who received it in a manner worthy of his station. The envoys, in their turn, discovered that all they had heard about King Hetel and Queen Hilde was true: they saw men everywhere with helmets and shields. Horant then gave orders to the escort that these travellers, Hartmuot's friends and kinsmen, should be accompanied to the court. His warriors readily agreed to do so.

When the Hegelings saw the envoys coming they all agreed that whatever the reason for their visit, they seemed to be men of power. Full details of the embassy were then brought to the king.

The Normans were given comfortable quarters, and orders were issued that servants should attend to all their needs. Hetel did not yet know what it was that they wanted in his lands, and on the twelfth day he sent for Hartmuot's ambassadors.

One of these was an earl, a man of the highest rank. The clothing that he and the others wore was extremely costly, and they rode the finest horses that could be found anywhere. Thus they went to the court in the best possible style.

King Hetel gave them a courteous and formal welcome, and his men did the same. However, once he realised that they had come to woo Kudrun, they were treated with nothing but contempt, and Hetel showed very little goodwill towards Hartmuot.

A clerk read aloud the letters.[3] King Hetel was angry that the great and powerful warrior Horant had provided these men with an escort. Had he not done so, they would not have escaped without trouble.

'It was hardly to your advantage, my good envoys, that Prince Hartmuot sent you here,' said King Hetel, 'and you will have to pay for it. Hartmuot's wishes anger both myself and Queen Hilde.'

One of the envoys replied, however: 'Be that as it may: he commanded us to give you the message that if he should be pleasing to the girl, and if she is willing to share the Norman crown before his kinsmen and his allies, then Hartmuot would offer you great service. He is a warrior of impeccable character.'

But Queen Hilde replied: 'How could she possibly become his wife? His father held a hundred and three castles in Garadie in fief from my father, Hagen. It would not be right for *my* family to receive these fiefs back from Ludewic's hands! Ludewic held lands in Scotland, and once he deservedly incurred the hatred of King Otto's brother, who was another vassal of Hagen, my father. He was Ludewic's bitter enemy, and he suffered greatly at the hands of that king.[4] You may tell Hartmuot that Kudrun will not be his wife, and that he will never be able to claim her love. If he is looking for a queen to rule in his lands, you may tell him to look elsewhere.'

The envoys were greatly displeased by these words, and angry that they now had to make the many days' journey back to their far-off Norman kingdom with much hardship, in sorrow and in shame. Ludewic and Hartmuot were bitterly disappointed when they heard of their lost labours.

'Tell me,' said young Hartmuot, 'did you see Hagen's granddaughter? Is Kudrun really as beautiful as they say? May God curse Hetel for being so ill-disposed towards me!'

'I can assure you', replied the noble earl, 'that anyone who set eyes upon that most lovely girl would have to agree that she stands far above all other maidens and ladies.' 'Then she shall still be mine!' replied Hartmuot.

Thereupon Queen Gerlint complained with tears in her eyes: 'Alas, my son! We should not have sent envoys to woo her in this way. May I live to see the day when we have her in our country!'

CHAPTER 11
Herwic and Hartmuot Both Come to Woo Kudrun

Some years went by after the visit of Hartmuot's envoys, and a new situation arose – which must be recounted now[1] – involving a young king whose name was Herwic. He sought after honour, and he is still held in esteem as a great warrior. He, too, began to pay court, to see whether the lovely maiden would take him as his love. He made a number of approaches, undergoing many setbacks, and employing much of his wealth, but even had the girl been in agreement, King Hetel was not inclined to give her to him. However much the young warrior complained and however many envoys he sent, they always went in danger of their lives, and this made him very angry, and weighed his proud heart down with sorrow. It was clear that he wanted Kudrun very badly indeed.

Meanwhile it came about – though it is not clear how – that proud Hartmuot appeared amongst the knights, the maidens and the fine ladies of the Hegeling court. Hetel would not have believed it, had he known. The bold and resourceful man had come to that country, but he and his men, the noble strangers, were known to no-one. Hartmuot and his warriors were all entertained well. He still cherished the hope that the girl would become his queen.

Noble women showed their interest when he came before Queen Hilde, with his fine manners and bearing. It was plain from the behaviour of the mighty Prince Hartmuot that he could very easily win the pure love of some noble lady. He was a man of some stature, handsome and brave, generous and courageous. Indeed, it is not clear why he had to suffer the indignity of Hetel's and Queen Hilde's refusal when he sought the hand of their lovely and royal daughter. Nevertheless, it distressed Hartmuot a great deal.

He had, however, now set eyes upon the lady who was the desire of his heart. They exchanged many covert glances, and he sent messages in secret to let her know that he was called Hartmuot and that he came from the land of the Normans. But she sent replies to the warrior that she was sorry – noble maiden that she was, she certainly had no wish to see him killed! – but that he should get away from the court as fast as he could, if he wanted to avoid being killed by her father and his men. She found him so handsome that she followed her heart in sending such a message, even though his envoys had been dismissed with contempt. The lady that he desired so much behaved graciously towards him, even though she gave Hartmuot nothing of what he actually wanted.

And so the courtly stranger left, carrying with him a great burden: how could he take revenge on Hetel for the wrongs done to him, and at the same time not forfeit the goodwill of the beautiful princess? The warrior Hartmuot left the land of the Hegelings in a state of mind that was sometimes hopeful and sometimes pessimistic about how he might gain success in wooing the lady. Later, many a helmet was to be hacked through on her account.

When he returned to his own lands, where he had left his father and his mother, Hartmuot, who was now very angry indeed, began to prepare for war without quarter, urged on continuously to do so by Queen Gerlint, the old she-devil.[2]

CHAPTER 12
Herwic Makes War on Hetel and Wins Kudrun

We may leave the story of Hartmuot at this point. Brave Herwic was suffering just as much for the love of the noble Kudrun, and now he enlisted the aid of his kinsmen in an attempt to win the girl.

His lands bordered on hers, but even if he had sent a thousand messages to her on a single day the only answer would have been haughtiness and rejection. But however strong her resistance was to him at first, she nevertheless became his wife in the end.

Hetel advised Herwic formally that he should no longer pay court to his daughter, but the king was to get an angry response to this. Herwic had no intention of giving up until they had met on the battlefield, and this would bring great harm to King Hetel and to Hilde, his queen.

It is not known who his counsellors were, but Herwic raised an army of three thousand warriors in support of his cause, and with them he brought grief to the Hegelings, the very people he had wanted to win over with the hand of friendship. His attack took the men of Stormarn by surprise, nor were the Danes aware of it until Irolt of Northland realised that bold Herwic was marching in arms against Hetel.

As soon as Hetel himself heard that Herwic's army was advancing fearlessly upon him, he said to his vassals and to his queen: 'I understand that we are about to receive some guests! What do you say to that?'

'What can I say?' said Hilde. 'What must be, must be. It is right and proper that a warrior should behave in a manner that will bring him honour in the eyes of the world, whether he is our friend or our enemy. How can he fail? Herwic is a brave and resourceful man. What we have to avoid', continued the noble lady, 'is that he should put our warriors in peril of their lives. I have heard that he and his warriors have already reached the outer defences of your fortress in their attempt to gain the favours of your daughter!'

The king and his men had hesitated just a little too long, and it was Herwic who opened the hostilities. In the cool of an early morning, he and his allies approached Hetel's fortress. In the battle to come, Herwic himself would fight most bravely of all.

The warriors in Hetel's great hall were still asleep when a sentry on the ramparts shouted down to them: 'Up, up, all of you in the hall! Uninvited guests are upon us! Arm yourselves! I can see the light glinting from many helmets!'

Without a moment's hesitation they were out of their beds. Every warrior in the castle, of whatever rank, was now concerned for his honour and for his very life. That is how Herwic launched the attack to try and win himself a wife.

King Hetel and Queen Hilde came to the window. Herwic had with him a troop of men from the mountain country of Galeis,[1] men that bold Morunc, who came from the adjacent land of Waleis, had recognised all too easily.

Hetel looked on as they stormed the gates, and although Kudrun's father was a brave man, he was relieved not to be there at the forefront. But the intruders made him angry, even though his own men served him well. He had more than a hundred men within his walls, and now the king took arms himself, and fought bravely. His men fought strongly, but there was no help for it; Lord Herwic inflicted great losses on Hetel. Herwic himself struck sparks from many a helmet. Hetel's daughter, the lovely Kudrun, saw this, and was much taken by his prowess. She thought that the warrior was a brave and noble fighter, and the sight of him brought her both joy and sorrow.

Hetel, by now in a grim mood, stood ready for the fray – he was a powerful man both in status and in physique. But he did not do well in the battle. He allowed the fighting to come so close to the fortress that everything could be seen clearly. And then, when his men tried to bar the gates, the defenders found themselves unable to do so, and the fighting moved after this defeat into the very gates themselves. Herwic's hopes were still firmly fixed on winning the love of a beautiful woman.

The two valiant warriors, Hetel and Herwic, now fought at the forefront of their men, and sparks flew from the iron facings on the shields they held before them. It was not long before they had the measure of each other. Now that King Hetel had experienced for himself the bravery of the proud warrior Herwic he shouted out, over the noise of battle: 'The people who would not let this knight be my friend did not know him! The wounds he cuts are deep ones!'

The beautiful Kudrun, meanwhile, saw and heard the fighting, and she knew that fortunes can change as easily as a ball spins round. The princess herself could not separate the men, and she wanted both of them to win. She shouted across the great hall to her father: 'My Lord Hetel, blood is running down the mail-coats of our warriors, and the walls are wet with it. Herwic has proved to be a bad neighbour. For my sake, proclaim a truce and rest your limbs and spirits for a while, and let me ask you both who Prince Herwic's closest kinsmen are.'

Noble Herwic responded: 'There shall be no peace unless you let me approach you unarmed, my lady, and then I shall tell you who my kinsmen are. If we can agree on such a peace, then you may ask me what you like.'

For the sake of the lady, the battle was ended. The weary warriors stripped off their armour and washed away the stain that the mail had left on them. For these were fine-looking men, and they deserved to live.

Herwic came forward, with a hundred of his men, until he found Kudrun, Princess of the Hegelings, whose emotions were now so torn. She and her ladies received him, but the brave and noble warrior was a little wary of them.

The lovely princess invited them to sit down, for Herwic's courage had endeared him to her. His courteous behaviour now commended him both to Queen Hilde and to her daughter, and these two were now advised that the battle should be brought to an end right away.

'I have been told', said Herwic to the two ladies, 'that you look down on me because my family is inferior – although I must say that my efforts in battle ought to weigh against that. However, those of the highest rank often do very well to ally themselves with the less well connected.'

'What woman', replied Kudrun, 'could possibly look down on or despise a warrior that had fought so hard to win her? Believe me, I do not look down on you. No woman has ever been more favourably inclined towards you than I am. If my kinsmen will give me their blessing, then I will gladly be yours.' He looked at her with love in his eyes, and she, too, took him to her heart, and said so openly before the assembly.

The valiant knight now asked formal permission to seek the hand of the princess. Hetel and Hilde granted this, and asked whether Herwic's proposal was agreeable to their beloved daughter.

Herwic soon received her reply. The brave warrior was Kudrun's ideal – he seemed to her to be the very picture of a noble knight.[2] 'If you will have me, most beautiful of maidens,' said Herwic, 'I shall be yours to command with all my heart and mind. My castles and my kinsmen shall all be at your service, and I shall never regret my choice.'

'I do confess my love for you,' she replied. 'Today you have earned by your deeds that I should bring to an end the enmity between you and my kinsmen. I, too, shall have no regrets. We shall be happy, you and I.'

Hetel was sent for, and he joined the queen, and thus the quarrel was reconciled. With Hetel came the finest warriors of the Hegelings, his best men, and there was an end to all hostilities.

On the advice of his men, Hetel asked Kudrun publicly and formally if she would take the worthy knight Herwic as her husband, and the beautiful maiden replied that she could not imagine a more noble lover.

The lovely girl was betrothed right away to the warrior who would give her a crown in his own country. She was to bring him both joy and sadness when she became his bride, and many good warriors were soon to face war after this betrothal.

Herwic intended to take Kudrun home with him, but her mother would not permit it, and it was because of this that he was to suffer greatly at the hands of other warriors. But Hilde told the king that she wanted some time to prepare Kudrun for her rôle as queen. Herwic was advised, then, to leave her for one year, and to while away his time in the company of beautiful ladies elsewhere. The men of Alzabey soon heard of this, and at once began to plot against Herwic.

CHAPTER 13
Sifrit, King of the Moors, Attacks Herwic[1]

Sifrit, King of the Moors, called his allies together and began to arrange for the acquisition of ships, which he quickly armed and filled with supplies, all destined for an attack on Herwic. He summoned his men in secret. He had twenty strong vessels built, but those he told about the proposed journey were not pleased when they heard that he wanted to attack Zeeland.[2] The journey was to begin as soon as the rigours of winter were over.

He raised an army of eighty thousand warriors, and the whole land of Alzabey was drained of its peoples now that the King of the Moors had sworn himself to war. Only a few remained behind, and the rest followed the will of the king.

He declared war on Zeeland. Herwic, the prince of that land, was greatly troubled, and complained rightly that he had done nothing to incur the wrath of the mighty King of the Moors. He had extra guards mounted on his frontiers and in his fortresses. He let his allies and kinsmen know – as far as he could – that his land was being threatened with fire and the sword. He paid out a large amount of his riches to ensure service from warriors in support of his cause, and there were men who were glad to receive this payment.

Towards May, an army of warriors from Abakie and Alzabey crossed the sea, and they were so strong that they looked as if they could travel to the very ends of the world. Among them were many who set off lusting for battle, but who were later to lie in the dust on the battlefield.

They put Herwic's lands to the torch. Such allies as he was able to raise were summoned to ride with him, and they fought hard. The rewards that these warriors received – be it gold, silver or jewels – were sometimes paid for with their lives.

Herwic of Zeeland was greatly angered by the attack. What a brave warrior he was, and how valiantly he fought! His fields were watered with the blood of the enemy dead,[3] and old men felt young again under his inspiration. But many a head was struck off in the fighting. The battles went on for a very long time, and a great many men lay dead. The noble Herwic came under such great pressure that he was forced back to his border territories. Fire raged from one end of his lands to the other, and so he sent word to Princess Kudrun. He despatched envoys to Hetel's country, and the men he sent rode there in great sorrow. They found the mighty King of the Hegelings and made their report, giving him a full account of their apparently unrelieved plight.

As soon as Hetel saw their crestfallen appearance he received them with kindness, as one should receive one's allies in a foreign land. He asked how they had escaped from Herwic's lands, since the borders were aflame and the castles destroyed. They replied that they had managed to get away only with great difficulty. 'Day and night,' they said, 'Herwic's soldiers earn their pay with their lives! They are fighting bravely and honourably, but many women have been given cause to weep.'

'Go to Lady Kudrun,' said King Hetel. 'Whatever she commands, shall be done. If she asks us to avenge the wrongs done to Herwic, then we shall be glad to serve you, and those wrongs will be avenged in full.'

Before the envoys went to the noble lady, their pitiful state had become clear to everyone, and lovely Kudrun did not even wait, but sent for them herself, for she mourned for her lost lands and lost honour.

The envoys came to the noble maiden, who sat there with tears in her eyes. She asked them if they had left her beloved lord alive.

'He was alive and well when we left him,' said one of them, 'but we do not know what has happened to him, since the time we left, at the hand of the Moorish warriors. Many of the Moors have been killed, but still they have done nothing but burn and pillage. This, most noble lady, is the message our lord sends you: He and his warriors are in the greatest danger, and go daily in fear of their lives and lands. King Herwic asks now for a token of your loyalty to him.'

The beautiful Kudrun stood up from her throne. A report was made to the king that her people were being killed and the castles destroyed, and she asked her father, King Hetel, to ride to Herwic's assistance. With tears in her eyes she embraced her father. 'Help me, most noble of fathers! My sorrows will be too great for me to bear unless your warriors come to the aid of my dear ones, and do so with a will – no other men could do the task so well!'

'Nothing shall stop me doing so, I promise you! In a few days we shall reach Herwic, and to the best of my ability I shall put an end to the sufferings inflicted on him. I shall summon Wate the Old and my other allies. Wate will bring all the men he has from Stormarn, and when Lord Morunc hears how things are in Herwic's country, he will raise a thousand good warriors. The enemy will soon learn how we can carry ourselves in arms. Horant of Denmark will also bring three thousand warriors to the fray. Irolt will rally his men to the colours as well, and Ortwin, your brother, will fight too. My daughter, you will praise us for the help we provide.'

The messengers now sent out by the princess rode swiftly, travelling as fast as they could. Kudrun offered rich rewards to all those who promised to help her avenge these wrongs. So gracious was the greeting she gave to the warriors that she was able to win even more support.

Hilde, the mother of the princess, also said: 'Anyone who rides in arms, and is willing to help our allies shall have a share in the spoils of battle.'

The armouries were thrown open, and the things in them were brought out to the court – hauberks with rivets of steel and silvery mail-coats – and were given to the warriors, while the young princess watched with approval. The king armed and provided horses for a good thousand warriors. The horses were led out from the stables – as often before – ready for the long road with those who were prepared to fight. The king had a great many, and he left very few in reserve.

Hetel took leave of his wife, and both Hilde and his daughter began to weep, but they saw with approval the warriors who rode with him, and prayed that God should grant him praise and glory in the battle.

They reached the great gates, and the squires all sang, riding in front of the warriors as they set out with thoughts of fighting and of booty. They had a long journey, for the enemy were far away from them.

At dawn on the third day, Wate the Old joined them with his thousand men, and on the seventh Horant with his four thousand, just as Kudrun had requested. Lord Morunc came from the marches of Waleis, also ready to fight at the behest of the lovely princess. He brought a full two thousand warriors, all well armed, who rode cheerfully into battle. The princess's brother, the knight Ortwin, brought four thousand men or more, by sea this time. If the men of Alzabey had known this, they would have been very afraid.

By the time all these came to his aid, Herwic was under great stress. Every one of his attempts to counter the attacks upon him had failed, both for himself and for his companions in arms. The enemy were at his very door. The King of the Moors was causing havoc in his lands. His treacherous and arrogant behaviour had led him to break down fortified camps and castles.[4] Treachery and arrogance must always be condemned, in whomsoever they are found.

The envoys quickly returned, and reported to Herwic. Filled with hatred, the enemy began fighting late in the evenings and also in the early morning, but by now fresh support for Herwic was openly advancing. When the men of Karadie heard of this, the news was very unwelcome to them. Two kings fought amongst their numbers,[5] but their efforts proved in the end of no avail, now that Lord Hetel with his brave warriors had moved in upon them, from his own far-off country.

High-handed and confident as they were, the attackers now began to defend themselves. The Moorish army took up positions from which they could carry on fighting, and not give way to anyone. Any resistance to them would be very difficult indeed.

The brave warrior Wate was there with all his forces – the lovely Kudrun had provided for great support in arms for Herwic, her betrothed. But even though they accomplished much on this occasion, there was still to be sorrow when they returned home at last.

Even though they were not Christians, the men of Moorland could not be forced back, and they were known to be amongst the finest fighters in the world. Others had discovered this before, to their cost.

Herwic of Zeeland[6] now wanted to make up his disadvantage and take revenge on the men of Alzabey, and this soon led to suffering on both sides. Kinsmen and allies of both leaders received many wounds, and King Hetel became very angry.

When the forces already mentioned came together, they had to face great and prolonged hardships, with very little respite. The warriors went in fear of night-time attacks, wondering if they would see the light of morning. Three separate pitched battles were fought with the Moorish armies, and according to the rules of war, the cities at least enjoyed a respite during these periods.[7] But on the battlefield sword was set against sword and spear against spear. Neither side would sue for peace, and the numbers of wounded grew and grew.

Neither the invaders, nor the defending armies would give way, and they fought on and on. Their finest warriors lay dead on the field, but still they would not stop fighting. When the news from the war was brought to the womenfolk they could do nothing but weep and weep.

How valiantly Wate the Old fought in these battles! His long experience often brought sorrow and great harm to his enemies, and he could always be seen with his warriors attacking the best men in the enemy forces. Horant of Denmark was another bold fighter – and how many helmets did he cleave in two with his own sword! Nor did he neglect the rest of the enemy's armour. He thinned out their densely packed ranks! Brave Morunc was also well able to strike out, shield in hand, with great valour. He never gave way to the mighty King of the Moors, and he helped Herwic to take revenge on him.

Because his beautiful daughter had sent him into Herwic's lands to restore peace and order, the great Hetel fought with such vigour that anyone who valued his life would want to leave his border territories well alone!

Herwic himself fought better than any others, both at his gates and out on the battlefield. His body was wet with sweat under his mail, and he killed a great number of the men who had thought that they would overcome him.

The fine warrior Wigaleis inflicted many wounds on the invaders, and Fruote of Denmark fought so valiantly that he deserved praise and honour. He was forceful in the attack, and no-one had ever heard of such a brave warrior of his age.

Young Ortwin, the warrior from Northland, was said by many to have shown unsurpassed bravery in his bearing on the field, and all said that he inflicted grave wounds on the enemy.

For twelve days they fought hard. Hetel's warriors could be seen beside their king, hacking grimly at the shields of the enemy. The proud Moors were given good reason to regret their attack on Herwic's lands. Very early in the morning on the thirteenth day, Sifrit said sadly: 'Look how many of our brave warriors lie dead. The King of Zeeland[8] is fighting to the utmost for the sake of his love.'

He held a council of war with the men of Karadie, who were glad to do so, as were the men of Alzabey. They fell back to one of their own fortified camps, where they could make a recovery, before every one of these warlike intruders into Herwic's lands was killed. They withdrew from the battle to a place of security protected on one side by a river. When they retreated to this place of safety, their opponents tried to prevent them from doing so, and harried them along the way.

The King of the Moors rode towards King Hetel. It was well known that he considered the fighting so far to be just a beginning, now that he had found the man who had inflicted such grave wounds on his men. King Hetel and King Sifrit fought like the proud warriors they were. In this combat, shields of shining metal were hacked to pieces, but the King of the Moors had to give way to the overlord of the Danes.

Now the Danes were able to set up a siege-camp. It cannot be denied that after this things went very badly indeed for the bold invaders.

Although their place of retreat was a strong one, every man of them would rather have been at home! Sifrit's brave men were now besieged by their enemies, so that they were unable to fight on the open battlefield, even had they wanted to. They had no alternative but to defend their position as best they could.

CHAPTER 14

Hetel Sends Reports Home from Herwic's Lands

Hetel was now able to send messages home that there should be no more weeping, and he had his messengers report to the noble ladies that both the experienced and the younger warriors had acquitted themselves well in sorties and on the battlefield itself. Now they were to wait in peace for their return. He sent word, too, of how his men were laying a siege, and how he and all his men were serving the lovely Kudrun and Herwic of Zeeland, and were doing their best for them at all times. Hilde, his beautiful queen, wished that Hetel and all his men should enjoy good fortune, and that their cause should prosper as their honour deserved. 'May God grant', said Kudrun, 'that they bring back our friends safe and sound.'

Meanwhile the men of Stormarn made sure that the army from the land of the Moors and from Alzabey could not reach the sea, and could do no more than wait in fear. They now had most unwelcome neighbours in the persons of Wate and Fruote!

Hetel swore an oath that he would never leave that heathland until he and his men had taken hostages from the Moors. This was ill conceived, and they all had to suffer later because of this campaign.[1]

Hartmuot had sent out spies from the Norman Kingdom, and they were on the lookout for trouble. They kept a continuous close watch on everything that was happening, and they wished for the worst for Hetel in the attacks and in the pitched battles.

They saw how the King of Karadie, the noble Lord of the Moors, lay under siege, in such a dangerous position that no help could possibly reach him, since his own lands were too far away. The spies that Ludewic and Hartmuot had sent then returned to the Norman Kingdom with all speed, and brought back the welcome news that Hetel and Herwic were very heavily involved in a campaign of war.

The Lord of the Normans thanked them for their report, and asked: 'Can you say how long the men of Karadie will have to stay in Zeeland, locked in this combat with their enemies? Or when Hetel and Herwic will be fully avenged of the wrongs done to them?'

'My Lord King,' replied one of the messengers, 'I am quite sure that they will have to stay there for more than a year. The Hegelings will not let up, and they have besieged the others so securely that they will never find a way of escape.'

'A new hope has freed me from sorrow!' exclaimed bold Hartmuot, Prince of the Normans. 'They are so firmly entrenched with their siege that there will have to be another battle. Before Hetel can return home we shall make our attack on the land of the Hegelings.'

Ludewic and Hartmuot agreed that if they could raise ten thousand men, they would be able to abduct Kudrun before Hetel and his soldiers returned to the Hegeling homeland. The old queen, Gerlint, was particularly concerned as to the vengeance she would be able to take for the fact that Hetel had so scornfully refused Kudrun to her son, Hartmuot. She wanted to see both Wate and Fruote hanged!

'I shall give great rewards', said the old she-devil, 'to anyone who rides with you! My silver and gold shall be given to warriors, not to my women. Nothing else matters, as long as Hetel and Hilde are made to suffer.'

'We shall prepare, then,' announced King Ludewic, 'to leave our Norman lands for a campaign of war, my warriors and I. I am sure that I can muster a force of twenty thousand in a few days, and with them we shall abduct Kudrun.'

'If I could only see Hilde's daughter here,' replied his son, Hartmuot, 'I would give up the greatest kingdom in the world just for the chance to live together with her in peace.'

Councils were now held and discussions began as to how Ludewic could raise an army that he could lead to the land of the Hegelings. And all this time, Hilde remained quite unaware of the misfortunes to come! Ludewic's queen was completely occupied with thoughts of how she would have Kudrun there amongst the Normans, and how the princess would lie with Hartmuot.[2] All her efforts were directed towards the time when he would be able to take the girl in his arms.

'Bear in mind, my brave warrior,' said Ludewic to his son, Hartmuot, 'that we shall have much to endure before we can carry these people away from their home. You must pay for any additional troops that we bring in, and I shall pay our own soldiers.' And so they gave to many brave warriors great gifts of horses and mules, saddles and shields, the likes of which have never been seen in Germany.[3] It was all done with a will, and Ludewic had never behaved so open-handedly before.

They made themselves ready for the long journey as fast as they could. Ludewic obtained the services of the best mariners, who knew the sea-routes well. To earn their payment they would have to work hard at sea. Soon they were completely ready.[4] The news was out that Ludewic and Hartmuot were about to leave their lands, but they were still concerned as to how they should best approach the country of the Hegelings.

They came down to the shore and found the ships that were to carry them lying ready. They were strongly built, paid for by Gerlint's gold. Meanwhile, Wate the Old and Fruote of Denmark were in complete ignorance of what was going on.

There were twenty-three thousand warriors with them when they left. Hartmuot was still longing for Kudrun – that was quite clear from his behaviour. And so, with his kinsmen and allies, he began to wage war against Hetel.

They reached Hetel's lands in the best way they could (and many a mother's son was to suffer as a result!). The waves had borne them nearly to Northland and they could already make out Hilde's fortresses before Hetel got word of their coming.

Hartmuot's force had left the open sea and was within twelve miles of Hegeling territory. They were so near that they could see the great hall and the towers of beautiful Queen Hilde's castles. Ludewic the Norman had them drop anchor on that shore and ordered them all to disembark as quickly as possible. They were so close that they were much afraid of discovery by the Hegelings. But then they were ashore, armed with shields and good helmets. They prepared for combat, but first sent envoys, to see if they could find any support in Hetel's lands.

CHAPTER 15
Hartmuot Abducts Kudrun by Force

Hartmuot sent envoys to the beautiful Hilde and to her dear daughter with the message that, for the love of Kudrun, he would, with their permission, arrange things to the satisfaction of them both. If she would consent to love him – he had asked her before, and his thoughts had so often been with her – then he would serve her as long as he lived, and would give her his entire inheritance. But if she would *not* agree, then he would be her sworn enemy. He made this request to Kudrun in the hope that he might be able to bring the lovely maiden back to his own country without a battle. That, at least, was what bold Hartmuot had in mind.

'If she refuses,' said Hartmuot to his envoys, 'then tell her that nothing will turn me from my purpose, and before I leave this land she will be treated to the sight of my warriors! Furthermore, my valiant envoys, you should also say that I shall not put to sea again, but would sooner allow myself to be hacked to pieces than return without taking with me the noble Princess of the Hegelings. And if she still maintains that she will not agree, then she will soon see me and my warriors coming for her. The road to her castle will be lined on both sides with twenty thousand Hegeling dead. The fact that Hetel chose to follow the advice of Wigaleis and of Wate the Old, leaving us no alternative but to undertake these long journeys to the land of the Hegelings, means that many a child will be orphaned. I want to bring this matter to an end.'

There was not much time. The envoys rode swiftly, as Hartmuot had commanded, to the great fortress named Matelane, where Queen Hilde and her beautiful daughter, the young princess, were in residence. Hartmuot had sent two powerful earls, who had come with him across the seas from the Norman lands, to declare to Hilde that he was at her service, and to say that he was prepared always to do her bidding. They were to say that Hilde should give him her daughter, whom he placed above all other women, for he was still filled with the noblest love for her. Kudrun would benefit from this because of her high birth. He would – the envoys were told to say – never be weary of serving her.

The men charged with guarding the Hegeling ladies were told that a Norman embassy was riding towards Matelane. When the news was passed on, Queen Hilde told her men to be silent, and the beautiful Kudrun became nervous.[1]

Hilde's men opened the gates, so that the new arrivals need not wait any longer outside the castle. The gates were opened wide, and Hartmuot's envoys entered Matelane. They requested an audience with King Hetel's queen, but the men set to watch over her highness refused this, in keeping with the king's honour. The noble ladies, Hilde and Kudrun, were never left without guards. However, the beautiful Hilde came forward and welcomed Hartmuot's envoys, now that they had come to her court, and the noble Kudrun – that good and honourable lady, who loved Herwic so much – did the same in formal style.

However hostile the Hegelings might have felt, orders were given that the envoys be offered wine before they delivered their message. Queen Hilde allowed them to take their place before herself and her daughter, and the queen then asked them what it was that they wanted, for now it was time to break their silence.

The whole group rose in formal array from their seats, as ambassadors should, and stated what had brought them to the land of the Hegelings: that their lord, Hartmuot, had sent them for the beautiful Kudrun.

But the princess replied: 'I have no wish whatsoever that our kinsmen and allies should see me share a crown with bold Hartmuot. All my affections are for Herwic. I am betrothed to him. I have sworn to have him for a husband and he has likewise sworn to take me as his wife. Whenever he wins great honours, that pleases me. For all my days I shall never desire any other lover.'

At this, one of the envoys replied: 'Hartmuot instructed me to tell you that if he hopes were not fulfilled, then you would see him with his warriors at Matelane within three days.' But the lovely Kudrun merely laughed.

The envoys now wished to take their leave. The two powerful earls would gladly have been dismissed, but even though they were unwelcome visitors, Queen Hilde ordered that they be given rich gifts. However, they were careful to refuse them.

Hetel's warriors told the envoys that they were not in the least afraid of their anger or hatred, and that if they would not drink King Hetel's wine in friendship, then they and their soldiers would be poured instead a drink of blood.

The envoys returned with their message to Hartmuot, to where they had left him. He ran forward and asked how things had gone, and whether the noble Kudrun had received them and their request at all kindly.

'You have been turned down', said one of the warriors, 'because the princess has someone in her heart that she loves above all others. If you will not drink their wine, then you shall be given blood instead.'

'The shame of such an insult!' exclaimed Hartmuot. 'These words bring sorrow to my heart. But I shall never ask for better friends than those who help me fight now.' The men who were still resting on the shore now sprang to their feet. Ludewic and Hartmuot set off with their army, war-pennons flying, in a very angry mood. Their banners could be seen glinting in the sunlight from Matelane, far away, and when she saw them, the beautiful Kudrun shouted: 'All is well! Hetel and my Lord Herwic are approaching!'

But then they saw that these were not the king's banners. 'What great misfortune is upon us now! Enemies have come in pursuit of Princess Kudrun. Many a war-helmet will be hacked to pieces before night falls.'

The Hegelings promised Hilde: 'Whatever Hartmuot's troops may do today, we shall try and stop them, and shall inflict deep wounds upon them.' The queen at once gave orders for the great gates to be barred.

However, King Hetel's bold warriors would not do so. The men he had left to guard his lands raised his war-banner and prepared to leave the fortress. These warriors wanted to attack their worthy opponents.

The great beams that ought to have been lowered to bar the gates were raised instead, because of their over-confidence. Nor did they take any account of Hartmuot's look-outs. As Hartmuot's vanguard reached the fortress his men quickly closed up behind him.[2] There were already a thousand men with drawn swords standing before the gates, and now Hartmuot himself rode up with a good thousand of his men. They dismounted on the heathlands and quickly had their horses led away. In their hands they held long-shafted spears with sharp heads. There was now no way of averting the battle, and soon these men were inflicting severe wounds on the defenders of the fortress. Then suddenly Ludewic the Norman and his warriors rode up to join the attack.

The women were very much afraid when they saw him ride up. They saw clearly his broad banners as they fluttered in the wind, and beneath each ensign, three thousand or more men were advancing grimly, although many of these warriors were later to fall. There was great turmoil everywhere. No braver warriors were ever seen than those from Hetel's fortress. They were bent on giving wounds, and did so to Hartmuot's soldiers.

But just as the defenders thought that they were safe Hartmuot's father, the Lord of the Normans, came upon them with his brave warriors. His one concern was to aid Hartmuot, and that is certainly what he did on that day.[3] The blows of bold Ludewic, Lord of the Normans, struck fire from the iron shield-bosses with all the bravery and strength in his valiant breast – and those beside him fought fiercely and well.

The brave defenders now began to suffer for having ignored the advice that Hetel's lovely wife, Queen Hilde, had given them. Many a shield became dull under a rain of blows, and many a man lost his life. By now, Ludewic and Hartmuot had closed in, bringing their forces together, and they observed that the defenders were trying to close the gates of Queen Hilde's fortress. Accordingly they mounted an attack behind a wall of shields, and broke through to plant their banners in the castle itself. They paid little heed – full of fighting spirit as they were – to the many arrows and missiles that rained down on them from the ramparts. Nor did they pay any attention to their dead, though many a warrior was struck down by one of the great stones.

Ludewic and Hartmuot entered the great gates, leaving many badly wounded men behind them. This caused Kudrun to weep bitter tears. But still greater damage was to be done to Hetel's fortress.

The King of the Normans was delighted when he and his men brought their standards into the very hall of King Hetel. They had their banners raised to fly from the battlements, and brought great sorrow to the noble queen.

We can only guess how things would have gone with the invaders if the ferocious warrior Wate had seen how Hartmuot's soldiers walked with Ludewic through these halls, and how they took the beautiful Kudrun prisoner. If word had been brought to them, Hetel and Wate would have put up such a defence and would have hacked through so many helmets with their good swords that Kudrun would never have been carried off, a captive to the land of the Normans.

The people in the castle were full of fear and sorrow, as they would be now if such a thing were to happen. Those soldiers who were bent on looting took, as may be imagined, a great deal of things from the castle. Hartmuot's men made themselves rich.

The valiant Hartmuot went straight to Kudrun and said: 'Noble lady, you have always treated me with scorn. Now I and my friends might very well treat with scorn any prisoners we take, and could slaughter or hang them all.'

Kudrun said nothing, except: 'Alas, my father! If you had known that your daughter would be taken by force from your lands, this shame and disaster would never have happened to the poor Princess of the Hegelings!'

When the invaders had taken treasures and rich garments, they led Queen Hilde by the hand out of the castle. They intended to burn down the great fortress of Matelane. What became of it was of no importance to the Normans. However, Hartmuot gave orders that the fortress should not be fired. He was very eager to get away from these lands before Hetel's vassals and kinsmen, whose forces were occupying the border-lands of Waleis, should hear what had happened.

'Enough of the plundering!' said Hartmuot. 'When we return home I shall reward you with treasure of my father's. That way we shall be less heavily laden for the sea-journey.' Ludewic's show of strength caused Kudrun great sadness.

The fortress had fallen and the surrounding town had been put to the torch, while the finest of all had been taken prisoner. Sixty-two of the women, all of them most lovely maidens, were abducted, to the great sorrow of the noble Hilde.

In what a sorrowing state did they leave behind them King Hetel's beloved wife! The queen ran to a window from which she could look down on the girls as they were taken away, and many other noble ladies were left to mourn in the land of the Hegelings. The weeping and wailing was loud, and there was nothing but sadness as Hilde's daughter and her retinue were taken away across country. This act was later to prove a cause of suffering for many a son of noble birth.

Hartmuot brought his prisoners to the seashore, and ordered that Hetel's lands there should be burned and laid waste. Things had gone well for him, as he had planned, and he took Kudrun and Hildeburc[4] away with him. He was well aware that Hetel was still campaigning in a far-off country.[5] He left the shores, but he had hardly sailed from the land of the Hegelings when Queen Hilde sent word of the events to Hetel and his allies.

In what great misery did she send word to the king that at home his warriors were lying dead, that Hartmuot had left them to die there in their own gore, and that his daughter had been taken prisoner, with a great number of noble maidens!

'Tell the king, my envoys, that I stand alone and that great misfortune has befallen me. The mighty Ludewic has made an arrogant attack on Hetel's lands, and left a thousand or more dead at our gates.'

Within three days, Hartmuot and his army were at sea again. His soldiers had taken in booty as much as they could carry with them, and Hetel's warriors had been completely defeated.

Who can say how they fared after this? A roaring and rushing wind filled their sails as they turned away from Hetel's shores and headed towards an uninhabited island. It was called the Wülpensand.[6]

Chapter 16
Hilde Sends Her Messengers to Hetel and to Herwic

The noble Queen Hilde devoted herself heart and mind to the question of how she could get her messengers to King Hetel. The great agony of mind that Hartmuot had inflicted upon her left her with nothing but tears. She told her envoys to report to her husband and to Herwic that her daughter had been abducted, that their warriors were dead, and that she had been left alone in her anguish. Her gold and jewels, too, had been carried off by the Normans.

The messengers rode swiftly, hurrying across country. Their queen had despatched them in great distress, and on the seventh day they came in great sorrow to the place where they found the Hegeling forces besieging the men from the land of the Moors. They were giving evidence daily of their prowess in combat, but you could also hear the sound of musical instruments from their camp, for they needed to while away the time during the siege. They also engaged in sports, with foot-races, jumping and frequent contests in throwing the spear.

Lord Horant of Denmark saw Queen Hilde's messengers arrive. 'They bring us news,' he said to the king. 'May God grant that no harm has befallen those at home.' King Hetel went to meet them as soon as he saw the distressed envoys, and he greeted them formally: 'Welcome, sirs, to this country. What is the news from my queen, Hilde? And tell us, who sent you to us?'

'My lady herself sent us,' replied the messenger. 'Your castles have been destroyed and your lands burned. Kudrun and her retinue have been abducted. I do not know how your country can ever recover from such great disaster.' And he went on: 'There is more to tell you, though I speak in great sorrow. More than a thousand of your allies and vassals lie dead. Your wealth has been carried off to foreign lands and the treasury has been despoiled. Brave warriors can feel nothing but shame for all this.'

The king asked for the names of those who had done all this, and one of the retainers answered him: 'One of them is called Ludewic of the Normans, and the other is named Hartmuot. Their warriors brought disaster upon us.'

'It is because I denied him my beautiful daughter,' said Lord Hetel. 'I knew very well that the Norman king held his lands in fief from Hagen, and that is why Kudrun is too nobly born to be a bride for Hartmuot. Our present enemies must not hear of this! A secret report of this misfortune must be made to our allies, and our friends and kinsmen must be summoned quickly. Our warriors at home could hardly have suffered a worse tragedy.'

Word was sent to Herwic that he should come to the king, with Hetel's allies, relatives and vassals. As soon as they arrived they saw that King Hetel was very troubled.

'I must reveal to you a great sorrow,' said the Lord of the Hegelings. 'Trusting in your loyalty to me, I shall tell you the cause of my distress. My queen, Hilde, has sent word to tell me that things have gone very badly indeed in the homeland of the Hegelings. My lands have been burned, my castles left in ruins. It seems that my country has not been guarded well by those we left behind. My daughter has been carried off, and my kinsmen, who were left at home in charge of my lands and honour, have been slaughtered!'

Herwic wept when he saw Hetel's eyes full of tears, and those who saw this wept with them. Those who were closest to the king were in a very sombre mood.

'We must let none of this become known,' said Wate the Old. 'We shall be able to make good the misfortune that has come upon our friends and relatives, and we shall rejoice later! Then Ludewic, Hartmuot and their kin will be sorry!'

'How can this be done?' asked Hetel.

'We must make peace with King Sifrit of the Moors and his followers,' replied Wate the Old, 'and then we can take those warriors with us in search of your lovely daughter Kudrun. Early tomorrow morning', continued Wate with his wise counsel, 'let us engage with the invaders from the land of the Moors in such a way that they realise that they are never going to bring their men out alive unless we permit it.'

'That is good advice,' said bold Herwic. 'Let us prepare ourselves, then, to deal tomorrow with the enemy in such a way that we can make that clear to them. I do not care how we get away from here. I am gravely concerned for Kudrun and her ladies.'

They prepared themselves for battle, with horses and armour, readily following the advice of Wate the Old. In the morning they launched a fierce attack on the men of Abakie, and won praise and renown in the fighting. The war-banners were carried into the thick of the fighting, and many a strong man was cut down. The men of Stormarn shouted 'Onwards!' and their opponents were drawn all the more quickly into the fray.

Irolt shouted out from behind his shield: 'Why not make your peace with us, you Moorish warriors! My lord, King Hetel, has commanded me to ask you. You are too far from your own country. You will lose both men and wealth!'

But King Sifrit of the Moors answered: 'If you win the victory, then you will be able to take valuable hostages. Meanwhile, I will treat with no-one, and have a care for my own honour! If you have it in mind to defeat us completely, then there will be greater losses yet on both sides!'

'Just give us your word that you will support us,' called out the warrior Fruote, 'and we shall let you leave my lord's lands, free of any further attack.'

The men of Karadie raised their hands in token of peace.

In this way, therefore, the two forces were reconciled. The warriors came together, happy at this outcome, and the erstwhile enemies now offered service to each other. Now that their quarrel was resolved, they planned a campaign against the Normans.

Only now did Hetel tell the King of the Moors of the sad news that the messengers had brought him. And then Hetel swore that if Sifrit helped him to punish Hartmuot for the shame he had brought him, then he would be Sifrit's faithful friend for the rest of his life.

'If we can catch them it will be their doom,' declared King Sifrit of Alzabey, and Wate the Old said: 'I know their sea-route. It is not far from here. We can easily catch them if we take to the water.'

'Where can I get ships?' Hetel asked the company. 'I want to attack, but how can it be done? If I were in my own lands I could make preparations to follow them to the Norman kingdom, and if I could meet them there I would have my revenge for the injury and insult they have caused me.'

'There may well be a way,' said Wate the Old. 'God provides help when needed![1] Not far from here I know of at least seventy good ships, ready and victualled, lying in harbour. They are pilgrim ships, and we shall have to take them somehow or other. The pilgrims will have to wait patiently on the shores until we are reconciled with or have fought our enemies.'

With this, the bold warrior Wate hurried off with a hundred of his men. The others followed. Wate asked the pilgrims if they had any food to sell, for he wished to buy it. Because of his act, many of his kinsmen were to die, and he himself was later to suffer misfortune.

There were about three thousand men on the beaches – that fact is certain – but they were unable to prepare themselves for a struggle quickly enough, and by this time the king and his great army had reached them. The pilgrims were quite unable to prevent their silver and gold being unloaded from the ships – Wate did not want it – and put on land. Wate gave orders that the food should be left on board, and said: 'We shall make the loss good to you when we are able to return.'

The pilgrims protested and cursed them – this was a great setback for them – but whatever they said about the situation, bold Wate did not care a jot. He told them with a grim face that they had no option but to give up to him their ships and galleys, and all the food.

Hetel, too, was not concerned whether the pilgrims would ever be able to set sail under the cross. He pressed from their number five hundred or more of the best men that he could find, and few of these came back to the land of the Hegelings alive. It is not known whether Hetel and his men were ever punished for the injuries done to these pilgrims, who were carried off to a strange country away from their companions. But surely God in His heaven took vengeance for the wrongs done to His faithful!

Hetel and his men had a favourable wind, and set sail as soon as they could. They set off in pursuit of their enemies, bent on taking revenge for the insult and the injuries wherever they caught up with them.

CHAPTER 17
The Pursuit of His Daughter
Brings Hetel to the Wülpensand

By now, King Ludewic and Lord Hartmuot, with their men, had made camp beside the sea on a deserted shore. Although their numbers were great, this did not help them. Ludewic's army of Normans had made camp for themselves and their horses on a broad island called the Wülpensand, but this respite was to lead to terrible disaster.

The noble captives from the land of the Hegelings had been taken out on to the barren sandstrip. The bearing of the lovely maidens was as noble as it could possibly be. They were very unhappy there amongst their captors.

Camp-fires had been lit all along that shore, and the warriors, far from home as they were, took their rest. They thought that they could stay there with the beautiful ladies for a week or more, but this was not to be. While Hartmuot and his kinsmen and warriors were at ease on this uninhabited mooring, they were deprived of any hope they had of staying there for seven days with the lovely maidens.

They had brought the beautiful Kudrun so far away from Matelane by now that Ludewic's men had no fears at all for their own safety, nor did they suspect that Wate and his allies might cause them any harm. But then one of the sailors noticed a ship with richly decorated sails bobbing on the waves, and he sent warning to the king. When Hartmuot and his men saw that the sails had crosses on them, they assumed that the ship belonged to pilgrims.

Almost at once they saw three fast ships and nine powerful galleys coming towards them, and these ships bore across the waves a great number of men who had never taken up the cross in God's name! The Normans would soon have to suffer. And then the ships were so close that helmets could be seen shining on board. Ludewic and his men were now in great peril. 'Up!' shouted Hartmuot. 'Our deadly enemies are upon us!'

The Hegelings hurried to reach the shore, and oars creaked in the hands of many strong men. Those who waited for them on the beach, experienced fighters and younger men, knew only that they had to jump up and prepare to fight.

Ludewic and Hartmuot grasped their shields. They had had easier passages back to their own country on other occasions, but this time their pause for rest on the way had undone them. They had imagined that their enemy Hetel had no allies left. Ludewic shouted out to all his men – everything that had gone before was just a game compared to this! – 'Now I really *shall* have fierce warriors to fight. I promise great rewards to those who dare stay beside me under my banner.'

Hartmuot's war-flag was brought forward on to the sands. The ships had come in so close to land that they were within range of a spear-throw from the shore. Lord Wate the Old certainly did not fail to use his shield!

Never was any territory so fiercely defended. The Hegelings forced their way towards the shore and fought grimly with spears and with swords. They paid each other in coin that no merchant would be inclined to accept![1]

Everyone crowded towards the thick of the battle. No alpine wind ever drove snow so thickly as the spears now flew from men's hands. Even if they had so desired, the battle could not now have been averted. Spear was thrust against spear, and it was a long time before the Hegelings could even fight their way to the shore. Wate the Old hurled himself fiercely upon the enemy, so close was he to their lines. He was in a grim fighting mood, and it was quite clear what his intentions were.

Ludewic the Norman threw himself against Wate and hurled a well-sharpened spear at his man, but the shattered pieces flew from Wate's shield into the winds. Ludewic was a brave warrior. Wate's supporters now closed in round him, and he brought his sword down on to Ludewic's helmet so that the blade's edge grazed Ludewic's head. But Ludewic had under his armour a tunic and hood of the best silk from Abalie, and but for this thin layer he would surely have been killed.[2]

Ludewic barely escaped from this with his life and he had to take flight. Wate was a less than welcome guest as he sought victory over his enemies. A great many brave warriors fell at his hands.

Hartmuot and Irolt ran at each other, and the weapon of each clashed against the helmet of the other so hard that the noise could be heard right across the battlefield. Irolt was a valiant fighter, but Lord Hartmuot, too, was a brave man.

The famous and bold warrior Herwic of Zeeland could not jump right on to the shore, so he leapt into the waters and stood breast-high in the waves. But brave Herwic was mindful of a noble woman's honour.

The enemies of this brave man wanted to drown him in the sea, and many well-aimed spears shattered against his shield. However, he quickly reached his enemies on the shore, and the wrongs done to many of his warriors were soon avenged.

By the time the Hegelings reached land, the sea all around was already running red with the blood of those who had been killed, red with blood further than a spear's throw out to sea. No warriors had ever had to face such a fierce battle, nor were so many warriors ever before thrown down than on this occasion. Those men alone who died by drowning[3] were enough to populate an entire country, and the men who brought death to them perished in their turn.

Hetel and his followers were fighting for his beloved daughter. Great wounds and injuries were dealt out on all sides by his own men and by those who had joined with him. Very many men fell that day on the Wülpensand.

The hands of the Normans and of the Hegelings did great violence in the battle. The Danes, too, fought valiantly, and no-one stood in their way for long if he wanted to remain alive! Ortwin and Morunc held their ground with such honour that there were few indeed who could have fought with fiercer spirit against the foe. These two warriors and their followers wounded their enemies severely.

It is said, too, that the proud Moors sprang from the ships on to the enemy. Hetel hoped that they would help him in his adversity. They were courageous fighters, and blood soon spurted through iron helmets.

Who could have been more valiant than their overlord, Sifrit? Because of him, many a shining mail-coat was stained with blood, and in the thick of battle he fought with consummate courage. And how could Wate the Old and Fruote of Denmark have fought any more boldly than they did?

Spears flew everywhere. Ortwin and his men, too, forced their way through the field of battle, and many a helmet was split that day by these men. Kudrun wept bitterly, and so did the other women. The fierce fighting lasted for the whole day, the two sides always eager to be at one another, and the noise of the battle was enormous. Brave warriors suffered great misfortune when Hetel's allies tried to help him rescue his daughter.

Night began to fall, and this was to bring even greater disasters for King Hetel. Ludewic's men fought on grimly, and besides, there was no place of retreat for them. They inflicted deep wounds on their enemies in the defence of their captive, the princess.

The battle lasted in all its horror from early morning until darkness made it impossible to fight on. All the warriors, the seasoned fighters and the younger men, fought to the utmost and acquitted themselves without shame. And then King Hetel forced a way to the King of the Normans.

CHAPTER 18
Ludewic Kills Hetel and Makes off under Cover of Night

Hetel and Ludewic faced each other with their sharp swords held high, and soon each of them learned the true strength of the other. But Ludewic killed Hetel. News of this caused heartbreak and sorrow.

The beautiful Kudrun quickly learned that the Lord of Matelane was dead. The lovely princess and all her ladies bewailed the fact, and could not be comforted.[1] Men on both sides were saddened by his fall.

Then the fierce warrior Wate heard of the king's death, and he let out a mighty roar, and helmets became as blood-red as the setting sun from the force of his swift blows. He and all his men fought grimly in their anger. But whatever these bold warriors accomplished, now it was of no avail. The sands were soaked with warm blood, but the Hegelings wanted no truce; their aim was to rescue Kudrun there on the Wülpensand. The men of Waleis took vengeance for the death of the king in their fierce onslaughts, and the men of Denmark battled beside the Hegelings and the men of Northland in their distress. These valiant warriors fought on until the weapons broke in their hands. Brave Ortwin wanted to avenge his father. At that point Horant moved in, too, with a large body of his men. But the day was over, and night had begun to fall when the warriors began to inflict deep wounds in deadly earnest.

One of the Danes leapt upon Horant, and his sword rang out loudly in his hand. He had taken him for one of the enemy, and Horant was quick to retaliate, causing the other great suffering, and giving him a mortal wound. Having struck down one of his kinsmen in this way, Horant at once ordered the man's war-banner to be carried as a trophy with his own, but then he recognised the voice of the man he had laid low in his eagerness for battle, and he bewailed the death of this man very bitterly.

Herwic shouted out: 'This is murderous. Without light we are killing one another, friend and foe alike. If the battle goes on until morning, not one man in three will be left alive.'

It was foolish for anyone to stand in the way of the brave warrior Wate in the thick of battle. His wild fury could be withstood by no man, and he sent many men to the place from which there is no return.

Nevertheless, they had good grounds for halting the battle until daybreak. Men on both sides lay with terrible wounds given to them by their enemies. There was no moon, and the daylight had gone. It was because of this that the Hegelings lost the victory. With some reluctance the fierce warriors withdrew from battle and moved apart, weary in every limb. However, the two sides remained close enough to see the glint from each other's helmets and shields by the light of the campfires.

Ludewic and Hartmuot the Normans held a council of war. The king asked his followers why he should stay here, near such a bold warrior as Wate, who was intent upon killing him.

Cunningly he told his men: 'Go back and sleep for a time with your heads on your shields. Then make a great amount of noise, so that the Hegelings do not realise that I am trying, if I possibly can, to get you all away from here.'[2]

Ludewic's kinsmen and followers did as he said. They sounded horns and trumpets, just as if they had taken the whole land by force of arms. All this was part of Ludewic's crafty deceit. There was great tumult of shouting and wailing, but the captive girls were forbidden to cry out. They were told that if any of them refused to keep silent, she would be drowned – any that made a noise would be thrown into the sea.

They then carried to the ships everything that they could gather together in the way of belongings. They abandoned their dead, those who had fallen in the battle. To their great sorrow, many of their friends were no longer with them, and because of this many of the ships were left behind, empty.

With this trickery, then, the Normans took to the sea. It was a great hardship for the women to have to keep silent and conceal this flight from their relatives. The Hegeling warriors knew nothing of what was going on as they rested there on the Wülpensand.

The very men that the Danes expected to fight were off and away before daybreak. Wate had his great battle-horn sounded, and wanted to set off quickly in pursuit of the enemy, eager to cut them down with severe wounds. The Hegeling warriors, mounted and on foot, sank into the sand as they pursued the Normans. But Ludewic and the men with whom they wished to fight had already sailed some distance away.

The Hegelings found the ships empty, with all their gear and many unclaimed weapons scattered about, lying on the Wülpensand. They had slept too long to be able to reach the enemy now. When this was reported to Wate it caused him great distress. He bewailed most bitterly the death of King Hetel, and the fact that he had not been able to avenge this deed on the person of Ludewic. But many helmets had been split, and many a lady at home would have cause to mourn.

With what bitterness and with what inner anger did Ortwin bewail the loss of his brave fighters! 'On, on, my warriors!' he said. 'Perhaps we can still catch them before they reach the open sea! They are still close to the shore.'

Wate the Old was keen to follow, but Fruote tested the wind. 'Hurrying will be no use,' he said to the company. 'Mark my words, they will be thirty miles off by now. In any case, we have not enough men for the task, and if we did give chase we would not be able to harm them. Believe me,' he went on, 'there is no point in discussing it. You will never catch them now. Instead, have the wounded brought to our ships, and gather our dead together and let them be buried on this deserted shore. All their friends are here – why should they not be given this last service?'

They stood with empty gestures of despair. It would have been enough to have suffered just one of the misfortunes – that of losing the young princess – but what news did they now have to take home to Queen Hilde!

'If only we had to bear all these heartaches and sorrows alone,' said Lord Morunc. 'But we shall be unwelcome messengers indeed when we bring the news to Queen Hilde that Hetel lies dead. I would sooner ride away than go to her.'

They searched the beach and gathered the dead together. Wate, Lord of Stormarn, gave orders that those who were Christians should be brought to one place, however they had been found. There was a discussion with the younger warriors as to where these dead should lie. Lord Ortwin said: 'We should take care to bury them in such a way that they have a memorial: a grand monastery shall be built as a memorial for them, and the kinsmen of each one shall contribute to it a part of his wealth.'

'That is well advised,' replied the Lord of Stormarn. 'And the horses and trappings of those who lie dead here must be sold and the profits given to the poor, so that they can have their share in these men's wealth after their deaths.'

Lord Irolt added: 'Should we also give burial to the men who fought against us, or should they be left as food for the ravens and wild wolves on this sandy island?' The wise warriors advised that no-one should be left there unburied.

Now that they had time to do so after all their tribulations, they buried the king, who had met his death on those sands for the love of his family and friends. All the dead, no matter who they were, received the same treatment.

The Moorish dead were buried individually, as were the Hegeling warriors. So, too, the Normans were given their places and buried separately. There were both Christians and pagans amongst the dead.

The work occupied them for six days, and they did not spare themselves for a moment. They had no time yet to think how the Hegelings might win their way back to God's grace after the great guilt that they had incurred.[3]

So many masses were said and requiems sung that never anywhere had so much service been offered to God in the presence of men killed in battle. They left many priests behind on the Wülpensand with the dead. Some warriors, too, had to remain behind to guard them. Charters were drawn up granting them three hundred hides of land.[4] These men became Hospitallers,[5] and the story became known far and wide of how the monastery had been founded. All those whose kinsmen had fallen here, men and women alike, sent their tributes for the benefit of the souls of those who lay buried there. Later on it grew to be a very rich monastery, with the income from three hundred farms.

May the Lord have mercy on those who lie there, and on those who watch over that place. Those who had survived on the Wülpensand now set sail, and after these great disasters returned safely to their own country.

CHAPTER 19
The Hegelings Return Home

Hetel's men had left so many of their number lying dead that brave warriors never had to return to their home in such great sorrow; and when they did return, lovely women wept and had to wring their hands in sadness.

Ortwin, the Lord of Northland, did not dare for pain and shame to face his dear mother, the beautiful Hilde, who was waiting every day to see if they would bring back the Lady Kudrun.

Wate rode fearfully into Hilde's lands. The others did not dare to do so. His own strength and prowess in arms had been a poor defence in the grim battle, and he was sure that it would be a long time before he regained the favour of Queen Hilde.

When it was reported that Wate had returned, many of those waiting at once despaired. They knew that whenever Wate rode home from the wars, he did so with a great clamour. He had always done so. But now everyone was silent.

'Alas,' said Queen Hilde, 'what has happened? The shields borne by the followers of Wate the Old are dull, and the pack-mules are making their way along painfully slowly, so heavily are they burdened.[1] Their very bearing speaks of some disaster. I should like to know where King Hetel is.'

Almost as soon as she had spoken, people began to run towards Wate, wanting to question him about their own dear ones. He told them the news, and it filled them with sorrow.

Wate of Stormarn spoke: 'I cannot conceal things from you, nor can I lie. They are dead.' This was a shock to them all, the old and the young. No unhappier a group could ever be imagined.

'Oh my sorrow, my sorrow,' said King Hetel's wife. 'My own lord, the mighty Hetel taken from me! All my glory is gone! I have lost them both. I shall never see Kudrun again.'

Warriors and ladies alike beat their breasts and tore their hair in anguish and in pain. The great hall echoed with the lamentation of the king's wife for her dead husband. 'I am lost,' said Queen Hilde, 'if Prince Hartmuot goes unpunished.'

However, the brave warrior Wate said to her: 'My lady, you should weep no longer – the dead will not come back. Later, when the youngsters of this land have grown to manhood, then we shall exact vengeance from Ludewic and Hartmuot.'

'May I live only to see that day!' replied the weeping queen. 'I would give all that I have, poor wretched woman that I am, to be avenged and to see my daughter Kudrun again.'

'Weep no longer, lady,' said Wate to Hilde. 'In the next twelve days, let us send messengers to all your military allies, as many as we can muster, and discuss a plan of attack that can strike hard at the Normans.

'This, my Lady Hilde,' he went on, 'is what happened. I took nine ships from a band of pilgrims. Those poor men must be given recompense, so that if we fight again, things may go better for us.'

'It is my will that their loss be made good,' replied the sorrowing queen. 'To rob a pilgrim is a sin of great gravity. Let each of the pilgrims be given three marks of silver from my treasury for every one mark that they lost.'

They restored their ships to them as the lady had ordered. Before any of the pilgrims left that shore they were so well recompensed that they complained no more of anyone, and they had no cause to reproach Hilde, the daughter of King Hagen.

The next day bold Herwic, King of Zeeland, came to Queen Hilde as she mourned bitterly the death of her husband. Although she was in such distress, she welcomed the warrior in courteous fashion. Finding the queen in tears, Herwic, too, began to weep, and the young man said: 'Not all of the men who are able and willing to help you have been killed – as many of the enemy found to their cost! However, I shall never be at ease in mind or body until Hartmuot is made to suffer for daring to take away my bride and to kill our warriors. I will come so close to him that I shall take him in his own castle!'

Although they were very sad indeed to do so, the allies rode to Matelane. The queen asked that those who wished to remain loyal to her should not stay away, whatever had happened to them.

The Frisians came, and so did the men of Stormarn. She summoned the Danes, too, and Morunc's warriors came from Waleis. Then the Hegelings who received them rode with them to the castle of the beautiful queen.

Then came her son, Ortwin of Northland, and they mourned together, as was fitting, for the death of his beloved father. The warriors held a private council with their queen, and the decision that these brave warriors reached was to make war.

'This cannot be', said Fruote the Dane, 'until the city is full of men again, so that we can raise an army and ride out, whatever the enemy may do in the meantime.'[2]

'When will that be?' asked the queen. 'If my dear daughter has to remain in the hands of the enemy for so long, captive in a foreign land, then all happiness is taken from me as I wait on my lonely throne.'

'It can only come about', replied Wate the Old, 'when the many noble orphans, who are children now, grow up and reach an age at which they can bear arms. They will remember their fallen kinsmen, and they will be glad to help us on this mission of war.'

'May God grant that I live to see that day,' answered the queen. 'For me, unhappy woman that I am, the time of waiting is a long one. Anyone who has me and my poor Kudrun in their thoughts cannot but pity me, I am sure.'

The warriors sought leave to depart. 'May good fortune go with those who have me in their hearts,' said the noble queen. 'You will be welcome, my valiant warriors, at my court; and in the meantime, prepare for our campaign of war as best you can.'

Then Wate, the brave and wise old warrior, said: 'We should turn our attention to the forests of the West.[3] Since we are making plans for war, you must give orders that each country should provide you with forty galleys.'

'I shall have twenty strong ships, sound and good, made and berthed by the shore,' she replied, 'and I shall have them equipped, as I am sure will be possible, so that they will carry my friends easily to fight our enemies.'

And so they took their leave. The Lord of the Moors came and addressed himself courteously to the queen. 'Inform me', he said, 'when the ships are about to sail, and I shall not need to be asked twice before I join you.'

She gave them leave to depart in friendship. Her brave guests and the beautiful ladies all mourned her misfortunes. They talked continually of their plans – plans that were not even imagined in the Kingdom of the Normans.

When they had all left, to return with heavy hearts to their own lands, Queen Hilde in her great wisdom ordered provision to be made for those who said masses for the dead on the Wülpensand, so that they might remember her in their prayers. In addition, she ordered the building of a great church, and she had monastery buildings and hospices built as well. The church became famous in later years in many countries, on account of the dead who lay there, and came to be called the Minster of the Wülpensand.[4]

CHAPTER 20
Hartmuot Returns Home

Let us turn from Queen Hilde now, and from the work of the chantry-priests on the Wülpensand, and hear instead about Hartmuot, and how he brought all the high-born and noble maidens back to his own country.

When the Normans sailed, they left behind them, as we have already heard, many warriors who were mortally wounded in the battle. Their orphaned children would later have cause to weep for them without ceasing, when the news reached their land.

The Normans crossed the seas in some distress. Throughout the journey many good warriors, both young and old, felt constantly a great shame at having run away, even though things had gone well for them otherwise.

They approached King Ludewic's land, the kingdom of the Normans, which was soon recognised by the bold sailors. In the midst of their distress they sighted their homeland, and they said to one another: 'Those are Hartmuot's towers! We are not far from home!' Favourable winds now helped them towards the country of their prince. The Normans were delighted that they would see their wives and children again, because they had thought that their fate would be to lie dead on the battlefield.

When King Ludewic[1] saw his fortresses, the Norman lord said to Kudrun: 'Do you see those towers, my lady? You should be happy, too! If you behave graciously towards us, then we shall reward you with rich lands to rule over.'

But the noble princess replied sadly: 'To whom should I behave graciously? I have been taken ungraciously from my own happiness, very far away indeed, I fear.[2] This is a constant sorrow for me.'

'Do not be sad,' replied Ludewic. 'Love Hartmuot – he is a fine warrior. We are offering you all our lands and properties, and you would enjoy honour and delight with the worthy prince.'

'Why can you not leave me alone?' answered Hilde's daughter. 'I would rather be dead than take Hartmuot. Even if his father's family were of high enough standing for him even to pay court to me, I would give up my life before I took him as my love.'

These words made King Ludewic very angry, and he seized Kudrun by her long hair and hurled her into the sea. But the brave Hartmuot acted very quickly to save the noble princess from the wild waves. She was just about to go under when Lord Hartmuot reached her, and she would have drowned had not the bold prince grasped her golden braids with both hands and pulled her to him. There was no other way in which he could have prevented her from drowning.

Hartmuot managed to get her on to a ship. Ludewic's behaviour towards the fair sex could be less than gentle! After she had been rescued from the waves, Kudrun had to sit there in her shift. Treatment like this was quite new to her! And how sorry for herself she felt! Every one of the lovely captives began to weep – none of them could feel anything but sadness. If a king's daughter can receive this kind of punishment, they thought, we could not be in a worse situation. 'We shall be made to suffer even more,' they said to themselves.

'Why did you try and drown my bride, the beautiful Kudrun?' exclaimed Prince Hartmuot. 'She means more to me than my very life. If any man other than my father Ludewic had done this I would in my anger have taken his life and his honour!'

'I have lived a long time without suffering insult,' replied Ludewic, 'and I should like to live on in honour to the end of my days. And so you must ask Kudrun not to vent her scorn upon me.'

Advance messengers had reached the kingdom of the Normans in good spirits. They offered Queen Gerlint the loving and willing service of her son, Hartmuot, and asked her to prepare a welcome in her lands for a great number of noble warriors. Hartmuot had instructed them to say, too, that the Princess of the Hegelings was being brought with them across the sea, the lady for whom Hartmuot had longed so fervently, even before he had set eyes on her. When Gerlint heard this news it was more pleasing than any news had ever been. 'My lady,' went on the messenger, exulting in his news, 'you are asked to receive the princess outside the castle with affection, although she is very unhappy. You and your daughter are to ride together down to the shore, taking with you a retinue of ladies and unmarried girls, as well as the finest warriors, to where she will be waiting at the harbour, our guest in a strange land.[3] You are to welcome her, and her ladies-in-waiting, with words of love.'

'I shall be glad to do so,' replied Queen Gerlint. 'It will give me great pleasure to see Hetel's daughter and her retinue here in our country. Indeed, may I often have such occasion to see her happy with Hartmuot.'

Orders were given for horses to be saddled in readiness. The young princess, Ortrun,[4] was very happy and excited since she was at last to meet Kudrun, whose praises she had so often heard sung in her father's country.

They searched the royal wardrobes until they found the finest garments there – the finest that could be found anywhere. Orders were issued that Hartmuot's men-at-arms should be well turned-out, and the king's household rode out of the castle in finery and splendour. Three days later the men and women that Gerlint and Ortrun had called together as their retinue were also ready for the joyful reception. Now they did not linger at court any more, but rode together out of the fortress.

By this time, the guests they had come to welcome had arrived in the harbour. Their belongings had all been taken ashore, and the Normans were glad to be back in their own country. Only Kudrun and her ladies were unhappy as they left the ships.

The noble Hartmuot led her by the hand, something which she would gladly have avoided, had this been possible. The poor girl allowed him to do so merely out of politeness, although he for his part was delighted to serve her in this way, and in any way he could. The ladies-in-waiting, sixty of them, followed behind her, bearing themselves just as if they had left their own country with all the proper dignities. On earlier occasions, indeed, they had been received with honour in other lands, but now they felt only sorrow and no joy at all.

Hartmuot's sister, escorted by two princes,[5] came to offer a formal welcome to Queen Hilde's daughter. The Norman princess kissed the captive maiden, who stood there with tears in her eyes, and she took Kudrun's white hands in her own.

Next, Ludewic's queen made to embrace her, but Kudrun would

not accept this kiss. 'Keep away from me,' she said to Gerlint. 'I shall exchange no kiss with you, nor need you offer me any greeting. It was at your instigation that I, poor wretch that I am, have had to suffer great hardships, heartaches and shame, with more sorrows to come.' The queen, however, made every effort to win Kudrun's favour.

Gerlint welcomed the other ladies, one by one. A very large and noisy crowd of people now came up, and orders were given for tents with silken ropes to be erected there on the shores for Hartmuot and his men. The people worked busily until everything had been unloaded from the ships. It hurt Kudrun very much to see her ladies-in-waiting surrounded by Normans, and she herself was well disposed only towards Ortrun.

They had to remain for the whole day on the shore. Kudrun's eyes were constantly filled with tears. In spite of everyone's efforts, her eyes and cheeks were never dry. Hartmuot made many attempts to comfort her, but her pain was to last for a long time to come.

Ortrun, who recognised Kudrun's steadfast and noble bearing, was completely free of any malice towards her. In spite of the others, she enjoyed being with her, and did what she could to make it more pleasant for her to be in her father's lands. The poor princess mourned for the friends she missed so much.

When the Norman warriors and their squires showed them the things they had brought back from the land of the Hegelings, the people to whom they had now returned were, of course, delighted, and gave the warriors a warm welcome. They had not expected to see them again in their homeland!

Once they had rested after their journey across the wild sea, Hartmuot's men, though pressed to stay by the local people, now dispersed throughout the land, some in a cheerful, others in a very unhappy frame of mind.[6] Lord Hartmuot also left the encampment on the shore[7] and brought Kudrun to a fine castle – a place where she was to stay longer than she would have wished, and where she was to undergo much fear and discomfort.

When the noble princess – whom they thought to crown queen there – was installed in the castle, Hartmuot gave orders that everyone should serve her diligently, and they all complied. She was offered rich gifts. The old queen, however, Ludewic's wife Gerlint, wanted to know: 'When will Kudrun take the mighty Prince Hartmuot in her arms? He is her equal in rank. It would hardly hurt her to do so!'

Kudrun, a maiden held prisoner in a strange land, heard this. 'My Lady Gerlint,' she said, 'you would not like to be forced into the arms of a man who had caused the loss of so many of your kinsmen. Could *you* love such a man?'

'If a thing cannot be changed, then it has to be faced,' replied the queen. 'Embrace Hartmuot! I swear that I shall never cease to reward you for doing so. And if you wish for the title of queen, then I shall gladly relinquish my own crown!'

'I shall never wear that crown!' replied the unhappy princess. 'However much you might tell me about his wealth and power I shall never love that warrior. I am here against my will, and every day I think only of escape.'

Young Lord Hartmuot did not like these words and became angry. 'If I am unable to win the noble lady over,' he said, 'then, beautiful as she is, she will not be able to count on my goodwill.'

Queen Gerlint[8] said to Hartmuot: 'It is the duty of the wise to bring foolish children to their senses. Lord Hartmuot, if you will let me teach her manners, then I think I can see to it that her haughtiness is moderated a little.'

'I am quite willing', answered Hartmuot, 'for you to take the good princess under your tutelage, according to her honour and yours, too, regardless of how things turn out for me. Nevertheless, the girl is away from her own country. Teach her with kindness.'

Before he left, the prince thus gave the beautiful Kudrun into the charge of his mother, so that she could teach her. This pleased the young princess very little indeed! Whatever Gerlint did, Kudrun was not inclined to follow *her* instruction. And so the devil-queen said to the lovely girl: 'If you reject pleasure, then you must have pain. Look around – who is there that you can turn to? You will have to tend the fireplace and light the fire in my chambers.'

'I am quite able to do that,' replied the noble princess, 'and any other tasks you might set me, until God in heaven puts an end to my suffering, even though I, the daughter of a queen, have never been used to making and tending the fire.'

'On my life,' replied Gerlint, 'you are going to have to do things that no other princess has ever done. I am sure that I can break down your arrogance! You shall see the last of your maidens-in-waiting, too, before tomorrow is out! I gather that you consider yourself to be of the very highest rank, and it is because of that that your sufferings will be all the greater. I am certain that I can break your grim-faced haughtiness. I shall wear you down until you have given up every scrap of hope.'

Wicked Gerlint returned angrily to court, and said to Hartmuot: 'Hetel's daughter holds you and your friends in scorn. Rather than listen to that I would sooner never have set eyes on her!'

'Regardless of how the maiden behaves,' replied Lord Hartmuot to his mother, 'you must, my lady, treat her with kindness, so that I shall have cause to thank you. I have brought her a great deal of suffering, and she may well be reluctant to accept my service.'

The queen, however, answered: 'Whatever anyone does, still she refuses to do as she is told. She is so stubborn that unless someone manages to break her will she can never become your wife in proper fashion. And that is what we shall have to do, rather than leave her as she is.'

The Prince of the Normans, however, who was a noble lord, replied: 'My lady, show respect for my wishes, and instruct her in such a way that she will not reject my friendship altogether!'

The wicked devil of a queen stormed away to find the Hegeling maidens. 'You girls', she said, 'are going to be put to work! Whatever I command you to do must be carried out without fail.'

With that, the girls were separated and did not see one another for a long time. Maidens who had been noblewomen of the highest rank now had to wind yarn, and they were very unhappy indeed. However noble their families were, some of them were now reduced to spinning and combing the flax. Those who could embroider with gold and silk, and could sew on precious stones, now had to endure a great amount of hard work.

One of them, who should have been the highest lady at court, was ordered especially to make sure that the maidens took water to Ortrun's rooms. Her name was Heregart. None of them profited from the fact that they were nobly born.

Another lady was from Galicia, and misfortune had carried her away from her native Portugal. She had come from Ireland to the land of the Hegelings with Hilde herself, and was now amongst the women taken prisoner by the Normans.[9] She was the daughter of a prince who owned lands and castles, but now she had to light the stove with her own fair hands, when Gerlint's women went into their quarters – and they did not even thank her for carrying out this service.

The tale of their miseries is an astonishing one. Even if the least important of Gerlint's women told them to do something, they had to carry out her orders, no matter how mean the work. Their noble families were of little use to them there in the kingdom of the Normans.

The women were all treated badly by Gerlint during their time of captivity – except the one called Lady Heregart, who fell in love with the king's chamberlain and who wanted to become a powerful countess. This made the daughter of the beautiful Queen Hilde very

89

unhappy indeed – and it was to prove disastrous for the lady herself, later on, that she would not share in the discomforts suffered by the others. By then, however, Kudrun did not care about Heregart's fate.[10]

For three-and-a-half years, we are told, the Hegeling ladies had to perform the most menial tasks, until Lord Hartmuot came home again after fighting three campaigns. Throughout those years the captives had had to act as servants.

Hartmuot asked that his beloved Kudrun should be brought to him. It was clear from her appearance that the noble lady had been deprived of proper food and lodgings. She had been made to pay for her steadfastness and her virtue.

When she came before him, the young prince asked: 'Kudrun, most beautiful of all ladies, how have you fared whilst I and my warriors have been away?' 'I have had to be a servant,' she replied, 'to your shame and degradation!'

'Gerlint, my dear mother, why have you done this?' asked Hartmuot when he heard these words. 'I left her in your care, in the expectation that your grace and kindness towards her would ease the great sorrows she has had to bear in this country.'

But Gerlint the she-wolf replied: 'How else was I to teach Hetel's daughter a lesson? Let me tell you that however much I begged and entreated, I could never bring her to do anything but pour scorn on you, your father, and all our kin.'

'That is because of her pitiful situation,' countered Hartmuot. 'We killed so many warriors amongst her kin, and deprived the noble Kudrun of a father, when my father killed hers. The slightest provocation might easily wound her.'

Nevertheless his mother replied: 'My son, I can assure you that if we begged Kudrun for thirty years, or if we used the birch or the whip on her, we should never induce her to become your wife. Force will not bring her to agree.[11] Nevertheless, I shall treat her better in future,' went on Gerlint to Hartmuot. The bold warrior was not to know that she treated her worse than before in every respect, and no-one could prevent her doing this to the poor girl.

Gerlint went to where Kudrun of the Hegelings was sitting and said: 'If you do not change your mind, my fine lady, you will have to dust the benches and the chairs with your long hair. You will have to clean out my rooms three times every day, I tell you, and light the fire for me.' 'I shall do all those things,' replied Kudrun, 'rather than give my love to anyone but my betrothed.'

Without complaint, the noble maiden carried out all the tasks that were given her, and she neglected nothing. For seven full years she suffered these tribulations, a captive in a foreign land, with treatment that ill suited a princess.

Towards the beginning of the ninth year, Hartmuot, who was a wise lord, began to think that it was shameful to himself and to his allies if he did not assume the crown, since he was lord over a king's lands. He and his men rode back from a campaign in which his prowess at arms had won him great esteem. He thought that he would now become betrothed to the beautiful Kudrun, whom he desired more than any other woman.[12]

He came in, and took his seat, and ordered that she be brought to him. The wicked Gerlint did not permit her to wear anything but the poorest of clothing. However the warrior behaved, though, Kudrun still scorned everything he said, so steadfast was her sense of honour and loyalty.

At this, his friends advised him that he should try to persuade the beautiful girl to agree to his wishes by any means he could find, whether his mother liked it or not, for if he did, he would be able to enjoy many happy hours with the maiden. On this advice from his closest friends, he sought Kudrun out in her room, took her by the hand and said: 'Most fine and noble lady, love me and be my queen! My brave warriors will be yours to command.'

'I can never bring myself to do that,' replied the lovely girl, 'because wicked Gerlint has treated me so badly that I desire no warrior's love. With all my being I hate you and all your kin!'

'That troubles me greatly,' said Hartmuot. 'If it is within my power I will endeavour to make good the wrongs done to you by Gerlint, my mother, and this service will be to the honour of us both.' But the princess replied: 'I can never believe any of your assurances again.'

'You well know, Kudrun,' said Hartmuot, the Prince of the Normans, 'that this land, its castles and its people are all subject to me. No-one would send me to the gallows if I simply took you as my bedfellow.'

'I should call that a very great crime,' replied Hetel's daughter. 'I have never thought that you would do such a thing. Other princes, too, might have something to say if they heard that one of King Hagen's family had been taken as a concubine in Hartmuot's kingdom.'

'It is of no importance to me what they say or what they do,' answered Hartmuot. 'Nevertheless, you have only to accept willingly, and I could be king and you my queen.' 'Be assured that I shall never love you,' was her reply. 'You know full well, my lord Hartmuot, how things stand, and how your force of arms hurt me when you abducted me and took me prisoner, and of the harm your men

91

inflicted on my father's warriors. You also know very well – and it is the greatest sorrow that I have to bear – that Ludewic, your father, killed my father. If I were a warrior, he would never dare to come near me unarmed. Why should I ever consent to share your bed? It has long been the custom that no woman need accept a husband unless the match is desired by both parties. That was an honourable practice.'[13] The beautiful Kudrun still mourned greatly for her father.

'I no longer care how people treat you,' replied the warrior Hartmuot angrily, 'since you are not prepared to wear the crown by my side. You will get what you deserve, and you will be rewarded daily for your behaviour.'

'I will earn my keep as I have done up till now. Whatever work I must do for Hartmuot's vassals and Gerlint's women I shall carry out without complaint, since God has forgotten me. But I have many sorrows to bear.'

Still, they[14] wished to try a kinder approach nevertheless, and so Hartmuot summoned to the court the lovely and noble lady Ortrun. He asked her if she and her ladies-in-waiting could, by kindness, change poor Kudrun's mind. Lord Hartmuot said to her quite openly: 'I shall reward you richly, sister, if you can help me make the noble Kudrun forget her great sorrows and cease to mourn so bitterly.'

'I and my ladies will serve her', replied Princess Ortrun of the Normans, 'in such a way that she will forget her sadness. I and my maidens will bow to her wishes, and will serve her as if we were her vassals.'

Noble Kudrun thanked her. 'I cannot but praise you', she said, 'for your honest desire to see me crowned at the side of King Hartmuot, living with him in honour. But still it cannot be, since my very position as a captive in this land is a constant source of distress for me.'

CHAPTER 21
Kudrun Is Forced to Become a Washerwoman

Kudrun was offered lands and castles, but when she refused them, she was made to wash clothes every day from dawn to dusk. And it was because of this that Ludewic lost the battle that he was later to fight against Herwic.[1]

The noble maiden Kudrun was invited to rise and go with Ortrun, to take her ease and drink good wine. But the captive princess said: 'I will not be a queen in this country. You know very well, my lord Hartmuot, that whatever your wishes might be, I am betrothed to a king, bound by solemn oaths to become his lawful wife. While that man lives, I can share no other warrior's bed.'

'All your longing for him will not help you,' replied Prince Hartmuot, 'and nothing can separate us except death. Be friends with my lady Ortrun, and she will make you feel better, I am sure of that.'

Hartmuot was convinced that her obdurate constancy would be weakened if his sister shared with her all that she had. Indeed, they both thought that they might win her round.

Kudrun welcomed those who now offered to serve her. Ortrun sat beside her, the food and drink that they now gave her – there was plenty of it – brought colour back to her cheeks. But poor Kudrun was not sure how to respond to this treatment.[2] When Prince Hartmuot offered her politeness and courtesy, she did not respond. She thought all the time of the suffering that she and her ladies had undergone in this country of exile, and she took vengeance for that hurt with short and harsh words to Hartmuot.

She kept this up for so long that the prince became angry and said: 'My lady Kudrun, surely I am the equal of Prince Herwic, whom you took as your love, in spite of the great honour I offer you? You scold me too often and too harshly. Please do not. It would be by far the best for both of us. It hurts me greatly when someone makes you suffer, or when your heart and mind are troubled. However much you have hated me in the past, I still want to make you my queen.' And with that, Hartmuot left and went to join his men, giving them instructions to keep his lands and honour in their charge. He began to think to himself: 'I am hated so much, that I may suffer harm in the future.'[3]

The wicked queen Gerlint ordered Kudrun to be her servant, and hardly ever gave her a chance to rest, so that someone who by rights

93

should have been found amongst the children of kings was found instead amongst the lowliest. The old she-wolf said to her maliciously: 'I propose to have Hetel's daughter as my maid-servant, and because she is determined to carry on being so stubborn, she will have to work for me as she has never worked before.'

'I am prepared to work day and night, willingly and assiduously at all times, in whatever way I can do you service,' replied the noble maiden, 'since it is my fate to be separated from my friends and family.'

'Every day', said the wicked queen Gerlint, 'you shall carry my clothes down to the shore, and you shall wash for me and for my household – and take care not to be caught idle at any time!'

'Most mighty queen,' replied the noble maiden, 'arrange to have me taught how to wash your clothes. I am not fated to be happy, and I should not care if you treated me even worse than that. If I am to be a washerwoman, however, let them show me how to do it. I do not consider myself too high and mighty to learn such a skill. If I have to earn my keep in this way, then I shall not refuse.' Kudrun's response was a wise one.

Orders were given to a washerwoman to carry the clothes with her down to the seashore and to teach her what to do. Only now did Kudrun, in bitter sorrow, really begin her service. Gerlint tormented Princess Kudrun, and there was no-one to defend her.

They taught her within sight of Ludewic's walls, and she worked for his warriors so well, that no-one in the entire kingdom of the Normans could wash clothes better. Things had never seemed so bleak to her ladies-in-waiting as when they saw her working on the shore.

One of their number was also a princess, daughter of a king.[4] However much they all wept, their complaints went unheard. The indignity of seeing their royal lady washing clothes in such wretchedness touched them all. Hildeburc, Kudrun's loyal friend, said to them: 'Those of us who came with Kudrun to this country have good cause to be sad – and may our complaints rise up to God above! The rest of us can hardly expect to be treated well when our mistress herself is washing clothes on the seashore.'

Gerlint heard this, and said evilly: 'If you do not want your mistress to do this work, then you may take over all her tasks yourself.' 'If I am permitted to do so,' replied Lady Hildeburc, 'I should gladly do it for her. In the name of almighty God, Queen Gerlint, you ought not to let her do this work alone. She is a princess. My father, too, wore a crown, but I will work at her side. Let me wash with her, for good or ill. Although my own sorrows are great, she has all my pity on account of the high position that God granted her. Her forefathers were all mighty kings. This work is not for her, but I am prepared to share it with her.'

With that, the wicked queen Gerlint replied: 'You will have to suffer a great deal. However harsh the winter's cold, you will have to go out in the snow and wash clothes in the icy winds, no matter how much you might long to be in a warm room.'

Hildeburc could hardly wait until nightfall, for now some small comfort could be offered to Kudrun. Lady Hildeburc went to the princess's room and both wept bitterly over their servitude. With tears in her eyes Hildeburc said: 'Your great distress so touched my heart that I begged the she-devil not to let you wash clothes on the seashore alone. I will share the burden with you.'

'May God reward you for your concern over my misfortune,' replied the poor exile Kudrun. 'If you will wash clothes by my side, that will bring some comfort to us both, and will help the time pass. We shall be far happier.'

Although Hildeburc was permitted to go down to the sands with Kudrun, helping her to carry the clothes for washing, any joy they had soon gave way to sorrow. No matter how much work the others had to do, these two had more and more washing to do together.

In every free moment that they had, Kudrun's ladies wept bitterly to see these two, washing clothes on the seashore. They looked on with anguish, even though they, too, had to suffer under a harsher yoke than anyone in the world has ever known.

Kudrun and Hildeburc were forced to wash clothes and make them white for Hartmuot's warriors, for a full five-and-a-half years. No women had ever suffered more greatly, as they stood there in their pitiful state outside the castle walls.

CHAPTER 22
Hilde's Campaign to Rescue Her Daughter

Let us leave for the time being the tale of their servitude. Queen Hilde never let out of her mind for a moment the thought of how she might rescue her beloved daughter from the land of the Normans. She had already ordered the construction of seven strong warships at her sea-port, firm and well built, and also twenty-two new and powerful supply-ships, well provided with all the equipment they needed. Her pride and joy were the forty galleys that she had on the water. She waited for an army that she could send. She had fine provisions for that army, gathered in from all quarters, for she always rewarded her warriors in the most generous manner.

But now the time was approaching when they would delay no more, but would take to the seas in pursuit of Kudrun, who was suffering great hardships in a strange land. The beautiful queen Hilde ordered that her envoys prepare themselves well and put on fine garments. It was at Christmas that she announced the day to those who had sworn to avenge the death of Hetel. She told them to pass on the news to their kinsmen, allies and vassals that they were to rescue her dear daughter from the Normans.

First of all, she sent her envoys to Herwic, to remind him and his men how they had sworn solemnly long ago to a campaign against those enemies who had left the Hegelings with so many orphans of noble birth.

Hilde's envoys made their way quickly to Herwic's lands. He knew well why they had been sent, and came to meet them as soon as they were recognised, and welcomed them formally. Then they gave him Queen Hilde's message: 'My lord, you are well aware how things stand, and of the oath sworn in the land of the Hegelings. Queen Hilde trusts in your aid more than any other, for no-one else has greater cause to regret the abduction of Kudrun.'

'I am indeed aware of how things stand,' replied the noble prince, 'and that Hartmuot has criminally taken my bride a prisoner, because she refused him and chose me instead, and how, because of this, my Lady Kudrun also lost her father, Hetel. Envoy, you are to declare my service. Hartmuot shall not go unpunished for having kept my lady prisoner for so long! This is a task better suited to me than to any other man. Envoy, report to Hilde and her court that after the feast of Christmas I shall ride within twenty-six days to the land of the Hegelings, bringing with me three thousand men.' Hilde's ambassadors waited no longer, but returned to her at once.

And so Herwic prepared himself for battle, along with those followers who had done great deeds at his side in the past. He equipped for the campaign all those who agreed to go with him and to fight beside him in that cold winter.

In her search for the assistance she needed, the lovely Queen Hilde sent word to her allies in Denmark, asking that those most courageous of warriors who were prepared to ride against the Normans to rescue Kudrun should come without any delay.

She sent word to Horant that he should remember that he was a kinsman of King Hetel, and that he and his men should have pity for her beloved daughter, who was herself prepared to die before she would lie in Hartmuot's arms.

'Report to Queen Hilde', replied the noble lord, 'that I shall seek this vengeance, and many a widow will be left to weep. I shall come gladly, with all my followers, and we shall hear many people weeping in the kingdom of the Normans. Say further to my lady the queen that I shall be happy to come to her in a few short days only, and tell her that I am prepared for war and shall bring ten thousand of my men from Denmark.'

The envoys took leave of him and went, with his permission, to Waleis, to the border lands where they sought out the powerful Margrave Morunc, with all his men. He was glad to see the envoys and welcomed them graciously. 'I shall be happy to come and help win back Kudrun,' said the valiant warrior to the envoys. 'It is thirteen years since we swore our oath to fight against the Normans, when Hartmuot and his allies escaped from us with Kudrun.'[1]

Morunc had word sent to Holstein[2] that Queen Hilde had summoned her allies. He gave them news of the campaign, and the message was also brought to brave Fruote of Denmark. Lord Irolt declared: 'Now that I have heard the news I shall ride in seven weeks to the land of the Hegelings with as many of my warriors as I can raise, and I shall do so willingly, whether things turn out well or ill for me and my men in the end.'

Wate, the warrior of Stormarn, was also ready to join them. He brought them his support even though he had not yet had word from the envoys of the Hegeling queen. He rode as fast as he could with as many warriors as he could muster.

Thus they all prepared themselves for war. Wate of Stormarn was ready, with over a thousand warriors from amongst his vassals and allies, all prepared to fight against Hartmuot the Norman.[3]

As we have heard, the Hegelings were themselves busy with preparations. However, the sufferings of their country had never really been alleviated, and they thought often of their great sorrow. The warriors decided that they should send for Kudrun's brother. The messengers rode swiftly to Northland, and there on the plains they found the young prince, by a river where fowl were plentiful. The prince and his falconer were out hawking, something at which they excelled.

He saw the envoys hurrying towards him, and said at once: 'Some men are riding towards us, and my mother, Queen Hilde has sent them, my valiant warriors! She doubtless thinks that we have forgotten the campaign against Hartmuot.'

He let his falcons fly free, and rode quickly to the place where he was soon to hear news that would make his mood dark indeed. He welcomed the messengers, and they at once told him that the queen spent all her days weeping. They assured him of her friendship, good faith and loyalty, and asked whether he was of a mind to join them, and which of his men he would bring, for the Hegelings wanted to mount a campaign of war against the Normans.

'That is right,' declared Prince Ortwin. 'I shall lead from here a great army of my boldest warriors, twenty thousand strong. I shall lead them into this battle, even if none of them ever return.'

They could be seen riding in from all directions, the men summoned by Queen Hilde. These warriors offered her their service readily, in the name of honour, and the force that she was able to muster numbered sixty thousand or more.

Lord Morunc of Waleis had at least sixty stoutly built and seaworthy ships on the water, and he brought as many men as these could carry across the sea to the land of the Hegelings, ready to join in the rescue of the Lady Kudrun. Powerful ships came from Northland, too. Everything was in perfect order – from the warriors' horses to their battle-gear. All was ready for war, and the men were in full battle-armour, with swords and helmets.

A shield-count was taken to see how many men had come to help bring the noble princess from the mighty kingdom of the Normans back to the beautiful queen Hilde. There were seventy thousand of them, and Hilde rewarded them with rich gifts. Every one of those who had come or was now arriving at her court was welcomed punctiliously by the grieving queen, and each one received her individual greeting. She presented garments to these noble warriors that were of a richness almost beyond belief.

Hilde's ships were ready and would be able to set sail at a day's notice, well equipped and suitable for her worthy allies. But they would not leave until every place had been filled.

Queen Hilde gave the order for the weapons to be put on board, and she had a large number of helmets made from the finest steel. She also arranged that mail-coats of white steel for five hundred soldiers should be taken with them as reserve arms, in addition to what they already had.

The anchor-cables were of the finest silk rope, and the sails, too, were of the best quality, so that those who were eager to bring Kudrun back to Queen Hilde could cross the seas from the land of the Hegelings to the kingdom of the Normans. It is reported that the anchors were not made of iron, but rather were cast from bell-metal, and the shanks were bound with rings of Spanish brass, so that the magnetic rocks in the sea would not prove dangerous to the brave warriors.[4]

The beautiful queen Hilde gave Wate and his men a great number of valuable arm-rings. But many of the warriors would lie dead when he and the Hegelings brought the lovely princess back from Hartmuot's fortress.

Then Hilde exhorted the Danes: 'If you have fought bravely in pitched battle in the past, fight again and I shall reward you. Follow my standard-bearer, and he shall lead you well!'

They asked who that was to be, and she told them. 'Horant,' she said, 'Lord of Denmark. His mother was the sister of the great King Hetel. Trust in him, and do not leave his side in the thick of battle. Nor should you forget my own dear son, a very valiant warrior. He is just twenty, barely come to manhood, and if he is in grave danger, my bold warriors, then come to his aid and help him escape.'[5]

Every man of them agreed that he would do so. If they were at hand, then Ortwin would escape alive and return to his homeland, as long as he followed them. The young warrior Ortwin was happy to hear this and was in the buoyant mood of youth.

Supplies were brought down and loaded on to the ships, and their value could never be reckoned! Then the men took their leave to set out on their task. The lovely Hilde implored the almighty Christ in Heaven to be their guide.

A good number of men whose fathers had been killed went with the expedition. These valiant orphans would suffer their wrongs no more, and many a woman amongst the Hegelings wept, not knowing when the Lord in Heaven would send their beloved sons back to them again.

The warriors, though, could endure this no longer, and would not permit the people to weep over them any more. With great rejoicing and with much noise they set off, and the brave warriors could be heard singing as they marched to the ships. Now that the men had taken their leave, many of the women could be seen standing at the windows until they set sail, following them with their eyes from the castle at Matelane until they were out of sight.

The great masts creaked, a favourable wind sprang up and the sails filled. Many a man set sail in the hope of winning fame and glory. The chance to do so would come their way, but they had to struggle hard to earn them.

Indeed, it would be impossible to say how things went with them on the whole journey, except that Sifrit, King of Karadie, sailed with his men to meet them, bringing from his lands a good ten thousand fine troops. The King of the Moors was well received. He brought twenty-four galleys filled with men, and enough food and drink to last for twenty years. They were eager for the attack on the Normans.[6]

All of them, from every country, decided to hold an assembly on the Wülpensand, where the battle had taken place so many years before. The monastery had become rich from the gifts of young and old. Some disembarked and went down from the harbour, and many a son left his father's grave with a grief so great that the enemy known to have caused these deaths would soon be sorry.

They set off again from that shore as soon as the ships were ready to sail. Later they were to suffer great hardships on the high seas, even though Wate the Old and Fruote of Denmark were their leaders and guides.

Southerly winds drove the noble company out to sea, and this was to prove dangerous for them. They were driven so far off course that a thousand anchor-ropes would not have reached the bottom. Even the best of the mariners that had sailed with them wept for fear.

Hilde's fleet lay beneath the cliffs at Etna, and no matter how carefully their anchors had been made, the magnetic rocks had drawn them across the ocean to the Sea of Darkness, and their proud masts were bent and broken.[7]

In the midst of general despair, Wate the Old declared: 'Drop our heaviest anchors into the bottomless deep! I have heard of many places where I would rather be than this, but since our queen's fleet had been blown so far off course to the Sea of Darkness, I shall tell you that I heard as a child stories and tales told by sailors of how there was a great kingdom established on the cliffs of Etna. A fine race lived there, and their land is so rich that the rivers flowed down and deposited silver on the sands. They built their fortress walls of that silver, and for stones they used the finest gold. There was no poverty in that country! And I can tell you more, for God works many wonders! For example, if the magnetic rocks pull someone towards these cliffs, provided they can survive until the winds change, then they and their families will be rich forever. So let us eat our provisions,' went on Wate, 'and if we are lucky, we can fill our fine ships with precious stones. If we reach our homeland with that cargo, we shall live in luxury.'

Fruote of Denmark, however, said: 'Rather than have my companions becalmed in such misery here, I would swear a thousand oaths never to bother about wealth again, if only a favourable wind would get us away from these cliffs!'

Those amongst them that were Christians began to pray. By the time the ships had been stranded in the same place for at least four days and probably more, the Hegelings began to have real fears that they would never get away at all. But then the mists rose – on God's command – and the sea began to move, and they escaped from this great peril. Through the impenetrable dark they saw the sun, a west wind came up and their time of misfortune was over. That wind soon drove them along the cliffs of Etna for a good twenty-six miles, and they humbly acknowledged the hand of God and His aid. Wate and his men had had a narrow escape from the magnetic rocks.

Soon they came into a sea-current. They were not to be punished for their sins after all, and much of their anxiety was taken from them. God granted them this, and now the ships were on a proper course for the kingdom of the Normans.

But then a new danger suddenly arose. The ships' sides cracked, and a fierce undertow made them roll dangerously. 'The price we are having to pay for honour and glory is a high one,' said Lord Ortwin.

One of the sailors shouted out: 'Alas, this is a greater danger! It would have been better if we had been killed below the cliffs of Etna. Who can protect men whom God has abandoned? Most noble warriors, the sea will rage and the storm will be long.'

'Do not be afraid, men,' cried out brave Horant of Denmark. 'These are west winds, I know it, and they cannot hurt any of us.' This news encouraged the King of Karadie and his troops.

Bold Horant climbed up to the crows-nest and looked out across the waves. He let his eyes range far, and then the noble lord said: 'Calm yourselves: we are not far from the kingdom of the Normans!'

Orders were given for the whole fleet to take in the sails. By now they could make out a hill in front of them across the sea, and below the hill there was a great forest. Wate gave the command to his warriors to steer for that point.

CHAPTER 23
Landfall and Reconnaissance in the Norman Kingdom

They sailed for a long time beside that forest under the mountain, and the brave fighters now had to move with caution. They dropped anchor and lay up in a deserted area, so that no-one would see them. They went ashore on to the beach to rest a little, and what good things they found there! Streams of cold, fresh water running down from the mountains into the pines delighted these men, for they were weary from their travels across the ocean.

At the spot which they had chosen to use as a place to rest, Lord Irolt climbed a very high tree and looked around carefully to spy out the land. From that point he could see well into the land of the Normans.

'Good news, men,' cried the young lord. 'My fears are all past now, because I have seen at least seven fine palaces and also a great hall. We can be in the kingdom of the Normans before mid-day to-morrow.'

'Then we must bring our shields, weapons and armour ashore,' said Wate wisely. 'Rest yourselves and set your squires to work. Exercise the horses, and make sure that you give orders for the straps to be put on your hauberks and helms. If any of you has armour that does not fit perfectly, this is my advice: Queen Hilde sent five hundred extra hauberks with us, and these can be used by the brave warriors.'

The horses were quickly brought ashore, and the warriors and their squires took the fine horse-blankets and horse-cloths and tried them, to see which suited which horses, so that every one had the most appropriate covering. The horses were given their heads to exercise on the sands for long distances. Many of them were reluctant and could no longer gallop; these had been too long at sea, and had gone stiff, and Wate had them rubbed down with cold water.

The men lit camp-fires. Orders were given for food to be prepared for the travellers, the best that could be found there on that shore, for they all knew that they would not be offered hospitality anywhere in the neighbourhood!

They rested that night, until the next day dawned. Wate and Lord Fruote sought counsel with King Herwic[1] in private, so that there on the barren shore the leaders could discuss how best they could exact repayment from those who had destroyed their castles, now that they were in the enemy's land.

'We should send out scouts', said Ortwin, 'to try and get news of my sister and the other captives, to find out if they are even still alive. Whenever I think of them I am filled with heartache.'

They considered who might be sent on the mission to find out news and detailed intelligence as to where in that country the women were being held – someone who would be able to conceal the real purpose of his questioning from any enemy.

Eventually Ortwin, Lord of Northland and a brave fighter, announced: 'I shall act as scout. Kudrun is my sister by the same father and mother,[2] and therefore no-one is more suited to the task than I.'

'I shall be the other,' said King Herwic, 'and live or die with you. The maiden is your sister and she is betrothed to me, so I shall not deny her my service for a single day.'

Wate, however, became angry. 'This is childish!' he said. 'Most noble warriors, I must in all good faith advise you not to act in this way. Listen carefully to what I have to say! If Hartmuot gets any word of you, you will hang from his gallows!'

But King Herwic replied: 'For good or for ill, relatives should stand together without fear of danger, and so I and my kinsman Ortwin shall not hold back, whatever happens, until we have found Kudrun.'

Since both of them were resolved to undertake this mission, they called together their kinsmen, allies and vassals so that they could address them, and remind them that they should never forget the solemn oaths that they had sworn to the two bold warriors.

'I charge you by your faith', said Ortwin, 'that if we are discovered and taken prisoner, that you will ransom us with your wealth and property, selling your lands and castles, and doing so willingly. Most noble warriors, hear what else we have to say. If we are put to death or fall in fighting, then you must not, my bravest of fighters, forget us, until your wrongs have all been avenged by the sword in Hartmuot's lands.

'Worthy knights, we ask you further that whatever hardships it might cause you, that you do not leave the ladies captive here, as long as you still have the strength to fight, for their only hope will be in you.'

The very noblest of the warriors swore this on their honour, and gave their hand to the two princes, saying that they were prepared not to see their own lands again until they had brought the captive ladies out of the kingdom of the Normans.

The princes' most loyal friends were afraid of the wrath of Ludewic, and wept that there were no others who might undertake the mission, and some of them said: 'They are certain to be going to their deaths.'

They had debated the matter for a whole day, it had become late, and the light of the sun was now hidden behind the clouds that lay over far-off Gustrate,[3] so that Ortwin and Lord Herwic had to wait until the next day.

CHAPTER 24
Kudrun Is Told of the Coming of the Hegelings

Let us leave the deeds of these warriors now, and hear how things were with those who ought, by rights, to have been living in happiness, but who were forced to work as washerwomen in a country that was not their own. Kudrun and Hildeburc spent the whole time on the seashore, washing clothes.

During Lent, one day around noon, a bird came swimming towards them.[1] 'Most beautiful bird,' said the lovely princess Kudrun, 'I feel so sorry for you, having to swim so long and so wearily on these waters.'

But it suddenly answered her in a human voice, for it was an angel of the Lord, and spoke as if it were a man. 'I am a messenger from God, and if you would but ask, then I shall tell you, most noble lady, how things are with all your kin.'

When the princess heard the voice she could not believe that this wild creature, even if tame enough to approach her, could really speak. Yet she heard its voice, as if it had come from the mouth of a human being.

'Poor captive girl,' said the angel of the Lord, 'you may have good hope, for great joy shall come to you. You have only to ask me about your home. I bring you news of all your kin, for God has sent me for your comfort.'

The noble Kudrun fell down upon the sands, her arms outstretched in the form of a cross, as if she were making a prostrate supplication to the Lord. She said to Hildeburc: 'Blessed are we for the honour that God has shown us. Now we shall have no more cause for sorrow.' And then Kudrun, God's handmaiden, said to the angel: 'Since Christ has sent you to comfort us, exiles in a strange land, please tell me, most holy messenger, whether Hilde, whom poor Kudrun called mother, is living still.'

'I shall tell you', the high and holy one replied, 'that I saw Hilde, your mother, alive and well, when she sent forth to these lands the greatest army that any widow or kinsman ever raised for the sake of someone dear to them.'

'Most holy messenger,' asked the noble princess, 'I beg you, grant me leave to put another question. Is Ortwin, King of Northland[2] still alive, and also Herwic, my betrothed? This is the news I wish to hear most of all.'

'This too shall I tell,' answered the holy angel. 'Ortwin and Herwic are both well. I saw those noble warriors ride the mantle of the waves, pulling manfully at the oars across the sea.'

'Tell me more,' she said. 'Can you say whether Irolt and Morunc have come to this country, most holy messenger? That, too, I should dearly like to know, and I should dearly like to see them. They were kinsmen to Hetel, my father.'

'I will tell you,' the high and holy one replied. 'I saw Irolt and Morunc, both of them your willing servants, most beautiful of ladies, and when they come to this country they shall cause many sword-strokes to fall on the helmets of the enemy. And now I must leave', said the holy angel, 'for I have many tasks. May the Lord guard you in honour! To say more would go beyond my appointed task.' He vanished before their eyes, and the two ladies began to weep.

'My sorrow is now made greater,' said Hilde's daughter. 'What I wanted to ask must remain hidden from me. Angel, I beg you in the name of Christ our Lord to deliver me from my sorrows before you leave this place, unhappy princess that I am.'

Once again the angel shimmered before their eyes. 'Before we part forever, I shall serve you in any way I can, because you call me in the name of Christ our Lord. Because of that I shall give you news of all your kin.'

'I should like to hear', she said, 'whether you know if Horant of Denmark has come with his warriors, who last saw me in such a great plight? But I know him to be so brave a man that I, poor maiden, might be saved by him.'

'Horant of Denmark, your kinsman, has come to you with his warriors, ready to fight a fierce battle. He will bear in his own hands Hilde's war-banner, when the Hegelings come to the lands of Hart-muot.'

'And can you tell me', went on Kudrun, 'if Wate of Stormarn is still alive? If he is, then I shall be glad to hear it! We should all be overjoyed if we could see him and Fruote the Old riding under my mother's standards.'

'Wate of Stormarn has come to you in this country,' replied the angel. 'He pulled strongly at the oars beside Fruote in the same galley. Better friends in battle you could not wish for.'

Once again the angel wanted to leave, but Kudrun, the poor Christian child, said: 'I remain in sorrow, for I should like to know when it may be that I, an exile and a captive, shall see the envoys from Hilde, my mother.'

'You shall have great joy', replied the angel, 'for two envoys will come to you at dawn tomorrow – brave men both, who will not deceive you, and what they tell you shall contain no word of a lie.'

With that, the holy angel had to depart, and the two exiles asked no more questions. In their thoughts, though, they were both happy and sad, wondering where their kinsmen were, those worthy men who were to help them. They washed the clothes that day much more slowly, and they talked about the warriors that the great Queen Hilde had sent them from the land of the Hegelings. Anxiously they awaited the arrival of the princess's kinsmen.

The day came to an end. The captive maidens had to return, and they were received angrily by the evil queen Gerlint, who rarely failed to vent her fury on the noble prisoners.

'What possessed you', she said to the two ladies, 'to wash the linen and the other clothes so slowly? You took far too long washing my white silk. If certain people do not take care, then they will be made to weep for it!'

'We work as hard as we can,' replied Lady Hildeburc. 'You ought to temper your attitude towards us, my queen. We poor wretches are often freezing out there. If the winds were warmer, then we should be able to wash more for you.'

'Whatever the weather, you should not be wasting time,' snapped Gerlint at them, 'and you shall still wash my linen and my clothes. At dawn tomorrow you will come to my chambers. The time for a festival is coming closer, as you well know. It will soon be Palm Sunday, and we shall have guests here. If my warriors do not have white garments, then it will go worse for you than for any other washerwoman, in a king's hall or anywhere else in the world!'

They were dismissed, and went and took off their wet clothing. They should have been treated more gently, but no kindness was shown to them at all now, and they had good reason to be sad, for all they had for food was rye-bread and water. The poor unfortunates wanted to sleep, but their beds were not the most comfortable either, and they had on two grimy shifts. That was how much the evil Gerlint cared for them, letting them sleep on hard benches, quite bereft of love and care.

Poor Kudrun lay uneasily in her bed. They could both hardly wait for the morning, and slept so much the less, as they must have wondered constantly whether the angel-bird would lead the brave warriors to those shores.

Lady Hildeburc of Galicia, who had spent a very troubled night, went to the window as soon as dawn broke. It had snowed, and that was another bitter blow for the poor girls. 'We have to wash clothes today,' said Hildeburc the poor exile. 'The weather is such that if we have to wash barefoot today, unless God wills it otherwise, they may well find our corpses before night falls.'

However, they cherished the hope that they might that day see the envoys sent by Hilde, and when the lovely girls thought about the men who were to bring them solace and delight, then their sorrow was lessened. Hilde's daughter said: 'My friend, go and ask the wicked Gerlint to allow us to wear shoes when we go to the seashore today. She can see for herself that if we go barefoot we shall freeze to death.'

They went to the king and his wife in their chamber. Wicked Gerlint lay with her arms around King Ludewic and both were asleep. They dare not wake them – this was a bitter blow for Kudrun.

Half-asleep, Gerlint heard the two of them weeping, and she began to scold the lovely maidens: 'Tell me why you have not yet gone down to the seashore', she said, 'to wash my clothes and rinse them, so that there is not a speck of dirt left, and the rinsing water is flowing cleanly?'

'I do not see how I can get there,' said the poor princess. 'There was a heavy snowfall last night, and unless you want to preserve us from death, then today we shall die without shoes on our feet.'

'Nothing of the sort!' replied the she-wolf. 'You must go there just as you are, for good or ill, and wash the clothes properly, or I shall make you regret it! What do I care if you die?' The two maidens could do nothing but weep once more.

They took up the clothes and went. 'God grant that I may remind you of this one day,' said Kudrun. Barefoot the two maidens ran through the snow, in great sorrow at their lot. They reached the sands, as they did every day, and stood once more washing the clothes they had brought down to the shore with them. Their great hopes were still unrealised. Again and again they looked longingly across the sea before them, over which the envoys were supposed to come, those brave envoys that the powerful Queen Hilde had sent from their homeland.

CHAPTER 25
The Arrival of Ortwin and Herwic

They waited for a long time. But then they spotted two men, alone on the sea in a small boat, and Lady Hildeburc said to Princess Kudrun: 'I can see two men out there on the waves – perhaps these are your envoys?'

'Alas, poor wretch that I am,' replied Kudrun in great sorrow. 'I feel within me both happiness and pain, for if these *are* the envoys from Hilde, and they find me here in this pitiful state as a washer-woman on the seashore, then I shall never be able to bear the ignominy. Poor soul that I am, I do not know what to do. My dear friend Hildeburc, give me your advice. Shall I run and hide or shall I let them find me here in this shameful state? Rather than do that, I would sooner remain a servant for ever!'

'You can see how things are,' replied Lady Hildeburc, 'and you must not leave such a great decision to me. I shall gladly do whatever you do. I shall stay by your side for good or ill.'

They turned and ran away, but the two men were already so close that they saw the two beautiful washerwomen together there by the shore, and noticed that they were trying to run away, leaving the clothes they had been washing. They leapt from their skiff and shouted after them: 'Why are you in such a hurry, most lovely of washerwomen? You can see that we are strangers here. If you run away, you might very well lose these rich linens!'

The ladies behaved as if they had not heard this, but for all that the voice was music in their ears. Prince Herwic had spoken out loudly and clearly, and he did not yet know himself that he was so close to his beloved.

'Most lovely maidens,' said the Prince of Zeeland, 'tell us whose clothes these are. We ask this without any malice, on the honour of all maidens! Most lovely ladies, please come back to the shore.'

'I should be ashamed not to do so now,' replied Princess Kudrun, 'since I am a maiden, and since you have called me in the name of the honour of all maidens.' But still she added: 'I may have cause to regret doing so later.'

Dressed in their shifts, both of them wet, the ladies returned. They had enjoyed better times, these noble women, but now the frost made these poor serving-maids shiver. Their clothes were thin, and the March winds cut through them. It was the time of the year when winter was coming to an end, and the birds would soon be vying with one another in their songs again, when March was out. But now the poor fatherless girls were found amid snow and ice. Both maidens had beautiful faces, but the two men saw them with their hair unkempt, for the March winds had blown it loose. The two ladies suffered much in the rain and in the snow. There was ice on the sea all around, although it had begun to break up now, and the two girls were in a pitiful state indeed.[1] Their lovely bodies could be seen through their shifts, white as the snow itself, and they were greatly troubled by the situation, not knowing who these strangers were.

Noble Herwic bade the exiles good morning. They had long waited for such a greeting, for their mistress was so inhuman towards them that to hear 'good morning' or 'good evening' meant a great deal to them.

'Please tell us', said Prince Ortwin, 'whose fine clothes lie here on the sands, or for whom you are washing them? You are both so beautiful – how can your master treat you so badly? May the Lord in Heaven punish him for it! You are so lovely that you could well be princesses – if you had been born in that estate, you could quite properly be queens in your own lands. Has the person for whom you carry out this lowly service any other such beautiful washerwomen?'

One of the lovely girls replied sadly: 'He has many others, far more beautiful than we are. But now ask us what you want to know, for we have such a mistress that it will cost us dear if she sees us from the battlements talking to you.'

'Please do us the honour of taking this gold, these four fine bracelets, and let it be your payment, most lovely ladies. We give them gladly, if you will be so kind as to answer the questions we wish to ask.'

'In God's name, you may both keep the bracelets,' said the maiden, 'for we will accept no reward from you. Only ask now what you will, for we shall have to leave. I am terrified that we may be seen here with you.'

'Whose rich lands are these and who is their ruler, and to whom do these great strongholds belong? What is the name of the man who makes you do such humble service, so poorly clad? If he has any claims to honour – well, he deserves none if he treats you like this.'

'One of the princes to whom these vast lands and mighty fortresses are subject is called Hartmuot,' said Kudrun, 'and the other is called Ludewic, Lord of the Normans. They command a great army of warriors, and are both powerful rulers.'

'We should much like to see them,' said Ortwin. 'Can you tell us, most lovely ladies, where in these lands of theirs we might find the two princes? We have been sent to seek them out, for we, too, are servants of a king.'

The noble Kudrun replied to the warriors: 'I left them this morning, asleep in their fortress with their garrison of four thousand men. I do not know whether they have ridden out of the castle since then.'

'Can you say why these brave warriors have such great need of keeping so many warriors around them all the time?' asked Herwic. 'If I had so many in *my* halls, I should be able to conquer a king's lands.'

'We cannot say for sure,' said the young princess. 'We do not know where it is, but there is a country far away called the land of the Hegelings. Ludewic and Hartmuot are in constant fear that a strong enemy force might come from that country.'

The two maidens were shivering from the cold, and Prince Herwic said: 'If you most lovely ladies would not think it shameful, perhaps, noble maidens, you would wear our cloaks here on the sands.'

'In the Lord's name, keep your cloaks,' replied Queen Hilde's daughter. 'No-one shall ever see *me* wearing a man's clothing.' If the men had but known, far greater indignities had happened to these ladies than having to wear men's clothing.[2]

Herwic looked again and again at the one girl. She seemed so beautiful to him, and of such noble bearing that it touched his very heart, and he thought how much she resembled someone he had often thought of with longing.

Then Ortwin, King of Northland, said: 'Let me ask both of you maidens whether you know anything about a group of captives that once came to this land? One of them was named Kudrun.'

'I know very well about these captives,' replied the girl. 'They came here long ago, brought here to this realm after a fierce battle. The exiled ladies were very unhappy in this country. I saw the very person that you are seeking – she went on – 'that much I can tell you.' But the speaker was the very person that Hartmuot had carried off to that country, Kudrun herself, and she knew the story very well indeed!

'Listen, my Lord Ortwin,' said Prince Herwic, when he heard this, 'if your sister Kudrun is alive anywhere in any land on earth, then this is she! I have never seen anyone so much like her.'

'This lady is indeed beautiful,' Prince Ortwin replied, 'but she is not like my sister. I remember well from the time when we were growing up together that you could not have found a more beautiful child in the whole world.'[3]

As soon as it was revealed that the brave warrior's name was Ortwin, poor Kudrun looked at him once more. She wanted very much to be sure that this was her brother, for that would mean that all her sorrows had come to an end.

'Whatever your name is, sir, you are a noble warrior,' she said,[4] 'and you are very like a man I once knew. His name was Herwic and he came from Zeeland. If he were still alive he would rescue us from these cruel bonds. For I am one of those taken in battle by Hartmuot's forces and carried off over the sea. But if you are looking for Kudrun, your search is in vain. The Princess of the Hegelings is dead, and she died in great misery.'

At that, Ortwin's bright eyes filled with tears and Herwic wept with him when the princess told them that the beautiful Kudrun was dead. This was a great blow to both of the warriors.

When she saw them both in tears before her, the captive princess said: 'Your behaviour and response makes it seem as if you, most brave warriors, were related to the noble Kudrun.'

'I shall mourn her loss until the end of my days,' said Prince Herwic, 'for she was my bride, betrothed to me by the most solemn of vows. I lost her because of the trickery of the old King Ludewic.'

'You are trying to deceive me,' replied poor Kudrun. 'I have often heard that Herwic is dead. It would mean the world to me if he were still alive in some land, for he would have rescued me from this place.'

'Look at the gold on my finger,' said the noble warrior when he heard this, 'and see if you recognise this ring. I am Herwic, and with this ring I was betrothed to Kudrun in love. If you are indeed my bride, then I shall take you away from here for the sake of that love.'[5]

Kudrun looked at his finger and at the ring that shone there, and in the gold – it was gold from Abalie – was set the finest stone that her eyes had ever seen, and it was a stone that Princess Kudrun had once worn upon her own hand. With a smile of pleasure the maiden said: 'I know that ring, for once it was mine. Look, then, at this, which my love sent me in the days when I, poor wretch, lived happily at my father's court.'

He looked at her finger, and when he saw the gold that she wore, Prince Herwic said to Kudrun: 'You are indeed the child of a king, and of nothing but royal blood. After many troubles I have found my joy and my delight once more.' He took the lovely girl in his arms. It was a moment of sadness and of happiness for them both as he kissed the noble princess countless times, and then embraced as well the lovely lady Hildeburc, her fellow-captive.

Ortwin then asked the two ladies – and it caused them a great deal of pain, for they were very sensitive about it – if there was no other service they might have been put to in that country except working all the time as washerwomen, washing linen on the sands.

'Tell me, my sister, where are the children that you must have had by Hartmuot? Why do they permit you to wash clothes alone on the seashore? If you are a queen, they are treating you very badly.'

In tears she replied: 'How should I have any children? Every one of Hartmuot's people knows that he has never been able to persuade me to take him as a lover. That is why I have had to endure such hard work.'

'It is clear', said Prince Herwic, 'that our journey has been a success. It could not have been better. What we must do now is bring them both away from Hartmuot's stronghold as soon as possible.'

Lord Ortwin, however, said: 'I fear that we cannot. Even if I had a hundred sisters I would rather leave them to die than to hide in another man's land, and steal from my sworn enemies what they took from me in open battle.'

'What are you thinking of?' replied the warrior Herwic. 'I want to take my beloved away from here and then make arrangements to rescue our other women.' But Ortwin the warrior replied: 'I would rather that I and my sister were hacked to pieces!'[6]

Kudrun in her anguish said: 'What have I done to hurt you, Ortwin my dear brother? I have done nothing for which I could be blamed. I do not know, most noble prince, what you wish to punish me for.'

'I am not acting out of hatred, my dear sister. But all your beautiful ladies must be given a better chance of escape. I cannot take you away unless it is done honourably. You shall still have Herwic as your husband!'

At this, Herwic of Zeeland said: 'My fear is that if we are discovered, the ladies will be taken off to a place so far away that we shall never set eyes on them again, and this means that we have to act by stealth now.'

Ortwin, however, countered this with: 'How can we possibly leave the other ladies of the retinue? They have suffered for so long in this land of exile and they must be weary of it, too. All the ladies must be able to profit from the rescue of my sister Kudrun.'

They went down to their boat again, and the lovely princess wept bitterly, and said: 'How miserable I am. My sufferings are never-ending. I can now no longer have any faith in the one whom I had always trusted and hoped would rescue me. Good fortune seems a long way off.'

The brave warriors pulled quickly away from the shore and poor Kudrun cried out after Herwic: 'Once I was the highest and now I have been made to be the lowest in the land. Into whose care have you cast me now? And to whom can I, a fatherless child, turn for comfort?'

'You are not the lowest and you will be the highest. Most noble princess, keep this visit secret. Before sunrise tomorrow I swear that I shall stand before these walls with eighty thousand of my bold warriors.'

They rowed as strongly as they could away from the shore, and this parting was surely more bitter than any other that had ever taken place between kindred. The maidens followed the two warriors with their eyes as far as they could see them.

The two princesses forgot the clothes they had to wash, but the fact that the pair had been idle on the beach had certainly not escaped the wicked Gerlint, who was very angry indeed at the neglect of her laundry.

'Princess,' said Lady Hildeburc of Ireland, 'how can you leave these clothes lying there? Why do you not wash the garments for Ludewic's men? If Gerlint finds out, she will beat us more harshly than ever before.'

But Queen Hilde's daughter answered: 'I am too well-born ever to wash clothes for Gerlint again. From now on, such shameful servitude is not for me. Two kings have kissed me and have held me in their arms.'

'Do not be angry with me', countered Hildeburc, 'if I say that we should make these clothes whiter – we must not take them in such a dirty state back to the royal chambers, or both our backs will be sore from the beating we shall be given.'

'Joy, comfort and happiness will all be mine again soon,' replied the granddaughter of King Hagen. 'Even if I am beaten with birches until tomorrow morning I shall not die of it. Those who are doing us such wrong are far more likely to perish than I am. I shall take these clothes down to the sea' – went on the noble maiden – 'and they, too, can profit from the fact that I am a princess again. I shall throw them into the waves and they can float away to freedom.'

In spite of Hildeburc's protestations, Kudrun picked up Gerlint's linen and in fury swung the clothes high, and hurled them out on to the water. They floated about for a time, but who knows whether anyone ever found them?

The day was over, and it had begun to get dark. Hildeburc went, heavily laden, back to the fortress, carrying the rest of the clothes and seven pieces of fine linen. Ortwin's sister walked empty-handed at her side. It was very late indeed when they reached Ludewic's castle, and before the gates they found the wicked Gerlint waiting for them. She greeted her two noble servants harshly.

'Who gave you permission to take so much time?' said the queen. 'You will both be punished severely for wandering about so late on the shore. You are not fit to enter the chambers of a queen. Tell me at once', she continued, 'what you think you are doing! You have spurned powerful kings and are spiteful towards them, and yet you spend the evening gossiping with common peasants. If you are so concerned about your honour and esteem, this kind of behaviour is hardly appropriate.'

'What sort of slander is this?' replied the princess. 'Poor wretch that I am, I have never had any desire to stand and talk to anyone, nor have I held anyone dear enough to do so, except my kinsmen, and I am well entitled to speak to them.'

'That's enough, you spiteful bitch! Do you dare call *me* a liar? I shall teach you such a lesson tonight that you will not be quite so loud in your accusations in future. You shall feel it across your shoulders before I am done!'

'I would strongly advise against that,' replied the princess, 'and you had better stop beating me. I am of much higher birth and rank than you and your family. Such wild punishment might very well rebound on you one day.'

'And where', asked the she-wolf in reply, 'are my fine linens, since you are standing there with your hands folded so idly in front of you? As I live, I shall teach you that this is not the quality of service I require from you.'

'I left them', said King Hagen's granddaughter, 'down on the shore. When I was going to bring the linen back to the court it was too heavy for me to carry. I really don't care whether you see it again or not.'

'You won't get away with this,' said the she-devil. 'You are going to pay for this before the night is out.' And with that she gave orders that switches should be made out of freshly broken thorny twigs. Queen Gerlint had every intention of carrying out this extravagant punishment. Gerlint had Kudrun tied to a bedpost alone in the chamber. She wanted to take the very skin from the beautiful girl's body. Kudrun's ladies began to weep bitterly when they found out.

But then Kudrun said with great cunning: 'Let me say one thing. If I am beaten with these rods tonight, and if I am ever seen at the side of a mighty king later on, then you will certainly be made to pay for it. If you remit this punishment, then I shall choose as my love the one I have so far rejected. I will wear the Norman crown, and if I ever attain that position, *then* we shall see what things I shall accomplish!'

'Then my anger is all gone,' said Queen Gerlint. 'If I had lost a thousand pieces of the finest linen I would gladly suffer the loss. All will be well for you if you will take Prince Hartmuot of the Normans as your husband.'

'Yes,' said the beautiful girl. 'I want to make amends for my past mistakes. I can stand all these tortures no longer. Send for the King of the Normans. Whatever he wants me to be, that I shall be for evermore.'

As soon as this was made known, people quickly ran and told the brave warrior Hartmuot. He was sitting with some of the men of his father's household, and another of these came in and said that he should go to Kudrun.

'Give me my reward as a bringer of good news,' said the messenger in front of them all. 'The daughter of the beautiful Queen Hilde presents her compliments and requests that you come to her room. She will no longer reject you – she has changed her mind.'

'Why are you telling me these lies?' replied the noble prince. 'If these tidings were true, then I would certainly give you a reward – three fine castles and much land into the bargain, as well as sixty torques of solid gold. Yes, if it were true I should be happy forever.'

'I heard the news as well,' said one of the man's comrades, 'and I claim my share of that reward. You are to come to court – the princess says that she will be your love. If it is your wish, she will become queen of this country.'

Hartmuot thanked the messenger and sprang from his seat in great joy, thinking that God had granted him her love. He went to Kudrun's chambers in a very happy frame of mind. There stood the lovely girl in a soaking-wet shift. She greeted him with tears in her eyes, and went up to him, and stood so close that he wanted to take her in his arms.

'No, Hartmuot,' she said. 'You must not. If anyone sees you they will strongly disapprove. I am only a poor washerwoman, a servant-girl. You are a mighty king, and it would shame you – how would it look if we were to embrace? I shall certainly permit you to do so when I stand by your side, a crown on my head, in front of your fine warriors. Once I have the name of queen, then I shall not shame you. It will be fitting then for us to embrace, and then we shall do so.'

Because he was extremely courteous he stepped back, and said to Kudrun: 'Most beautiful lady, now that you have agreed to be my love, I shall reward you for it richly. I and my kinsmen are yours to command.'

'I have never been more content,' replied the maiden, 'and if I, poor wretch that I am, may now make demands, so let my first be that a fine bath be made ready for me after all my troubles, before I go to bed tonight. My second order is this: that my ladies-in-waiting be brought to me as quickly as possible, from wherever they have been placed among Gerlint's women. Let none of them be left in her private chambers.'

'I shall willingly arrange all that,' said Prince Hartmuot, and many noble ladies were brought from the queen's chambers to Hartmuot and Kudrun dressed in poor clothes and with their hair unkempt. The wicked Queen Gerlint had behaved without any thought for their well-being.

Sixty-three were brought before Hartmuot.[7] The noble Kudrun said gently: 'Look, noble prince! Is this honourable behaviour? How have these ladies been treated?' 'This shall be stopped at once,' said Hartmuot.

'Hartmuot, for my sake,' said the young princess, 'arrange that all my ladies-in-waiting, who have suffered so much here, be allowed to bathe tonight. Please do as I ask, and see to it personally that they be given fine clothing to wear.'

'Most dear Lady Kudrun,' replied the noble warrior Hartmuot, 'if any of the garments that your retinue brought with them have been lost, then they shall be given instead the best that can be found anywhere in the world. I shall be happy to see them, dressed in their finery and standing at your side.' The baths were quickly prepared, and many of Hartmuot's kindred acted as chamberlains, hurrying to serve Kudrun, in the hope that they might win her favour in times to come. The princess was attended well at her bath, as were her ladies-in-waiting. All were then brought the best clothing that anyone could wish for. Even the poorest of these clothes would have been fit for a queen to wear.

As soon as they had bathed, they were brought wine, the finest that was to be had in all the Norman realm. There was good mead, too – but Hartmuot had no idea of how he was soon to be repaid for this!

The lovely ladies now sat in a hall, and Queen Gerlint told Ortrun, her daughter, to dress formally and visit the daughter of Queen Hilde, together with her ladies-in-waiting. Lady Ortrun quickly put on formal clothes and went, with great delight, to see Kudrun. Kudrun herself, the kinswoman of Wate the Old, came to greet her, and when they came together their joy and happiness was clear to everyone. With chaplets of gold on their heads, they met and embraced, both of them shining like the gold they wore. But the pleasure they felt came from different sources. The noble Princess Ortrun was pleased to see the high-born washerwoman dressed in this sumptuous manner. Poor Kudrun, however, was pleased – as we already know – because she was going to see her noble kinsmen again so very soon. The two ladies sat and laughed together, and just to see them brought solace to the saddest heart.

'This is the happiest day of my life,' said Ortrun, 'now that you have agreed to stay here with Hartmuot. In gratitude for your goodwill, I want to give you my mother Gerlint's crown, the crown that I was to have worn myself.'

'May God reward you, Ortrun,' replied the princess, 'and I hope ever to be able to do your bidding. You often wept for my great misfortune. My friendship and willingness to do you service shall never fail.'

Then, with a child-like cunning, the noble maiden said: 'Lord Hartmuot, you must send envoys out into your Norman lands, and summon your closest allies and kinsmen here to court, if they will come. If there is peace in all your realm, then I say that I should like to wear the crown at your side in front of all your warriors. Then I shall be able to see just how powerful the man is who wishes me to be his queen! I can also present myself and my family to your warriors.' This was a well-thought trick. He sent out a hundred or more men as messengers, and therefore the enemy numbers were reduced – as Kudrun had intended them to be – when the Hegelings came in search of Hartmuot.

'My dear daughter,' said Queen Gerlint, when this had been done, 'it is time to withdraw. Tomorrow morning you will be together again.' She bowed to Kudrun, and commended her into God's keeping. Hartmuot also took his leave. Chamberlains and stewards were provided for Kudrun, and the service they gave was impeccable. They had been instructed to look after the well-born and noble ladies, and they provided the exiles with food and drink in plenty.

One of the Hegeling ladies, however, a very beautiful maiden, said: 'Our hearts are heavy when we think of the fact that we shall have to remain in sorrow with those who carried us off to this country. We never thought that this would happen.' She began to cry, in front of Kudrun, her lady. When others of the ladies-in-waiting saw this, they thought sadly of their own pitiful state and they, too, began to weep. But noble Kudrun laughed out loud.

The ladies-in-waiting thought that they would have to stay there for ever. Their mistress, however, had quite different ideas, and did not intend to stay even for a few days. Soon Gerlint was informed of what she had done. Kudrun, who had had no cause for amusement in fourteen years, now laughed, and in an unseemly manner! The wicked she-devil heard this, and gave a sign to Ludewic. Suddenly she was extremely uneasy. Quickly she sought out Hartmuot and said: 'My son, I am sure that troubles are in store for this land and its people. I do not understand why the beautiful Princess Kudrun should have laughed aloud. I do not know how it happened, or where she got word, but I am sure that a message has come to her in secret from her allies. Most noble warrior, take care that these allies of hers do not rob you of your honour and your life!'

'Let it be,' he replied. 'I do not begrudge her and her ladies any happiness they may have. Her closest relatives are far enough away! How could they harm me? I am sure they will not be able to do me any damage.'

Kudrun asked her attendants if their beds had been prepared, as she wished to sleep. On this one night she was free of all sorrow. Prince Hartmuot's chamberlains conducted her to her rooms. Norman pages carried lights for them – they had never done such service for her before. Thirty or more beds, with fresh linen, had been made ready for the noble ladies. Many-coloured quilts from Araby lay on the beds. The coverlets were richly made, edged with finely fashioned braiding, and gold thread shone brightly in the excellent silk cloths that hung round the beds themselves. The under-covers were made of otter-skins.[8]

Hartmuot loved the beautiful Princess of the Hegelings. He could not foresee the harm that her kinsmen were to inflict upon him.

'Go now, and sleep,' said the noble lady to Hartmuot's men. 'My ladies and I wish to take our ease this one night. We have not had such rest since we came here to this land.'

All the Normans, young and old, then withdrew, and Hartmuot's people hurried back to their own quarters and left the ladies. The exiles were well provided with mead and with wine. And then Hilde's daughter said: 'Bar the door.' They shot the four strong bolts, and the walls of the chamber were so thick that nothing they did could be heard outside.

First they sat and drank the good wine. Then the princess said: 'You all have good cause to rejoice, my ladies, after all that you have had to endure. I shall let you feast your eyes tomorrow on your friends and kinsmen. This very day I kissed Herwic, my betrothed, and also my brother Ortwin. Mark this: if any one of you would like me to make her so rich that she would never have another care in the world, then let her keep watch and tell us when the morning comes. Her reward will not be a small one. A time of happiness is approaching. I shall give her gifts of great and powerful castles, and much land. I shall have these to give, if I live to take the title of queen.'

They lay down to sleep in good spirits, for they knew that many valiant warriors were on their way, to help them escape from their wretched and pitiful state. They could hardly wait to see them when they came in the morning.

CHAPTER 26
Herwic and Ortwin Return to Their Army

Now let us turn to a new part of the story. Ortwin and Herwic had soon made their way back to their warriors, who were still on the deserted beach, and the Hegeling soldiers came running to meet them. They welcomed the two envoys with delight, and asked them what news they brought, wanting to know immediately. They asked bold Ortwin, one of the envoys: 'Is Kudrun still alive in King Ludewic's lands?'

'I cannot tell you all individually,' replied the noble warrior. 'No, I have to wait until my closest allies are here with me before I can tell you, and then we shall tell all of you what we saw by Hartmuot's stronghold.'

This was passed on amongst the warriors, and a great throng of them now assembled. Soon the envoys were surrounded by a mass of soldiers, and then Lord Ortwin spoke: 'My friends and allies, I bring news which I wish we could all have been spared. But still I have to tell you a most amazing thing. I have seen my sister Kudrun, and also Lady Hildeburc of Ireland.'

When he said this, there were some who did not believe him, and a few said: 'This is a poor joke. We have pondered for a long time on how we might win her back from King Ludewic's lands – Ortwin and his warriors still bear the shame of her capture.'

'Ask Herwic! He saw them too, and they were in a state which constitutes the gravest possible insult to us. Consider well, my kinsmen, whether this shames us: we found Hildeburc and Lady Kudrun washing clothes on the seashore.'

This news brought tears to the eyes of the kinsmen who were gathered there, but Wate the Old shouted angrily: 'You are all behaving like women, and with no real reason! This is not the way for warriors to behave. If you want to help Kudrun out of danger, you will have to stain with red those white garments that she has had to wash with her fair hands! *That* is how you can be of service to her, and that is how she can escape from this captivity.'

'How are we to do it?' asked Fruote of Denmark. 'How can we get to them before Ludewic's men and Hartmuot's warriors find out that Hilde's army is already on Norman soil?'

'I have a plan,' replied Wate the Old. 'I have every intention of fighting to my utmost right up to their fortress, if I am spared until we get there. Warriors, it is time to leave this place and make our way towards the Normans. The air is pleasant and the moon is clear and bright tonight – this is very fortunate. Now men, down to the shore as quickly as possible, so that we can reach Ludewic's castle before dawn!'

Wate's words spurred them into action. They loaded their horses and armour on to the ships, then made all speed through the night until they reached Ludewic's country. Before dawn they were on the shore in front of his fortress.

Wate told the entire force to keep silent and to rest on the sands. Tired after the sea-journey, the warriors were allowed to lay down their shields, and a number rested their heads on them.

'If you want to win the battle in the morning,' said Wate the Old, 'you must take care not to sleep too long. We have waited a long time for this attack, and so, when dawn breaks, make sure that not one of you brave warriors delays or hesitates. And one more word: wherever you are and whatever you are doing, when you hear the sound of my war-horn, prepare for battle immediately. That is the signal that dawn is about to break, and there must be no delay then. When I sound my horn a second time, make sure that your horses are saddled and that you are ready and waiting beside them until I see the first light of day, so that no-one is too late when the time comes for the attack.'

They all agreed to do what he asked – and how many beautiful ladies was he to deprive of all joy later, in the fierce fighting, with his deadly wounding blows! His men waited together, eager for the dawning of the new day.

'And when I sound my horn for the third time, my brave companions, then you must be armed and on your horses. But you must still wait, my warriors, until you see me ride out in arms under the banner of the beautiful Queen Hilde.'

The weary soldiers lay down on the shore, very close to Ludewic's great keep. Although the night was dark, they could all make it out, and so these brave warriors lay there without making a single sound.

The morning star had risen high in the sky, and to the window came a beautiful girl, who kept watch to see if it was daybreak, hoping to win thereby a great reward from Kudrun, her mistress. At last, this noble lady caught a glimpse of the breaking day, and reflected on the sea she saw the glint of bright helmets and of very many gleaming shields. The fortress was surrounded, and the plain all around shone with weapons.

She went back to her mistress. 'Wake up, princess. This country and this mighty fortress are besieged by enemy warriors. Our friends and allies from home have not forgotten us in our distress.'

Princess Kudrun leapt out of bed and ran to the window. She thanked her lady-in-waiting for this wonderful piece of news, and later she rewarded her richly. Still very much afraid, she looked eagerly for her kinsmen. She saw the great sails bobbing on the sea, and the noble lady said: 'Now for the first time I am faced with real misery, poor wretch that I am, and I rue the day I was born. Today will see the death of many a noble warrior.'

When she said this, most people in the fortress were still asleep. Then Ludewic's sentry shouted out in a loud voice: 'Up, up, brave warriors! To arms, to arms![1] Up, you Normans! You may already have slept too long!'

Gerlint, Ludewic's wife, heard this and got up, leaving the old king asleep. She hurried quickly to the battlements and saw the enemy army, which distressed the she-devil very much.

She ran back to the king. 'Wake up, Lord Ludewic! Your fortress and your lands are besieged by terrible enemies. Kudrun's laughter will cost your warriors dear today!'

'Enough!' said Ludewic. 'I must see for myself. We shall have to wait to see what happens.' He hurried to his great hall and saw from there that he had guests that day who were hardly welcome. King Ludewic saw the banners fluttering in front of his stronghold, and said: 'We must tell my son, Hartmuot. Perhaps these are pilgrims, who have stationed themselves in front of my castle and on my lands for purposes of trade?'

Hartmuot was wakened, and when he heard the news, the brave warrior said: 'Have no fear. I can recognise the war-banners and badges of princes from twenty different lands. But I am sure these must be our enemies, come to take their revenge on us for the old wrongs done to them.'

CHAPTER 27
Hartmuot Names for Ludewic the War-Banners of the Hegelings

Hartmuot left his men asleep and ran with Ludewic to look out of one of the windows, and when they saw the army Hartmuot said at once: 'These are a little too near my fortifications for comfort! Dear father, these men are no pilgrims. They must be Wate and his men, the warriors of Stormarn and Northland. I can see one banner fluttering there that seems to indicate as much. It is the tawny flag of Karadie,[1] and before it is lowered again, many warriors will suffer! The device on it is a Moor's head in gold. We could well do without such visitors to our country. The Lord of the Moors will have brought twenty thousand men with him, and I can see that they are fierce fighters, who will be bent on winning great honour in their struggle against us. And over there I can see another banner, with even more warriors around it. It is the war-standard of Horant of Denmark, and there with him I can see Lord Fruote – I know him – and also Lord Morunc of Waleis. He has brought a great number of enemies to our shores. And there is another banner, with red bars, sharply indented. That will bring trouble to our warriors – it is the banner of Ortwin of Northland, whose father we killed.[2] His mission is not one of friendship. Over there, too, I can make out a banner with a field whiter than any swan, and you can see devices of gold on it. That one has been sent across the sea to us by my intended mother-in-law, Hilde. By nightfall we shall have felt the hatred of the Hegelings.

'There are more. I can see a broad banner of sky-blue silk flying, and I can tell you that Herwic of Zeeland has brought that one to us – his sea-lilies are embroidered on it[3] – and he will be determined to take vengeance for the wrongs done to him. Lord Irolt is there as well, I am sure, and I would expect that he has many men from Frisia with him, and from Holstein too, skilled warriors all of them. The battle cannot be far off. To arms now,' shouted Hartmuot, 'all the men of the fortress. Up my men! I do not grant these grim strangers the honour of coming so close to my castle. Let us receive them at our gates with the sword!'

Those still in bed leapt up and called out for their bright battle-armour in their desire to help their king to defend his lands. Some four thousand soldiers were there, in good battle-order. Ludewic and Hartmuot now armed themselves. The exiled ladies had mixed feelings, as they had no friends inside the fortress. But one of them said: 'Let those who laughed last year shed tears now.'

Queen Gerlint, Ludewic's wife, hurried to Hartmuot and said: 'What are you going to do, my lord? Are you planning to throw away your own life and the lives of all these warriors? If you leave the fortress, the enemy will kill you.'

'Get back, mother,' replied the noble warrior. 'It is not for you to give advice to me or to my men. Go and give orders to the women – they may listen to you. Tell them how to embroider and sew jewels on to silk. You may as well make Kudrun and her ladies go and be washerwomen,' he went on, 'just as you did before. You thought that they had no kinsmen or allies! You will see today what swift thanks we shall get from our new guests!'

'It was for your sake that I made her do that,' said the she-devil. 'And now you should listen to my advice again. Your fortress is a strong one. Have the gates barred, and these intruders will get very little out of their journey here. You know very well, Hartmuot, that they hate you because you killed their kinsmen, and you should take all the more care for that reason. Beyond the castle you have no kinsmen to help you, and there are twenty proud Hegelings to every one of our men. Furthermore, my dear son, we have bread, wine and food enough in the castle for a whole year. If any of us is taken captive, that person will not be spared for ransoming.'

Ludewic's queen had still more advice for the prince. 'You can maintain your honour and not lose your life. Let your men inflict deadly wounds with their crossbows, from the windows. That will give the Hegelings' friends at home good reason to weep. Have strong catapults made, ready to welcome these guests of ours. The fortress is full of warriors. Rather than allow you to cross swords with the enemy, I and my women will carry slingstones in the wide sleeves of our white gowns.'

By now, however, Hartmuot was angry. 'Lady, get back! How can you presume to give me advice? I am quite able to think for myself. I would rather die out there at the hands of Hilde's soldiers than be found shut up in my castle.'

'I am giving you advice that will help you to save your life,' replied the old queen, with tears in her eyes. 'Nevertheless, all who appear today under your banner may count upon a reward from us. And now, to arms!' she said to the men, 'and follow my son. Strike sparks and fire from the enemy helmets and stand by your prince today. We must welcome these unwanted guests with deep wounds.'

'The queen speaks well,' said Hartmuot. 'My good warriors, if any man, who fights with a will today and helps me overcome the enemy, should fall, then I will make his dependants rich.'

Eleven hundred of Ludewic's own men were armed and in the fortress. Before these marched out of the king's gate, however, Ludewic arranged for a standing guard to remain, and five hundred brave warriors were left inside the fortress. Then the bolts were drawn on the four great gates. Those who were to fight alongside the young prince were fully armed, down to the last spur, and their helmets were firmly tied. Three thousand rode out with the young lord.

The time for battle was now very close. Wate of Stormarn sounded his horn, and it could be heard echoing across the sands for a good thirty miles. The Hegelings quickly began to assemble under Hilde's banner.

Wate sounded his horn a second time to give the order that all the warriors should be in the saddle and their troops drawn up in the direction of battle. Never did an experienced old warrior fight so valiantly as Wate in this attack.

Then he blew his horn a third time, with such force that the ground trembled where he stood, and the sound echoed across the waves, and all but shook the corner-stones from Ludewic's castle walls. And then Wate told Horant to raise up the banner of Queen Hilde.

The Normans were afraid of Wate, and no-one made a sound. You could hear the softest whinnying of a horse. Herwic's bride appeared high up on the battlements, while those bold men who were to fight beside Hartmuot rode out proudly. Hartmuot and his men appeared, fully armed, riding through the great gates. Those within the fortress could see from the window-slits how the sun glinted on the helmets of friend and foe alike. Hartmuot did not ride out to fight alone.

The Hegeling army made its approach on the castle from all four sides. Their armour was silvery, and the light could be seen gleaming on their burnished shield-bosses. Wate the Old was as fearsome as a great lion in the wild.

The warriors of Moorland rode at a distance apart from the rest, and hurled their strong war-spears. Many lances were smashed that day! When they joined battle with the Normans, their swords and armour gave off sparks from the blows.

Then the men of Denmark rode towards the castle. The powerful warrior Irolt deployed more than six thousand of his good and brave soldiers to one side of the walls, where they caused havoc for Ludewic's forces.

Another company was made up of Ortwin and his men – he had a force of about eight thousand under his command, who also brought great harm to the land of the Normans and to its people. Gerlint and Ortrun stood on the battlements and wept.

And then there came Prince Herwic, Lady Kudrun's betrothed, and because of him, many Norman ladies were to suffer great loss when he came to fight for his beloved bride. The noise of swords ringing on helmets was thunderous.

Then Wate the Old rode up, with his troops. His warlike mood was clear to all who saw him. With his spear still raised, he rode up to the very gateway. Gerlint was by now very much afraid, but Kudrun was grateful to him.

Now Hartmuot appeared before his army. He could not have been better equipped had he been an emperor. His trappings and his armour shone in the sun, and his spirit was undismayed.

Ortwin, King of Northland, saw him and said: 'Will anyone who knows tell me, please, who this knight may be? He rides as if he wanted to wrest a whole kingdom from us with his own hands.'

Someone answered: 'That is Hartmuot. Where feats of arms are recognised, he is known to be a great warrior. He is the man who killed your father,[4] and in battle he is always valiant and very daring.'

'Then he has a great debt to pay,' answered Ortwin angrily, 'and he shall settle the account in full today. What we have all lost because of him will now be made good. Gerlint will not help him come out alive!'

By now, Hartmuot had seen Ortwin. Although he did not know who he was, he spurred on his horse and it galloped towards Ortwin. Both men lowered their spears for the charge, and they struck fire from each other's armour.

Again and again they thrust at one another, and then Ortwin's horse went down on its haunches, knocked down beneath the fury of these two kings. But Harmuot's horse stumbled too. Both horses sprang to their feet again, and the sound of the kings' swords as they clashed together rang out loudly. They fought cleanly and admirably in valiant combat, for they were both brave men, and neither would give way to the other.

Their men rode on to each other with spears levelled, and many a mother's son fell. Deep wounds were inflicted on both sides by these brave fighters. All of them were valiant, and all were eager for honour in battle.

Thousands upon thousands of Hartmuot's men bore down on Wate's warriors. The Lord of Stormarn made sure that they suffered for this, and anyone who came within reach of Wate did not live to fight again.

By now, Herwic's troops were engaged in combat with ten thousand of the enemy, who had advanced grimly upon them. They would rather have perished there than allow themselves to be driven from the field of battle.

Herwic himself fought like a veritable hero! He strove in arms so that the beautiful princess might love him all the more. Unbelievable as it might have seemed to him, Kudrun was watching every blow.

Ludewic, the old king, had joined battle with the Danes by this time, and stood regally in front of his men with his mighty war-spear in his hand. But they had moved too far away from the gates.

Brave Fruote and the men from Holstein slew great numbers – he was a very valiant warrior indeed. Morunc, the young Lord of Waleis, could be seen before Ludewic's castle, watering the ground with the blood of the slain.[5]

Young Irolt was a bold warrior, and in the heat of the battle his sword-strokes made blood flow over the armour of the enemy. Wate's kinsmen fought hard under Hilde's banner, and the faces of the fallen grew pale in death as the throng of warriors became thinner.

Then Hartmuot and Ortwin met in combat again. Even the wind that blows snow into drifts was not as strong as the force with which these warriors wielded their swords. Hartmuot was hard-pressed by the King of Northland. Young Ortwin was a brave fighter. However, Hartmuot was very strong and struck through his helmet, drenching his bright armour with blood. Bold Ortwin's followers were dismayed when they saw this.

There was a great confusion now of hand-to-hand fighting, and many gaping wounds were struck through coats of ring-mail. Many a head was bowed under the blows of the broadswords, and Death himself was bent on snatching friend away from friend.

Horant of Denmark saw that Ortwin was wounded, and asked who had harmed his dear prince in the battle. Hartmuot had come close in the battle, and he laughed out loud. Ortwin himself told Horant: 'It was Hartmuot,' and with that Horant gave Hilde's war-banner, which he had carried well in great honour and to the detriment of the enemy, to another warrior, and he attacked Hartmuot with great vigour.

Hartmuot heard a great commotion beside him and saw how the blood of many of his soldiers flowed from their bodies and wet the ground. The valiant prince declared: 'I shall have to avenge the harm done to my men!' He turned to face Horant, and so fiercely did they fight that sparks soon flew from the mail-coats of each, flying up into their eyes, and their sword-edges were blunted against the bands on their helmets.

Horant was wounded at the hands of Hartmuot, just as Ortwin had been, and a stream of red gushed out over his mail-coat. Hartmuot was a fearless fighter – who would dare to lay claim to *his* lands!

In the force of battle many good shields on either side were cut to pieces from the blows that the men poured down upon each other. It was an hour of extreme peril for them all. Hartmuot defended his land with great honour.

Horant's and Ortwin's allies made sure that these two were able to retire from the battle and have their most severe wounds bound up. This was soon done, and they rode back to the fray and fought on once more – we may leave them as they fought with great valour. It was by no means clear yet who would be the victors and who would be the vanquished in this battle for Ludewic's stronghold. Ludewic's men put up a strong defence, and the attackers fought for honour and glory.

It would be impossible to mention every single warrior, but many who fell there are remembered to this day. The clash of swords could be heard all around, and the swift and the slow all joined in the fighting with equal vigour.

As might well be guessed, Wate did not stand idle! Many men received his grim greeting, which signalled the end of their lives as they were cut down by his sword. The warriors of the great Norman families were eager to take their vengeance for this.

Then, so it is reported, Herwic and a great troop of his men came up against Ludewic. He met the old king and his lords in full attack, so that many of the brave warriors under his banner were felled by them. Herwic shouted out: 'Does anyone know who this old man is? His sword and his strong arm have maimed and killed so many that he will give beautiful women cause to weep for the fallen.'

Ludewic, Lord of the Normans, heard him. 'Who is asking for me in this battle? I am Ludewic, King of the Normans. If I am to fight an enemy worthy of me, then I am ready to do so.'

'If you are Ludewic,' replied Herwic, 'then you have earned my hatred. You killed many of our men on that sandy island, and Hetel, who was a fine and noble warrior, also died at your hands. You did us still more harm, too, before you got away, and that hurt we still mourn, for it caused me great sorrow. You stole my bride and left my warriors lying dead on the Wülpensand. My name is Herwic. You stole my wife. You must return her, or one of us must die, and many of our men as well.' But Ludewic answered: 'You threaten me too much in my own country! You are wasting your breath telling me all this. Even if there are others here whose lands and kin I have taken, count on it that I shall make sure *you* never come to kiss your bride!'

With that, the two powerful kings ran at each other.[6] It was not easy to get the upper hand, and since neither of them gained the advantage, men from both sides ran towards them in the fight. Herwic was very brave and valiant, but Hartmuot's father struck out at the young prince, and he reeled under Ludewic's blows, and would have lost his life and lands but for the fact that his men were by now so near, and were able to help him quickly. Had they not done so, he would have been killed. The old King Ludewic was much feared by younger fighters, and with good reason!

Herwic's men helped him to escape death and to get back on his feet, and when he had recovered himself he glanced quickly up

127

towards the battlements to see if he could make out whether his beloved was standing there.

CHAPTER 28
Herwic Kills Ludewic

Herwic thought to himself: 'Fate has dealt me a cruel blow! If my lady Kudrun has seen all this, and we both live to see the day when I can embrace her, she will still blame me, even when I am lying by her side. I am thoroughly ashamed that this old greybeard should have knocked me down.' He called for his banner to be brought forward, towards Ludewic and his men. They pressed towards the enemy so that the Normans could not escape from the battle.

Ludewic heard the noise behind him, turned and went back down to face Herwic. Swords rang against helmets again, and those who were nearby suffered when they were caught up in the fury of the two kings. In the middle of the battlefield, where the two armies were fighting and there was a great tumult, they ran to attack each other. It will never be known how many died that day; and Ludewic, too, was to be defeated in the struggle against Herwic.

Kudrun's betrothed struck home at Ludewic with all the force of his hand, catching him in the gap between the rim of his helmet and the top of his shield and wounding him so badly that he could fight no more. He could do nothing now but wait for death at Herwic's hands. Herwic struck again with great strength, and took the king's head from his shoulders, paying him back for having been brought down. The king was dead. Many a lady would weep to hear of that.

Ludewic's warriors tried to bring their war-banner back to the castle when he fell, but they had moved too far from the gates, and their standard was captured. Many of them lay dead beside their lord. The castle sentries saw that he had been killed, and men and women alike wept when they heard that the mighty old king had fallen. Kudrun and her ladies waited anxiously inside the castle.

Hartmuot, however, had not yet heard the news that his father was dead, and many of their kinsmen with him. Nor did he know why he now heard loud cries and sounds of grief coming from the castle.[1]

'Turn back with me now,' said Lord Hartmuot to his men. 'Many of those who wanted to kill us in this grim battle themselves lie dead.

Let us return to the fortress and wait for a better opportunity to fight again.'

They followed him, and turned to ride back. With great efforts they hacked their way across the field on which they had struggled against a grim foe. Blood flowed from the wounds that Hartmuot and his men inflicted.

'Kinsmen and followers!' said Hartmuot. 'You have served me so well that I shall share the wealth of my kingdom with you! But now let us ride back to the fortress and rest. The gates will be opened for us, and we shall drink mead and wine.'

They had left behind them many of their fighters. His men could not have fought better in the battle if the lands had been their own. But now they wanted to get back to the castle, and Wate, with a thousand men, still harried them.

With a great number of his warriors, Wate had reached the gate that Hartmuot and his men now wanted to enter – but they could not do so. Nothing helped them, even though many great stones were hurled down from the walls as they watched. The defenders fired their arrows so fiercely at Wate and his warriors that they seemed like a rainstorm out of the sky. But Wate did not care who lived or died. His only thought was to gain the victory.

Hartmuot saw the gates in front of him and shouted out: 'It will be made very clear to us today just what we have earned from these men! Those of us who are still whole have cause to be afraid – many are doomed to perish yet. I am more than sorry that I ever made so many grim enemies. I can see Wate and his men with drawn swords at our gates, and if he is acting as gatekeeper, we can hardly expect him to be a good-natured one! See for yourselves, men! The walls and the gates are surrounded with a huge number of warriors, and all around us they hold the roads. Kudrun's people are bent on complete victory. Look for yourselves! You will see what I have seen. We are going to lose still more of our soldiers. I have no idea how it has come about, but I can see the banners of Sifrit of Moorland flying beside the outer gate, and my warriors are fighting hard against those who are carrying them.

'By the next gateway I can see still more of the enemy. A banner with jagged lines is billowing out in the wind – Ortwin, Lady Kudrun's brother is here, in service of the Hegeling ladies. Many more helmets will be split before *his* mood gives way to a calmer one.

'And by the third gate I can see Herwic standing, and he has about seven thousand men with him. He is fighting chivalrously, following the dictates of his heart. Princess Kudrun and her ladies will have been glad to see that today.

'My instinctive responses were too late. I and my warriors have nowhere to turn, now that Wate the Old has fought a way to the fourth gateway.[2] My people inside the castle will have to wait a long time for their menfolk to return. Whatever happens to me now, I have no wings and cannot fly, nor can I burrow under the ground. We cannot escape from our enemies by turning towards the sea. I shall tell you then, as clearly as I can, what seems to be the best we can do. There is no other way out, my noble warriors, but to dismount and do your best in drawing hot blood from their mail-coats! It is the only way!' They dismounted, and drove their horses away to the rear.

'Forward, my brave warriors,' said Hartmuot when they had done so. 'Make for the fortress. Come what may, I have to reach Wate the Old! Whether I can defeat him or not, I must try to get him away from the gates.'

With drawn swords the valiant Hartmuot and his men made for the gates. To his great credit, Hartmuot withstood the fierce fighter Wate. Swords clashed, and even more brave warriors lost their lives.

As soon as Wate saw Hartmuot fighting his way towards him – Fruote was carrying the war-standard at the time – the warrior said angrily: 'I can hear the ring of good swords coming in our direction. Fruote, my dear cousin, make sure that no-one gets past you and reaches the gates.'

Wate ran furiously at Hartmuot, but that valiant man stood his ground. A huge cloud of dust darkened the sun, but the two men fought on with undiminished vigour, both of them striving for honour and glory. For all that Wate was said to possess the strength of twenty-six men, young Hartmuot, the Norman prince, nevertheless managed to withstand him. In spite of the great deeds of their enemies, Hartmuot and his men fought back undaunted, for the prince was a true warrior, strong in battle. The dead lay in a vast mound all around them. It was a miracle that Hartmuot was not killed by Wate, who was fighting now in the grimmest of tempers.

Then Hartmuot heard Ludewic's wife cry out loud. His mother, Queen Gerlint, was bewailing the death of the old king, and she offered a great reward if there was anyone who would not just stand by and accept this loss, but who would put to the sword Kudrun and all her ladies.

And there was indeed one scoundrel who desired the reward so much that he came forward, striking terror into the hearts of the beautiful Hegeling ladies as they sat together. For the sake of a rich reward, he was ready to put them all to death.

When Queen Hilde's daughter saw a naked sword brandished in anger before her, she had good cause to regret the fact that she was so far from her friends! And if Prince Hartmuot had not seen what was happening, her head would have been struck off.

Forgetting her aristocratic breeding, she screamed out in pure terror when she seemed about to be killed. The other women who were with her screamed as well, high up at the windows. Their situation was desperate.

Lord Hartmuot recognised her voice, and wondered what was the matter. Then the noble warrior saw the wretch with the sword about to kill her, and he shouted out: 'Who are you, you filthy coward! How can you think of killing the Hegeling ladies? If you harm a single one of them, your own life is forefeit, and all your family will hang as well!'

The man sprang back in fear of Hartmuot's anger. Just then, King Hartmuot came close to losing his own life because of his honourable efforts to give comfort to poor Kudrun, saving her from grim death at a time when he himself was in peril of his life.

Ortrun, the young Norman princess, came running to the Lady Kudrun, wringing her hands. The noble young maiden threw herself at Kudrun's feet and wept bitterly for her father Ludewic.

'Noble princess,' said Ortrun, 'have pity for the fact that so many of my kinsmen lie dead here, and give a thought to how you felt when your own father was killed. Noble princess, today I have lost my father. Most dear lady, this is a disaster for us. My father and most of my kinsmen are dead, and now Lord Hartmuot is locked in deadly combat with Wate. If I should lose my brother I would be an orphan and all alone.

'Let it count in my favour', went on the noble Ortrun, 'that when you were shown no pity by any of the people here, no-one befriended you except me. Whatever they did to you, I wept for you constantly.'

'You did that often,' replied Hilde's daughter. 'But I do not know how I can stop the battle, since I am not a knight and have no weapons. I should be happy to stop the fighting and to prevent your brother from being killed.'

Still, Ortrun wept bitterly and begged and pleaded, until Princess Kudrun went to the window and waved her hand in a signal to the men, and asked them if anyone from her father's country was amongst them.

Herwic, the noble and brave warrior, shouted back: 'Lady, who are you? Who asks us this question? There is no-one nearby from the land of the Hegelings. We are from Zeeland. Tell us, my lady, how we serve you.'

'I want to beg you to stop the fighting,' said King Hetel's daughter. 'The battle has been a long one, and I would be indebted forever to anyone who can give me the comfort of seeing Hartmuot rescued from his struggle with Wate the Old.'

'Tell me your name, noble lady,' replied the Lord of Zeeland courteously, and she said: 'I am Kudrun, of the line of King Hagen. Once I was rich and powerful, but I have had little joy in this country.'

'If you are Kudrun, my own dear lady,' answered Herwic, 'then I shall do gladly anything you ask. It is I – Herwic, and you are my only love! I want to show you how ready I am to help ease your sorrows.'

'If you want to serve me, most noble knight,' she said, 'do not take amiss what I ask. The beautiful ladies that are with me here are begging that Hartmuot should be separated in the battle from Wate the Old.'

'I shall be glad to bring this about, my beloved lady.' And Herwic shouted out to his men: 'Carry my banner towards Wate,' and he and all his warriors moved in that direction. It was a fine deed of service to his lady that he accomplished there. Herwic shouted out to Wate the Old: 'Wate, my dear friend, put an end to this battle as soon as possible! Beautiful ladies are imploring you to do so.'

'Away with you, Herwic,' said Wate angrily. 'If I were to follow women's advice, then where would I be? If I spare the enemy it would mean my own death. I'll have none of it! Hartmuot must pay for his wrongdoing.'

But, for the love of Kudrun, bold Herwic sprang between the two, and there was a crash of swords. Wate was furious. He took great offence that anyone should dare to separate him from his adversary in combat. He struck Herwic a great blow when he tried to part them, and brought him down, but his men rushed in and helped him away. Then Hartmuot was taken captive in the sight of Herwic and his men.[3]

CHAPTER 29
Hartmuot Is Taken Prisoner

Wate was extremely angry. He fought his way past the gates and towards the great hall of the castle. From all around could be heard the sounds of weeping, and at the same time the clashing of swords. Hartmuot had been taken prisoner, and as a result things had gone badly for his men. Eighty good warriors were taken prisoner with the king, and the rest were killed. Hartmuot had been taken to one of the ships and put in chains. It was not yet all over, and they still had more to endure.

Although the Hegelings were driven back from the castle itself many times by spears and arrows, Wate managed nevertheless to take the fortress with his fiercely determined attack. And then the great bolts were hacked from the walls. Beautiful women wept to see that.

Horant of Denmark was carrying Hilde's standard. Many of his large following of warriors went with him past a great hall and up to the strongest tower that the Hegelings could find in the castle. The fortress had fallen, and this was a moment of great terror for those inside. Now the warriors forced their way in, eager for plunder, and the fierce fighter Wate shouted: 'Where are our squires with the sacks for booty?'

Many richly furnished chambers were stripped. A terrible tumult was heard throughout the castle, and the invading Hegelings were themselves bent on different things. Some of them were still inflicting wounds upon the enemy, while others were concerned for the spoils. It is said that they took so much from the castle that two heavily laden sea-going galleys could not carry all the rich cloths, silk, silver and gold.

There was no spark of hope in the hearts of any of the occupants of the fortress. The people of that country suffered very much indeed – men and women alike were killed, and many children were slaughtered in the cradle.

'Those children have not caused you the slightest harm!' shouted strong Irolt to Wate. 'They have no share of the guilt for our kinsmen's deaths. For the love of God, have mercy on these poor orphans!'

'You are thinking like a baby yourself,' replied Wate the Old. 'Do you think it is a good idea for me to let these infants, crying in their cradles, live? As soon as they grew up I would trust them no more than a wild Saxon!'

Blood flowed in streams from the chambers, to the great anguish of the watching relatives of those killed. Then noble Ortrun came in sorrow to find Kudrun, fearing that there would be even worse to come. She bowed her head before the beautiful princess and said: 'My Lady Kudrun, have pity on my bitter grief, and do not let me perish. It is your virtue alone which will decide whether or not I die at the hands of your friends.'

'I shall gladly save you if I can do so in accordance with justice, for I wish you nothing but honour and good. I shall make peace for you, and your life shall be spared. Stand here with me and my ladies, with your own ladies-in-waiting at your side.'

'Willingly,' said the young Princess Ortrun. In that way she and thirty-three of her ladies escaped. Sixty-two warriors stood beside the women, and if they had not retreated to that place, they too would have been cut to pieces by the Hegelings.[1]

Eventually, Wate the Old caught sight of them.[2] With his eyes flashing and his teeth grinding, and with his great broad beard he stood before them, and all were in great terror of the warrior of Stormarn. He was all bloodstained, and his surcoat was wet with it. Although she was pleased to see him, Kudrun would have been happier had he come to her in a less violent state of mind. No-one gave him a proper welcome, and this was certainly because they were all so afraid.

No-one, that is, except Princess Kudrun, who stepped forward when she saw Wate. The daughter of dear Queen Hilde spoke to him sadly: 'Welcome, Wate. How joyfully I would have greeted you if you had not caused the deaths of so many people here!'

'My thanks for the welcome, noble lady! Are you Queen Hilde's daughter? Who are these ladies who stand so close to you?' And Lady Kudrun replied: 'This is the noble Ortrun, and you are to spare her, Wate. All these ladies are in great fear of you. The rest are those unfortunate women that Ludewic's army brought with me across the sea, away from the land of the Hegelings. But do not come so near to us – we should be grateful if you would do us that favour.'

Wate went back to find Herwic and Ortwin, King of Northland, as well as Irolt and Morunc, and Fruote of Denmark. All of them were fully occupied as they fought and killed brave warriors.

Meanwhile, the young noblewoman Heregart came to Kudrun and said: 'Most gracious Kudrun, have mercy on me, wretched woman that I am. Remember that we were all part of your retinue – and we still are. Let me live, most noble lady!'

Princess Kudrun, however, gave her an angry reply: 'Keep your distance! You did not raise your voice to complain about the pains that were being inflicted upon us poor wretches, nor did you even care about them. And now I do not care whether things go well or badly for you.'

Then the wicked Queen Gerlint ran to Kudrun and submitted herself to Queen Hilde's child as a prisoner. 'Save us, Princess, from Wate and his men. It is within your power to decide whether I live or die.'

But Hilde's daughter answered: 'I am listening to your pleas for mercy, but how can I grant you that? Nothing that I ever asked you for was granted to me. You showed me no mercy. For that, I should hate you with all my heart. Nevertheless, stand with my women, closer to me.' Wate, meanwhile, was seeking out his enemies, and looking for the wicked Queen Gerlint, while the old she-devil was with Kudrun and her ladies.

Wate strode grimly across the hall and said: 'My Lady Kudrun! Hand over Gerlint and her friends, the woman who made you into a washerwoman, and whose kinsmen killed so many of our warriors at home.'

But the lovely princess replied: 'There are none of them here.' In his anger, Wate came closer and said: 'If you are not quick to point out the ones I am looking for, friends and foes alike will have to die!'

They soon realised how great his fury was, and one of the beautiful ladies-in-waiting gave a sign by glancing across, and from that he recognised which was the wicked she-devil. 'Well, Queen Gerlint,' he said, 'do you need any more washerwomen?' He grabbed her by the hand and pulled her away from the group. Wicked Queen Gerlint began to weep, and Wate stormed at her: 'Most noble queen, my lady will wash your clothes no more!'

When he had dragged her to the doors of the great hall – the others were all watching to see what he was going to do with her – he took her by the hair, asking leave of no-one, so great was his anger, and he struck off the queen's head.

The women screamed out, for this act terrified them, and he returned to them and said: 'Where are the rest of her tribe? Show them to me! Not one of them is so precious that I would think twice about cutting their heads off!'

King Hetel's daughter was in tears as she answered: 'For my sake let those live who have come to me in peace, and who stand here at my side. This is Princess Ortrun and her retinue of Norman ladies.'

Having been granted mercy, these were then told to stand back, but Wate now began to demand roughly: 'Where is Lady Heregart, the young noblewoman who took the Norman king's seneschal as her courtly lover?' They would not show him who she was, but he found her and said: 'Even if you had owned a whole kingdom no-one would have believed that you could behave so arrogantly! You gave very poor service to your mistress, Kudrun, in this country.'

The other women cried out: 'Let her live,' but Wate the Old answered: 'This cannot be. I am the lord chamberlain, and it is my task to look after the discipline and behaviour of the womenfolk.' He struck her head off, and the others fled to hide behind Kudrun.

Everyone was weary now, from the battle. King Herwic came, bloodstained, into Ludewic's great hall, with his companions-in-arms. When Kudrun saw him, she gave him a loving welcome. The warrior quickly took his sword from his side, stripped off his mail-coat and laid it on his shield. Then, still stained from his armour, he went to the princess, for it was for the sake of her love that he had fought his way through the battle that day.

Ortwin, King of Northland, joined them, and so did Irolt and Morunc, taking off their mail-coats so that they could be cooler out of armour. They wanted to see the women, and now their wish was granted. Tired from the fierce fighting, the two warriors from Denmark now laid aside their shields and weapons, took off their helmets and went to join the women. Kudrun welcomed them both in courteous fashion.

Irolt and Morunc at once bowed to the lovely lady. It was clear to see that she was delighted to welcome such a company of nobles. Hilde's daughter, the Princess of the Hegelings, was happy at last.

The King of the Moors[3] was also well received, as is fitting for a valiant knight. The brave warrior was thanked by the princess for having travelled so far from Karadie.

Next, the leaders and their men decided in council that, now that they had taken the fortress of Cassiane,[4] the other strongholds in that country might be seized. Wate the Old advised that they should burn down the towers and the great hall, but Fruote of Denmark said: 'That must not happen. My dear princess has to live here. Have the dead carried out of the great hall. Our own warriors, too, will be in far less danger here. This is a good castle, large and strong. Have the blood washed from the walls, so that the lovely ladies will not be too upset to stay here while we mount a campaign into Hartmuot's lands.'

Fruote was very wise, and they followed his advice. Many a good warrior, who had been cut down with deadly wounds, was carried from the fortress. Those that lay dead before the gates were carried down to the sea, and more than four thousand were thrown into the waves. This was no easy task, but Fruote urged them to do it. There was much that still had to be done, and in the meantime, Princess Ortrun remained a prisoner in the castle of King Ludewic. Sixty-two knights and thirty ladies-in-waiting were with her, all treated as hostages. Kudrun said: 'I shall have charge of the women – they were granted mercy at my request. Wate may do what he likes with his prisoners.'

Lord Horant was then given charge of all the hostages held in Cassiane. He was charged, too, with looking after Kudrun and all her ladies, since he was her closest kinsman,[5] and for that reason could best be entrusted with the task. He was put in command of the forty strong towers and sixty great rooms there by the sea, and also over three other palaces. He was the lord of all of these, and Princess Kudrun was to stay there with him.

A guard was also mounted on the ships down on the sea. Lord Hartmuot, too, was brought back to the fortress of Cassiane to join his kinsmen, where the women as well as the warriors were held prisoner. Orders were given for them to be guarded well, and a thousand brave soldiers were detailed to stay there under the command of Horant of Denmark, to watch over the women. Wate and bold Fruote were now eager to smash more shields.

They made ready for their campaign with thirty thousand men. At their command, the countryside was set on fire, and many parts of Hartmuot's kingdom were put to the flames. Now Hartmuot really felt true sorrow for the first time.

The warriors of Stormarn and of Denmark razed all the strong castles they found. They took more plunder than could be imagined, and many beautiful women, too, were taken prisoner by the Hegelings. By the time Hilde's army returned from their campaign, they had taken and destroyed twenty-six castles. They were fierce, and proud of their campaigning, and they brought back more than a thousand hostages for Queen Hilde. The standard of Queen Hilde was carried unchallenged through the land of the Normans, back to the shore where they had left the noble ladies of the Hegeling court. And now they all wished to leave, being reluctant to stay there any longer.

Those that had been left behind in Hartmuot's great hall rode out of the fortress down to meet the men. They welcomed them, both young and old, and Horant and his Danes asked: 'How did it go with you, my young warriors?'

King Ortwin replied: 'So well that I shall always be indebted to my kinsmen. We have paid off our debts with such vigour that we have paid them back a thousand times over for all that they did to us.'

'Whom shall we leave here to govern the country?' asked Wate the Old. 'Go and fetch the lovely Kudrun. We must return to the land of the Hegelings, and show Queen Hilde what we are bringing back to her country.'

Everyone, old and young, was of the same mind: 'Leave the Danes, Horant and Morunc, in command. Let them stay here with a thousand men.' These warriors could not but agree to do so. The leaders took many hostages away with them.

When they were ready to set off for the land of the Hegelings, they brought down to the ships a huge amount of goods of all kinds, things that they had taken as booty, and also their own equipment. The things they had taken from the land of the Normans would arouse great interest at home.

Next, orders were given for Hartmuot to be brought from the hall. The noble warrior and five hundred of his men were all held as hostages. They had many a hard day still in front of them in the hands of their enemies. The lovely Lady Ortrun was brought out as well, to her great sorrow, with all her ladies-in-waiting. When they had to leave their country and their friends they knew how Kudrun and all *her* ladies must have felt.

The prisoners were taken away, then, and the castle handed over to Horant and Morunc. These remained in the land of the Normans with a thousand of their best soldiers when the Hegelings set off.

'I implore you', said Hartmuot, 'to leave me in my father's country! I shall place my life and all that I own at your disposal.' But Wate the Old replied: 'No. We shall keep a close guard on you. I have no idea why my nephew Ortwin wants to take home to his own country someone who tried to take his life and property from him. If he wanted me to, I would soon make sure that Hartmuot need worry no longer about being a prisoner!'

'What good would it do', said Lord Ortwin, 'if we killed everyone in this country? Hartmuot and his men must be given some hope for better things. I want to bring them back honourably to the lands of my mother, Queen Hilde.'

They brought down to the ships a great amount of gold, jewels, horses and rich garments. They had succeeded in what they had hoped to do, and men who had had cause to weep before were now able to sing with joy.

CHAPTER 30
Envoys Are Sent to Hilde

The army of the Hegelings set out happily for home. More than three thousand of those who had come over the seas with them remained behind, dead or wounded, and their kinsmen mourned greatly for every single one of them. Their ships had a smooth passage. The winds were favourable, and those who were bringing back booty were in the best of spirits. Somehow they managed to send on advance messengers, who brought the news to Queen Hilde in the land of the Hegelings.

It is quite certain that these messengers made as much speed as they could, although it is not recorded how many days the journey home took them. Queen Hilde had never heard such welcome news as when they told her that King Ludewic had been killed.

'How are my daughter and her ladies?' she asked. 'King Herwic is bringing his loved one back to you,' they replied. 'Things could not have gone better for such fine warriors. They are bringing Ortrun and her brother Hartmuot back as prisoners.'

'That is indeed welcome news!' said the noble lady. 'I have suffered in mind and in body because of what they did to me. They shall be punished for it as soon as I set eyes on them. I have undergone private anguish and public shame. And I shall reward you, messengers, for bringing me the news that has banished my sorrow! I shall give you gold from my treasury, and do so willingly!'

'Noble lady,' they replied, 'it would not take much to make us very rich indeed, because we are already bringing back so much booty. If any of us refuses your gifts, this is not done disparagingly. It is just that our galleys are weighed down with bright gold, and trusty stewards are guarding it on the journey.'

Once she heard this, Queen Hilde gave orders that food and drink be prepared for the many guests that she was now expecting, and she arranged, too, for the provision of enough seating, making sure that everything was in accordance with her high status. And so the people of Matelane began to work busily. Carpenters were set to work on the plains and on the beach. They worked fast, so that Herwic and Kudrun might be enthroned in proper state.

The story does not relate whether those still at sea faced any dangers. But Ortwin's army was back within six weeks, bringing the princess and many beautiful ladies. It *is* known, however, that by the time they returned, their campaign had lasted about a year.[1] It was May when they came back with their hostages, and although they had memories of their troubles, they returned with a great noise and cheering. As soon as their galleys were sighted off Matelane, the sound of horns and trumpets could be heard, and there was piping, fanfares and the beating of drums. The ships of Wate the Old had now reached the harbour.

All the warriors of Northland were there, and Queen Hilde and her retinue rode out of the fortress at Matelane and down on to the beach to meet them. And then came Kudrun and all the beautiful ladies.

Queen Hilde and her retinue dismounted, and stood on the sands. Then the noble Irolt led Kudrun forward by the hand. Although Hilde had known them all, she could no longer distinguish between the ladies. The queen saw Kudrun and her following of a good hundred ladies-in-waiting, and said: 'Now I do not know which one I am to welcome as my own dear daughter! I cannot recognise her at all. Welcome, all of you, on your return from across the sea.'

'This is your daughter,' said Lord Irolt. She came closer, and now no amount of treasure could ever outweigh the joy that these two experienced when they embraced. Their sufferings were now at an end.

Queen Hilde next greeted Irolt and all his men, and then she bowed deeply to Wate. 'Welcome, warrior of Stormarn! You have served me well. How could you ever be repaid for this, unless it be with the gift of lands and a crown?'

But Wate replied: 'Whatever service I can do for you I shall be glad to perform, until my dying day!' With that, Hilde kissed him as a sign of her love, and she embraced Ortwin as well. Then Herwic arrived, with his brave and worthy soldiers.

He led young Princess Ortrun by the hand. Kudrun asked her mother gently: 'Dear lady, give a kiss of greeting to this noble maiden. In my exile she did me much honour and service.'

'I shall kiss no-one who is a stranger to me. Who are the kinsmen of this maiden that you want me to kiss in welcome, and what is her name?'[2] Kudrun replied: 'This is Ortrun, the young princess of the mighty kingdom of the Normans.'

'I cannot kiss her – how can you ask this of me? It would be more fitting for me to have her killed! Her family caused me great suffering, and they took great delight in my tears.'

'My queen,' replied Kudrun, 'this lovely princess never said a word that could have hurt you. And think, dear mother, of how guilty *I* should feel if my kinsmen were to kill anyone! Take pity on this poor child!'

Hilde would still not agree, but Kudrun begged her mother, in tears, to relent, and at last Hilde said: 'I have no wish to see you weep any more. If she helped you in any way, then she shall be rewarded for it in my country.'

And so the beautiful Queen Hilde kissed Ludewic's daughter. Then, for Kudrun's sake, she welcomed the other Norman ladies. After that, Lady Hildeburc, who had washed clothes with Kudrun and had now returned with her from out of exile, came forward. Lord Fruote led her by the hand.

'My dear mother,' said Kudrun, 'give your welcome to Hildeburc. Is anything greater than loyalty and true friendship? Hildeburc ought to receive for herself alone all the gold and jewels of an entire realm.'

'I have indeed heard how she shared your joys and sorrows with you,' replied the queen, 'and I shall never sit easy on my own throne until I know that she has been rewarded fittingly for the loyalty she showed you.'

She embraced the maiden – and the others as well – and then she said to Fruote: 'I am not ashamed to come foward myself to greet you and your warriors! You are all more than welcome in the land of the Hegelings, my brave fighters!'

They all bowed deeply to her when she greeted them. Then the King of Moorland came with his warriors on to the shore. There was a great fanfare, and the leaders of his troops sang a Moorish song. Queen Hilde waited until he reached the landing-place, and then she gave a courteous greeting to the Lord of Karadie. 'Welcome, Lord Sifrit, King of Moorland! I shall be forever in your debt for your help in avenging the wrongs done to me.'

'My lady, I shall do gladly whatever you desire of me. Now, though, I shall return to the country that has been mine for many years, since I was a young man, and from which I once rode out to fight against Herwic – though I shall fight against him no more!'

The galleys were unloaded, and many goods brought on to the beach – this was part of the plunder that they had brought home with them. When it became cooler, and evening came on, they all went to their lodgings at last.[3] Queen Hilde rode up to the plain with her guests. In front of the fortress at Matelane pavilions and tents, all decorated with gold, had been set up. Many richly decorated thrones had been placed in them, and there in the tents and pavilions they were all waited upon most attentively.

Queen Hilde had arranged for so many provisions to be brought there that her guests would have to pay for nothing. The world has never known a more generous hostess than this noble widow. Her guests paid neither for their food nor for their wine.

The weary travellers rested for five days. But however well all the others were being treated, Hartmuot was still fearful of what his fate would be, until the beautiful maidens begged Queen Hilde to pardon him. Her daughter and Ortrun went to her, and Kudrun said: 'Dearest mother, bear in mind that no-one should pay back evil with evil. Maintain your great virtue and position of esteem, in the case of King Hartmuot.'

Hilde, however, replied: 'My dearest daughter, you must not ask this of me. I have suffered great wrongs because of him, and in my dungeons he shall be duly rewarded for his arrogance.' Kudrun and Ortrun, with sixty other ladies, fell to their knees in front of her. Then Ortrun implored: 'My lady, let him live. I will guarantee that he will serve you willingly. Show mercy towards my brother. All the honour will be yours if he comes to wear his crown again.'

All of them wept to see him there as a prisoner in chains. Their tears fell for Hartmuot, king of the Normans, and for the great iron fetters that bound him and his men.

And then the queen said: 'Weep no longer. I shall permit them to come to court free of their chains, but they must give their solemn parole not to escape, and swear a binding oath that they will not go from here without my leave.'

The noble hostages were released from their chains, and Kudrun gave orders that the warriors be allowed secretly to bathe, and that they should be given fine clothes before they were brought to court. They were noble fighters, and all this would make a better impression.

When Hartmuot was seen, standing there with his warriors, everyone thought he was the most noble-looking of men. In spite of all his sorrows, he stood as if he had been finely drawn on parchment with an artist's brush. The ladies found him most attractive, and this made them accept him the more readily. The hatred that lay between them was wiped out, and they forgot that their warriors had ever fought against one another.

Then Herwic gave thought to how he might leave the land of the Hegelings with due ceremony. He arranged for trappings and cloths to be brought out for the horses, and his pack-animals were loaded up. Queen Hilde, however, did not want him to leave, and did her best to prevent it. 'My Lord Herwic,' she said, 'you must stay longer. You have brought me so much joy that I shall be in your debt forever. Do not ride away! Before the guests leave, I wish to hold a great feast with my friends and allies.'

'My queen,' said Herwic, 'it is well known that those who send their kinsmen campaigning in foreign lands all desire very much to see their own people home again. Our people can hardly wait for us to start out on our homeward journey.'

'Do not begrudge me the honour and happiness of it all,' replied Hilde. 'I could ask for nothing better. Most noble King Herwic, grant me – poor widow that I am – that my own dear daughter should be crowned here in my presence.'

He was reluctant to agree, but she begged and begged. Indeed, the hostages were eventually freed because of Herwic's decision. As soon as Herwic had agreed that he would stay, Queen Hilde was filled with great joy.

She gave orders for great seats to be set up for the warriors, even finer than before, and many brave fighters sat in honour close to her at the feast, reports of which were heard far and wide in later times. Lord Herwic gave the command that the beautiful Kudrun should be crowned queen.

None of the men who had come with Herwic left Matelane before the great feast. Hilde had rich garments presented to more than sixty lovely maidens. She was ever mindful of her own standing and esteem. Fine clothing was given, too, to a good hundred married ladies. Nor were those who had been brought as prisoners to that country neglected, and every one of them was given fine clothing as well. The gifts of the lovely Queen Hilde were a veritable wonder!

Irolt was the chamberlain, and he had to hurry back to Hilde's lands, though he appeared very soon. Wate, the warrior of Stormarn, was the seneschal and strong Fruote of Denmark was also sent for in great haste.[4] He was detailed to act as steward, and the warrior said to Hilde: 'I shall be happy to carry out this duty, my lady. If you want me to be steward, then you can give me the lands that go with that office, and twelve war-banners of my own. That will make me overlord of Denmark!'[5] Hilde laughed heartily at his joke, and said: 'No, no, no! Your kinsman Horant is Lord of Denmark, and you are to act as steward as his friend and in his stead. Even if he is away in the land of the Normans you must still think of him as if he were here at home.'

The servants were given instructions on how to look after the guests. Queen Hilde ordered the distribution of many bales of fine cloth that had been kept back for a long time in chests and cupboards. Under-stewards brought these out, and they were divided freely amongst the guests. There was not a single person, however low his standing, that did not receive rich garments. No-one can say why still more guests were invited from abroad to the land of the Hegelings, since those who had come back from the campaign against the Normans must have numbered thirty thousand!

Where else could anyone be found who was rich enough to provide finery for all these people? Even if a man were lord of all Araby he could still not have obtained better garments than those given to the guests at this great festival. Princess Kudrun helped in this, too.

The lovely princess was sitting with her own guests, and she sent for Ortwin. The reason for this was that she wished to commend to him the love of Ortrun. Ludewic's daughter was sitting there with her.

The Lord of Northland[6] came to her apartments, and all the beautiful maidens gave Ortwin a courteous welcome. His sister rose from her seat and took him by the hand, and then the noble Kudrun went with him down to the end of the great hall.

'My dear brother,' she said, 'take some advice from me. I want to say something to you in all loyalty. If you wish to gain any real joy in your life, you should pay court to Hartmuot's sister in whatever manner you can.'

'Is that such a good idea, do you think?' replied the noble warrior. 'Hartmuot and I are not exactly the best of friends! And we killed Ludewic! If she were to think of that when she was lying by my side I am sure that it would make her sigh with despair!'

'Then you will have to make her love you so much that she does *not* do so! I am giving you this advice in all loyalty – more than I have shown to anyone else in this world. If you can make her your wife, she will bring you great happiness.'

'If you consider her a lady that my people and country will accept as their queen,' replied the noble knight, 'and are sure that she is of such high breeding, then I shall be glad to pay court to her.' 'You will never have a moment's sadness in her company,' answered Kudrun.

Ortwin discussed this plan with his closest friends and relatives, but Queen Hilde was against it until Ortwin spoke to the warrior Prince Herwic about the matter. He gave the idea his firm support, and when Ortwin told Fruote, too, he said: 'Woo her! You will win many good warriors that way. Besides, the enmity that we have felt should now give way to reconciliation. And I shall tell you how we can bring this about,' went on the brave nobleman Fruote. 'We shall have Hildeburc marry King Hartmuot.'

Lord Herwic spoke frankly on the matter: 'I would advise Lady Hildeburc very strongly to give her consent. She would rule as a mighty queen in Hartmuot's lands – he has the overlordship of a thousand fine fortresses.'

The beautiful Kudrun spoke in private with the noble Lady Hildeburc so that she could arrange this life of ease for her. 'My dearest friend,' she said, 'let me give you your reward for what you did for me – you shall wear the crown of the Norman kingdom.'

The lovely Hildeburc, however, replied: 'I would not wish to love a man who never showed with heart or mind the slightest inclination towards me. If I were to grow old at his side, we should be forever at odds with one another!'

'It is up to you to guard against that,' replied Princess Kudrun. 'I will have Hartmuot sent for immediately, and ask him if he wishes me to release him from his captivity and send him home with his men to their own country. If he finds this agreeable, then I shall at once suggest that he may want to form a closer alliance, and I shall ask him if he will marry, and thus seal the friendship with my kinsmen and with me.'

Hartmuot, King of the Normans, was brought by Fruote to the chambers where Hilde's daughter sat with the two fine ladies. Thanks to Kudrun's intervention, Ortrun and Hildeburc were later to be very happy indeed.

When King Ludewic's son walked through the great hall, every single person, the greatest and the least, stood up from their seats in respect. He was a brave warrior and a great and powerful nobleman. The lovely Princess Kudrun bade him be seated – she had never refused him her greeting. 'You may take your place, Hartmuot,' said Hilde's daughter, 'beside that companion of mine who once washed clothes with me for your warriors.'

'Great queen, do not mock me with that reproach! The sufferings that were inflicted upon you were painful for me as well. My mother gave orders that these things were to be kept from me at all times, so that I never found out what was going on – and neither did my father nor any of his warriors.'

'There is nothing for it,' said Kudrun, 'I have to speak with you in private, Hartmuot. No-one is to hear – just you and I.' With this, Hartmuot thought to himself: 'I hope in God's name that she means me no ill.'

She allowed no-one but Fruote to accompany them, and then the lovely princess said to the king: 'If you take the advice I am going to give you, Hartmuot, and do so willingly, then all your troubles will be at an end.'

'I know that you are honourable,' said Hartmuot, 'and would give me no advice that was not sound and trustworthy. Nothing shall prevent my following your advice, whatever you want me to do.'

'Then I shall tell you how you can save your life,' said Kudrun. 'I and my kinsmen will provide you with a wife, with whom you can retain both your lands and your position, and the hostility that was between us will be forgotten forever.'

'Tell me, then, my lady, whom you wish to give me. I would rather die than take as a wife someone that my own kinsmen at home would think unworthy of me. I would far rather that they heard news that I was dead.'

'I wish to give Ortrun, your beautiful sister, to my dear brother as a wife, and you shall take the noble Princess Hildeburc. There is no better match for you in the whole world.'

'If you will arrange things as you have said, and if your brother Ortwin really takes lovely Ortrun as his wife, then I shall marry Hildeburc, so that there shall be an end to the hostilities for ever.'

'I have already seen to it that Ortwin agrees,' she replied. 'If you want him to restore your lands and titles, and all the fortresses of your realm to you, then be content with Hildeburc as your queen.'

'I agree willingly,' said Hartmuot, and gave his hand on the matter.

'As soon as my sister wears the crown of Northland, I shall at once give Hildeburc the right to sit at my side, and to confer fiefdoms and distribute largesse.'

When he had sworn this, the noble princess said: 'I should be happy to extend the bonds of friendship even further. In order that there should always be a firm alliance between us, we wish to give Herwic's sister as a wife to Sifrit, Lord of Karadie.'

Never had there been such a great reconciliation as that brought about by Kudrun on this occasion. The brave and noble warriors now assembled, and Fruote of Denmark said that Ortwin and Sifrit, King of the Moors, should be sent for. When these two men came to the court, dressed in their festival finery, Kudrun sent word to Wate, and the news was sent, too, to Irolt. These men discussed the plans with each other, and approved everything wholeheartedly. Wate the Old said, however: 'This reconciliation cannot be completed until Hartmuot and Ortrun go before Queen Hilde and prostrate themselves at the feet of the noble queen. Only if she gives her approval can all this be agreed.'

'She is not unmerciful towards them,' replied the noble Kudrun. 'Look, Ortrun is wearing the very garments that my mother provided for me and my ladies. I shall be glad to bring about the reconciliation. Our Norman hostages may trust me to do so.'

And so they brought Ortrun and lovely Hildeburc into the circle they had formed,[7] and Ortwin and Hartmuot accepted them as their brides. 'It is my wish', said Queen Hilde, 'that we should now enjoy a lasting peace.'

Ortwin took his betrothed by the hand, and led her out of the circle in courtly fashion. He placed a gold ring on the white finger of the princess, and with that the pain of her exile from her own country was brought to an end. Hartmuot similarly embraced the maiden from Ireland. Each placed gold on the finger of the other. There was nothing about Hildeburc with which Hartmuot could possibly find fault, and the two were now bound together in faith and love.

'Most noble husband,' said Hilde's daughter to Herwic, 'I wish that your kingdom was so close to ours that somehow your sister could be brought to my mother's country for the King of Karadie.'

'Then let me say,' replied King Herwic, 'that a man who rides fast can be there in twelve days. However, the young princess cannot be brought here unless I send my personal escort.'

'Then I beg you most strongly', replied Hilde's daughter, 'to do just that. If you do, you will be able to enjoy the festivities too. Besides, my mother will provide food and clothing for the messengers.[8] Have the girl brought here, and you will earn my undying gratitude and praise.'

However, Prince Herwic wanted to know: 'Where will she get proper clothing? The King of Karadie caused a great deal of damage in my lands, and he burned down my castles. She lost all her finery in the destruction.' However, the King of the Moors declared that he would marry her even if she stood there in nothing but her shift.

Herwic sent a hundred warriors to fetch her, and told his men to go as fast as they could. He asked Wate to ride with them, and bold Fruote as well. This was an imposition, but they agreed to do it for the good warrior's sake. They all rode as hard as they could, and when they reached the princess, Herwic's men had difficulty in preventing Wate from starting a fight with the men of Zeeland![9] However, Herwic's envoys brought the girl and a retinue of twenty-four maids-in-waiting from her homeland. Wate escorted her from her castle down to the shore, where he found two galleys and two transports. They took one of these and set off at all speed. With a favourable wind they were back – by sea this time – within twelve days.

When they brought the princess to the land of the Hegelings, the knights of that land certainly did not fail to hurry down to the shore with their banners, to welcome the beautiful maiden. All these knights kept their oath of chivalry and service to noble ladies.

Never had any royal princesses greeted each other more graciously! The ladies of the court came to welcome her, along with Hilde, the great queen, and her ladies-in-waiting. In spite of the fact that her own country had been devastated and burned, Herwic's sister did not come alone and unattended.

Three hundred or more men of the court followed Hilde, and when King Herwic himself came to welcome his sister he fought a number of fine jousts in her honour. The other knights did the same, and the clash of the warriors' shields could be heard once more.

All four kings rode to welcome her. When they all appeared together there was great debate amongst the warriors as to which of the four was the most splendid. All of them received great praise, however, and there the matter had to rest!

Lady Kudrun embraced her, and the others followed suit at once. They went then to where a pavilion of finest silk had been set up on the shore, and they went in. Herwic's sister was greatly surprised when she heard what had been proposed.

The King of Karadie was summoned, and they asked the princess: 'Will you accept this man as your husband? He will make you the ruler over nine kingdoms.' She noticed very many dark-skinned warriors in his retinue.

Sifrit's mother and father, however, had not been of the same race, and his colour was that of any Christian warrior.[10] The hair on his head was the colour of spun gold, and she would have been foolish not to take him as her love. She did, however, show some reluctance, as young women often do. When they offered her love to the noble warrior, however, he declared: 'She delights me so much that I shall not rest until I have proved myself of such worth that I may come to share her bed.'

And so the warrior and the princess were betrothed. The four couples could hardly wait for the night to come. All four marriages, then, were consummated in the same night, and four kings' daughters were anointed as queens in the presence of all the warriors.[11]

CHAPTER 31
The Four Kings Hold a Great Festival in Hilde's Country

The kings were anointed too, as was fitting and proper. More than five hundred youths were knighted, and a great feast was held in Hilde's lands at Matelane, on the grounds in front of her castle.

The beautiful Queen Hilde gave fine garments to all her guests. And how well Wate the Old rode before her throne, and Irolt and Fruote too, the warriors from Denmark! Many a lance levelled at each other by the warriors was broken in the tournament. The air was quite still, but the dust-cloud that they raised made it as dark as night. The valiant combatants gave no thought to the fact that they might cause the dresses worn by the beautiful ladies to become dirty. They fought joust after joust in the lists before Hilde's throne at Matelane.

But no-one wanted the princesses to be neglected. They were conducted into one of the wide window-bays, with Queen Hilde, to delight the eyes of the warriors. With the four princesses were at least a hundred ladies-in-waiting, all most beautifully dressed.

Travelling entertainers were, of course, also present on this occasion. All the various performances were presented in lively fashion. The next morning, after due honour had been paid to God at early Mass, the young knights were soon jousting again.

What else was needed at such a festival apart from general delight and the noise of enjoyment! The great hall rang with the sounds of all manner of music. All of this went on for fully four days, and the noble company never rested for a moment!

One man at the court was more generous than any other.[1] He knew about travelling entertainers, and how they were forever hoping for great riches, and he willingly helped the entertainers towards this end. That man was Herwic, Lord of Zeeland, and he was the first to toss out a purse of gold. All those who saw this, or received a share, thanked him. Herwic gave gifts of well over a thousand pounds worth of shining gold. His kinsmen and vassals made presents of clothing, and many a man who had not ridden before this time now gained a horse and a fine saddle. And then Ortwin saw all this, and he began to compete in generous behaviour.

The King of Northland gave out such rich clothing that it may be said with all certainty that no-one had ever worn finer garments. He and his knights were soon left without any more garments to give.

It would be impossible to calculate how many rich garments the men of Moorland – so the story relates – left there, and good horses as well! Those who were given these could have hoped for no better gift.

Young and old were made rich. Young King Hartmuot, too, behaved in the same way, acting as if his lands had not been devastated. He was seen to behave in such a generous way that no man could have given out more gifts than he did. He and his men – those who had been brought with him and who were, in fact, hostages – gave away willingly whatever was desired or asked of them. Hartmuot and his men begrudged nothing. The lovely Kudrun was very fond of Hildeburc of Ireland, who had so often carried clothes for washing down to the seashore with her, and she made sure that she helped Hartmuot win that lady's affection. She gave orders that a great amount of goods be brought from her own treasury for his use – so much, indeed, that it could well be said that the young queen could have given garments and heavy gold to anyone to whom she was so kindly disposed.[2]

The Lord of Stormarn stood before the royal thrones in such fine court dress that neither a king nor any of his men had ever looked so splendid. Those who asked for gifts from him that day did not have long to wait. Wate alone gave away clothing so fine that no sovereign ever wore better. His own garments were covered with a tracery of jewels and gold – that was the clothing that he wore to court! There was a precious stone at every stitch. The very names of these were unknown, but by the cut and faceting it was clear that they were stones from Abalie. The warrior kings all grasped Wate and his men by the hand. All who were present at the time had to admit to the brave warrior Wate that his largesse was far greater than a king's bounty. Anyone who received a share in it was a rich man for a long time to come.

Irolt, too, willingly gave evidence of his own happy frame of mind, and showed that he begrudged no-one any of the riches he dispensed. Fruote of Denmark acted as Hilde's chamberlain,[3] and he served his lady so well that men talked about it for many years afterwards.

Eventually the festivities had to come to an end, and the people all departed. Hartmuot was permitted to leave in appropriate style – once a peace-treaty had been concluded between the erstwhile enemies – now that he was married to Hildeburc. He and his men returned home in a far better state than they had anticipated!

Queen Hilde bade them a courteous farewell. She and her daughter rode out with Hildeburc from her castle, and with them went many of the court. Then, when they were about to leave, Lord Hartmuot made his formal farewell. Queen Hilde provided an escort for him on land and on sea, and in addition they were given a good force of soldiers to go with them, furnished by Ortwin and Lord Herwic. Thus the followers that Hartmuot and Hildeburc took back with them now numbered a good thousand.

Everywhere the ladies were embracing one another. Many of those that now took leave of each other were never to see one another again. Ortwin and the mighty King Herwic conducted them down to the ships. Irolt himself acted as their escort then, all the way back to their own country. Herwic gave instructions that he should report to Horant of Denmark all the things that had happened before they left the land of the Hegelings. Later on, Irolt brought back with him very many brave knights.

It is not known when they reached Cassiane, whether it took a short or a long time. But all the people there rejoiced, and after the great troubles they had seen, God now surely granted them His grace.

Once back in the land of the Normans, Irolt told Horant that the kings had sent him back as an escort. 'But now it is fitting', he said, 'that we should leave these warriors. They are glad to be home, and I, too, can hardly wait to see my own country again.'

Hartmuot was received formally, and then they left his lands. The story does not relate how he ruled after that. Horant and his men set off, and made all speed to get back to Denmark as soon as they could.

Now we have to leave them to their journey, with the comment that no warriors or their kinsmen ever parted from a great feast in such fine spirits as from Hilde's.[4] And now only the men of Karadie remained at the festival in the land of the Hegelings.

CHAPTER 32
The Others Leave for Home

These did not stay any longer in the land of the Hegelings. With great music they led Herwic's sister away to Alzabey. Their mission had been a success, and once they were on their way the warriors sang joyfully.

Queen Hilde bade them all a courteous farewell. Even though Herwic's men had been rich when they had arrived in her country, Hilde let none of them go without receiving a gift of some sort. It must be recorded as a real wonder that anyone could be so generous.

Queen Kudrun said to her mother: 'You must now be well content. Do not weep any more for the dead. I and my noble husband shall serve you so well that you will never know sorrow again. You will always have the support and love of Herwic.'

'My dearest daughter,' replied the old queen, 'do me the favour of sending envoys here to the land of the Hegelings three times a year, otherwise I shall not be able to contain my impatience for news.'

'Gladly, mother,' answered the noble Kudrun. And amidst laughter and tears she and her ladies-in-waiting left Matelane. Her sorrows were now all in the past, and no-one could imagine a more beautiful lady.

Fine horses, suitably saddled, were now brought out for Kudrun and her ladies to ride. These horses had bridles of shining gold, and elegant reins. By now, the ladies were ready to leave, all of them, wishing to delay no longer.

The unmarried maidens that rode with her wore gold circlets on their flowing hair.[1] They were not completely happy, as they were leaving Ortrun and her ladies-in-waiting. If any woman had outshone Ortrun in loveliness, Kudrun would have been very sad.

Ortwin's bride gave her thanks to the noble Kudrun, because it was through her that her brother, Hartmuot, had regained his Norman kingdom. 'May God reward you for that! You have made me free of sorrow for the rest of my days!'

She thanked Kudrun's mother, Hilde, as well, that she was now to wear the crown of Northland as the wife of King Ortwin. Queen Hilde replied that she was happy to see her take up this destiny.

Ortwin and Herwic swore a solemn oath to each other that they would carry out their princely duties in faith and loyalty, according to their high rank and position, and that if an enemy were to attack either one of them, that they would fight side by side to capture and kill him.

THUS ENDS THE STORY OF KUDRUN.[2]

NOTES

The Bartsch/Stackmann edition has been used as the primary text for this translation, and strophe and line numbers after individual notes refer to that text. However, on a (very) few occasions that strophic order is unacceptable, in which case that of the Symons/Boesch edition or of the MS has been adopted instead. Strophe numbers at the page-heads are those of the MS, which all editions at least indicate. Textual quotations are either from Bartsch/Stackmann or from the MS as printed in diplomatic form by Bäuml.

Chapter One

1   The work begins on fol. 140 of the MS with the title of the whole piece. Normally there is the word *aventiure* 'what happens', 'chapter' plus a brief indication of (some of) the contents, but a title has to be supplied here. (Chapter title)

2   The MS has *Eyerlanndt*, and in spite of attempts to see this as Frisia it may be taken as Ireland. There were Norse kingdoms in Ireland from the tenth to the twelfth centuries, and the first Irish coins were in fact issued by Viking rulers. (1, 1)

3   Up to this age he would have been brought up by the women, as is his son Hagen, later. (3, 1)

4   Of appropriate and equivalent rank. This theme is recurrent in the work and is of some importance. (6, 1)

5   The name Uote (identical with that of Sigebant's mother) is not given at this point, but is inserted for clarity. She is named in strophe 42. (8, 4)

6   The text has *Frideschotten*, the first element of which may be the word 'firth'. The name recurs in strophe 30, but its reappearance in strophe 611 may or may not refer to the same place. Uote is referred to in 8, 4 as being 'in Norway', rendered here simply as 'Norwegian'. Norway had Scottish possessions until the Treaty of Perth in 1266 and kept Orkney and Shetland until the late-fifteenth century. (9, 3)

7   Uote is spoken of as having been brought to land with the help of a westerly wind, and of arriving *ûf zweier lande marke*, 'on the border of two lands'. Others arrive by sea directly in Sigebant's (and later Hagen's) lands, but perhaps Uote is to be thought of as arriving, because of the winds, on the coast of one of the other kingdoms in

Ireland, which acknowledged Sigebant as overlord, and then being taken to his own kingdom. (13, 2f.)

8   An interjection in the text: 'now listen to a marvel'. (50, 1)

9   Literally 'unweighed silver', a sign of extravagant generosity parallel to the giving in the previous strophe of whole bales of (uncut) silk. (65, 3)

Chapter Two

1   The last line of this strophe is corrupt, making no sense in the MS. It is usually emended either to refer to Hagen (a solution I follow here), or (with some expansion) to take the meaning: 'many women left at home asked for news of them, and were saddened by what they heard'. Several strophes in this part of the text (88, 1; 90, 1; etc.) have been emended. (96, 4)

2   The beast killed by Hagen is referred to as being 'like a *gabilūn*' (and the MS is also slightly problematic at this point, reading *Seinem*, 'like *his*'). The word is probably a corruption of 'chamæleon' and the beast itself some kind of dragon. The episode recalls the exploits of Siegfried in the Nibelung story, though Hagen is not made invincible and has no vulnerable spot, nor can he understand the speech of the birds. (101, 1)

3   The whole incident with the lion is unclear. It has been suggested that the lion had been fighting with the dragon, and what actually happens is also obscure. In the romance of Yvain/Iwein, known in Middle High German in a version by Hartmann von Aue, the hero is befriended by a lion. Here, however, we have simply the juxtaposition of a dragon-like creature (with evil or satanic overtones?) and a lion, whose attributes are bravery and nobility. (102)

4   *Wild* is the epithet regularly attached to Hagen from this point onwards. I have translated it literally (though 'savage' might have served), and in order to preserve the point that it becomes a formula I have made it into a semi-formal title. (106, 1)

5   *Garadie* (in the MS in fact as Karade here, and elsewhere as Baradie, Gradie, Garadine and Garadie) cannot readily be identified as a real place, though it is spoken of as close to Ireland (110, 3) in a phrase which might mean that it borders on the lands of Sigebant. Although the name as such is really the same, this country has to be separated in the context of our story from Karadie (Karade, Karadine), the land of Sifrit, King of the Moors, mentioned frequently later. The

name may have been taken from Arthurian romance and may also echo a real place, several of which have been suggested, including Karrharde in Frisia and Cardigan in Wales. A location in Wales, with the first element being *Caer-* does no harm to the fictional geography. (108, 3)

6   Salmé is either another designation for the earl's homeland or more probably a part of it. Again the name may have a literary or a geographical origin, and this time suggestions include Soholm (in the Karrharde region of North Frisia) and the Solway Firth. (110, 1)

Chapter Three

1   Of the homelands of the three princesses, India regularly betokens 'faraway and exotic'. Iserland has as its first component a place-name element found in northern and in central Europe. The second princess, named rather later as Hildeburc, and who, like Hilde, the first princess, plays an extended part in the work as a whole, comes from Portugal, her homeland being referred to also as 'Galicia' later on (1008, 1196) – which is at least close. The *Portigale* referred to in 222,5 is clearly a different one. (118–120)

2   The MS reads *Ir mûtet*, a second person plural that would make Hagen refer to the whole company (and the possessive in the same line is indeed plural). The Bartsch/Stackmann text (but not most others) emends *Ir* to *Er*, the third person singular, which matches the reference to 'his help' in the second line. The emendation makes sense, and I have tried to make Hagen speak in a derogatory fashion. (134, 1)

Chapter Four

1   The town is called Balian in the MS. The first element is clearly the Irish *baile* (Bally-) 'town', and in spite of counter-claims for Boulogne, and the patently Irish but unknown Ballyghan, I have invented what is I hope a plausible-looking name adapted from a putative Irish one meaning 'the town of the king'. (161, 2)

2   This is strophe 164 in the MS. I adopt here the order in the Symons/Boesch edition (161, 164, 162, 163) in order to place the reference to the departing guests in a more logical position. (164)

3   The title or nickname given to Hagen has caused much critical speculation. The very phrase *Valant aller künige* (MS) 'devil of all kings' is unusual. Of the many discussions of the phrase, perhaps the

most useful is that by Ian Campbell (*Kudrun*, 1978, p. 75), who shows that *valant*, 'devil' can indicate not only the devil as such, but warriors of great stature (notably giants) and those who, like Hagen, have superhuman strength. (168, 2)

4   The addition of the three days appears to have been traditional. Cf. 'a year and a day'.

5   Even though Sigebant has not yet abdicated (as he does in 189), Hagen could take the title. The eldest son of Henry II of England was crowned king in his father's lifetime in 1170 (though he predeceased his father). Such a measure would secure a succession. In any case, the terms 'king', 'prince', 'lord' and so on are used relatively loosely throughout the work. Here Hagen is for the moment *a* (but not *the*) king. (176, 2)

6   The women are not referred to in the MS, but all the editions expand the otherwise metrically lacking line in this manner in view of the following strophe. There seems no reason to reverse the order of 183 and 184, however, as Symons/Boesch do. (183, 4)

7   We may recall that Scandinavia was not completely Christianised until the twelfth century. (186, 3)

8   This line is also corrupt in the MS, and there has been no agreement on its emendation or indeed its meaning. (196, 3)

9   The name possibly derives at some remove from Wales, though its location near Denmark is one of the many geographical problems in the work. The name has probably again been borrowed from Arthurian romance, and has therefore to be left as an unidentified Waleis near a rather more specific Denmark. It may also derive from the land near the river Waal, in the Netherlands by Nijmegen. Interestingly, it is part of King Hetel's territory and figures later. (200, 2)

10   The verb *hāhen* is emended here and in the three later cases where it occurs (228, 4; 229, 2 and 452, 4) from MS *haben* which *might* (but is unlikely to) mean 'to take prisoner' (rather than simply 'to have'). At the time of copying, the verb-form *hāhen* for 'hang' would not be a familiar one, so that a repeated error is quite understandable. (201, 1)

Chapter Five

1   Hetel rules over the Hegelings, the name of his people being the same

as that of his country, though I have tried to distinguish between the two consistently. The name itself is probably a variant form of 'Heteling' ('the people of Hetel'), possibly with counter-influence from the place-name Hegelingas (Högling, in modern Bavaria). His empire includes identifiably Denmark (which may itself be a subdivision of the 'land of the Danes'), Dithmarschen, Frisia (Friesland), Stormarn, and Holstein itself. Together with these we have the less easily identifiable Northland, Waleis and Nifland. Of these, the first appears in the MS not only as Nortlant, Nortrîche, Hor(t)lant, etc., but also as *Ort*lant – the title used by Hetel's son *Ort*win – and the names are clearly linked. I have translated it as 'Northland' consistently, although it may be Jutland. Waleis is the western frontier-territory and Nifland is enigmatic. The area, however, is that of present-day Northern Germany, Denmark and the Netherlands, including the Frisian Islands. Hetel's central kingdom has cities at Campatille and Matelane (if they are not in fact the same place), but neither is identifiable. The border territories are governed by allies, such as Wate or Horant, who are usually relatives, and the strongest of these is Wate, whose formulaic designation *alt* 'old' I have made into a kind of title. We may accept the identification of his country of Stürmen (or Sturmlant 'Storm-Land') with Stormarn (there are other claimants) as it retains the 'storm-' element so suitable to his character. The relationships of the warriors (and indeed their functions at Hetel's court) are neither clear nor consistent. Thus Horant is the son of Wate's sister (206) *and* Hetel's sister (1112), so that Wate may be an older (half-) brother, bringing Hetel up in Stormarn, where Ortwin, too, is brought up. (200–204)

2 Nifland is often identified as Livland, Livonia, but Morunc is associated also with Frisia, so that the Baltic province seems a little unlikely. Perhaps it is the Nibelung country on the lower Rhine. (211, 1)

3 The comment in the Bartsch/Stackmann edition on the first line of this strophe is misleading. (214, 1)

4 The name is the same as that of the home of the second princess carried off by the griffin. But where that was plausibly Portugal, this clearly is not, so that I have retained the MS name. (222, 2)

5 The MS has Agabÿ, though Abali(e) occurs elsewhere. At all events, an oriental location is intended, although the Algarve has been suggested, too. (267, 3)

6 The Bartsch/Stackmann edition reverses this and the preceding strophe, but the MS is followed here. (271–272)

7 This curious interjection is not typical, and seems to indicate other contemporary versions of the tale with a confusion between *Polan* and *Baljan*, although the MS versions *Baliane* and *Polaÿ* are less close. (288, 3)

8 An emendation to *Campanie* 'Champagne' has been suggested, but presumably an oriental location is once again thought of as a source of fine cloth. (332, 2)

9 A defective strophe, with two half-lines missing. Most editors add the idea that she is reluctant to kiss Wate, however. (341, 1–2)

10 Earlier editions by Bartsch reversed the order of this and the next strophe, although even that makes small difference, and later texts have not done so. There might be a case for moving the strophe two ahead, giving the order 350, 352, 353, 351. (351)

11 Some editors have wanted to read Wate instead of Hagen in the last line, but Wate has not yet taken the advantage, as he does when he declares a 'no-holds-barred' contest. (365, 4)

12 References to warrior tribes presumably neighbouring to Hetel's land. Saxons have a special reputation for wildness in other medieval writings. (366, 4)

Chapter Six

1 Again an unidentified place, probably oriental, and looking rather like Abali(e), a name which recurs. The Arab influence on medieval courtly love song is well known. The final part of the strophe is not completely clear, and the note in Bartsch/Stackmann a little far-fetched. (397, 1 and 3)

2 As the note in Bartsch/Stackmann points out, the change from a single speaker (the chamberlain) to this group of (presumably) three is somewhat abrupt. (420, 1)

3 Wate's 'just let me get at her' speech of action is typical of him, and his reference to Hagen's keeping Hilde locked up in a *klūse*, a monastic cell or hermitage is not, of course, literally meant. (427)

Chapter Seven

1 As the Bartsch/Stackmann notes point out, this is a precise time indication; early Mass is that held at the third hour (monastic Terce), that is, at 8 or 9 a.m. (440, 1)

2   The strophe (which is one of those with rhymes at the caesura as well) is problematic in having an identical rhyme in 3 and 4. Most (but not all) editors emend the second *ēre* to *hēre*, 'noble', and I have followed this. (441, 4)

3   Hagen calls for his *gērstange*, which I have translated as 'war-spear' or 'battle-spear'. It originally seems to have meant the spear-shaft, but here means the whole weapon. As a weapon it is both unusual and old-fashioned, in keeping with the role of Hagen as a massive, but conservative, figure. He also carries a sword, but he is the only figure who is associated with this weapon. (447, 3)

4   This strophe and the two which precede it are clearly in the wrong position in the MS, and nearly all editions rearrange them as here. The three strophes ordered here as 474, 475, 476 in fact appear in the MS as 476, 474, 475 – strophe 476 is simply misplaced. (476)

Chapter Eight

1   The MS has *Da es Abende begûnde*, 'towards evening', but the sense very clearly demands an emendation, even though the major editions do not now make one. If the text is left as it stands, the assumption must be made that Hagen's ships do not reach land until the next day, having been sighted on the evening before. (488, 1)

2   Earlier editors changed the order of these strophes (502–509) but Bartsch/Stackmann retains the MS order, which seems in any case to convey the heat and confusion of the battle extremely well. (509)

3   The MS reads *da kuelten nu die wunde*, but since the word *wunde* 'wound' has just been used it is reasonable to accept that in the second case the proper reading is *winde* 'winds.' (518, 3)

4   The strophe that follows this, strophe 524 in the MS, Hagen's answer to Hetel, comes better at a later stage, and most editors make the change, even though Hagen ought perhaps to have a response strophe here as well. (523)

5   528 = MS 524.

6   MS *von ainem Wilden waibe* 'from a wild woman', presumably an isolated cunning-woman. I have tried to avoid the word 'witch'. (529, 3)

7   The MS actually reads 'Hagen' and a case could be made for his

having now achieved the end of marrying his daughter well. However, 'Hetel' makes more sense, and most editors accept the change. (548, 1)

Chapter Nine

1 Horant's capital, *Gyfers* in the MS, is not the same as the mountain referred to by the same name in strophe 1128. I have accepted, though it is in Germany and not Denmark, the suggested identification with Jever in East Frisia, near Wilhelmshaven. It might be noted, too, that the heading given to this chapter is an extreme case of that title applying only to the first couple of strophes, and arguably just to this one. The birth of Kudrun and the suit of Sifrit are far more important. (564)

2 Ortwin is brought up just as Hetel was, by Wate in Stormarn. He takes eventually his father's subsidiary title of Lord of Northland (much as the son of a British monarch would take the title of Prince of Wales). (574, 2)

3 This means, presumably, the age when she reaches marriageability, rather younger than a boy would be when he was of an age to be knighted. The text does not say 'age'. Kudrun must be presumed to be rather young at this point, so that her chronology, at least, is acceptable. (577, 2)

4 Sifrit, King of the Moors, is an important character. Presumably conceived of within the context of the story as an Arab king, his lands and cities – whose spelling has sometimes had to be amended slightly to assist pronunciation – of Alzabey, Abakie and Karadie/ Karade are not readily identifiable. Ikaria, however, is the name of an island in the Aegean, and seems to be the name of an allied territory or part of a large empire, referred to as Moorland or the Land of the Moors. Although described as dark or swarthy in 583, 3, Sifrit is described at the end of the work as being 'of Christian colour', that is, presumably, white, so that he can be married to Herwic's unnamed sister (see 1664, 2). The name of this king, cast into a Moorish role, possibly derives from a genuine Sigifrid, a Viking leader who attacked France and the Low Countries in the ninth century. Only the name, though, has been borrowed. (580)

5 Wigaleis is presumably a vassal of Hetel's, though his name has been borrowed from Wigalois, who is the eponymous hero of an Arthurian romance by Wirnt von Grafenberg. (582, 2)

Chapter Ten

1 Hartmuot's country is usually given as Ormanie(lant) – with a great number of variations in the MS – or as Norman(d)ie(lant), again with variations, to say nothing of versions with an initial H-. It is tempting to identify it with Normandy, of course, the land in France settled by the Norsemen, and the conquerors of England in 1066. Geographically, however, the distances mentioned would not make a great deal of sense. The most attractive suggestion is that the poet has in mind that other great Norman kingdom, that of Sicily in the twelfth century (the island having been taken finally from the Saracens in 1090). See D. Blamires, 'The Geography of *Kudrun*', *Modern Language Review* 61, 1966, with reference to many other possible identifications in the Mediterranean. (587, 1)

2 As the Bartsch/Stackmann note indicates, the fear is based on the length and difficulty of the journey, although the envoys are later threatened by Hetel. (590, 4)

3 *einer der daz kunde* 'someone who was able (to read)', a skill that not many at the court would have. (607, 1)

4 The point of this somewhat complicated passage is, of course, that since Ludewic was a vassal of Hagen's, his son is inferior in rank to Hagen's granddaughter, and the match is therefore not possible. Garadie is possibly the same land as that referred to in 108, 3 as the home of the earl who brings Hagen away from the land of the griffins. The reference to Scotland is obscure, but Otto may be Otto IV, if the name has not simply been inserted as a caesura-rhyme here. Otto IV, who died as Holy Roman Emperor in 1218, received York as a fief from Richard Lionheart. It is sometimes difficult in this passage to gather who is meant by any one personal pronoun. (610–611)

Chapter Eleven

1 In the text this is a narrator-insertion assuring the audience of the complete truth of the tale. (617, 2)

2 Gerlint is referred to either as *vālentinne* or *tiuvelinne*, both of which mean 'she-devil', or as *wülpinne*, 'she-wolf', with a similar force. They are characterisations, rather than semi-formal nicknames, and are bestowed on her by the narrator, rather than reported as used of her by others (as was the case with Hagen's 'title' of Devil-King). (629, 4)

Chapter Twelve

1   *Galeis* (MS Galays) perhaps derives from Calais, but seems to mean a place on the frontiers of Herwic's territory adjacent to Waleis, which we have seen as the frontier of Hetel's empire. The reference to a mountain (I have made the translation more general) makes identification very difficult in a Northern European context! (641, 3)

2   The sense of the strophe is that Herwic was, for Kudrun, the very picture of a knight. The rather fuller original says that he stood before her 'as if he had been well-drawn by a master painter on a white wall'. Wall-paintings of scenes from epic and romance are still in existence in various places. (660)

Chapter Thirteen

1   The MS provides no title for this chapter, but it is clearly concerned in the main with Sifrit, King of the Moors, whose territories seem to cover various presumably Mediterranean lands, even though (North) German equivalents have been found for some of them.

2   Herwic's country is called *Sēlant*, the closest to which seems to be the province of Zeeland in the Netherlands, rather than Zealand in Denmark, though it might just mean any land by the sea, perhaps the Frisian Islands and the mainland nearby. The element '*Se-*' 'Sea-' ('Zee-') is clear, however. (669, 2)

3   Literally 'he dunged the fields with the dead'. (675, 3)

4   The strophe is somewhat unclear. The MS has the reading: *daz man do die* herten *und vesten purge zerprach* (Bäuml, although the editions give the MS reading as *horten und vesten*). Some editors have read the problematic word as *porten* 'gates' but the reading *warten* 'fortified camps' seems more reasonable. (700, 2)

5   Historical equivalents have been sought for the two kings, but presumably they are Sifrit and a second (client?) king of one of his lands. (702, 2)

6   Herwic's land is referred to here as *Sēwen*, but I have referred uniformly to the one place. The 'Sea-' element is retained (although in fact the MS reads *Seben* at this point). (706, 1)

7   According to the note in the Bartsch/Stackmann edition it would have gone against chivalric practice to attack towns left unprotected

while their armies were on the battlefield. The text reads 'according to chivalric custom'. (708, 2)

8   The MS refers in fact to *der künig von Morlannden* – that is, Sifrit himself – at this point, but most editors emend to *Sēlant*, and make the reference to Herwic. I follow this with a certain reluctance, but the tense in the last part of the strophe sounds more like Sifrit speaking than a narrator reporting on what Sifrit had himself done. (718, 3)

Chapter Fourteen

1   It is not clear to whom – Hetel or Sifrit – the word *unversunnen* 'ill-thought-out, foolish' refers. I have applied it to Hetel, and have taken the line as one of the frequent glances ahead. It might, however, mean that Sifrit's campaign had been a foolish undertaking, for which he and his men had to suffer. (729, 4)

2   Literally 'how Kudrun's body would be warmed by Hartmuot'. (742, 2f.)

3   The MS reads *ze Swabe*, edited usually to *ze Swāben*, 'in Swabia'. I have made it a little more general, but the text probably read in its original form either *zer welde* 'in the whole world' or *ze Ormanie* 'amongst the Normans'. (744, 2)

4   The text in fact has *Etelīcher māze* 'more or less' (ready) at this point, but we may follow Bartsch/Stackmann in taking this as litotes. This sort of irony is not uncommon in Middle High German. (746, 1)

Chapter Fifteen

1   The final comment in the strophe is unclear, and it is not even entirely certain that the phrase *diu wol getāne* 'the beautiful one' does refer to Kudrun. The women are, however, rightly apprehensive about the Norman embassy. (763, 4)

2   Once again this is an obscure line, since it is not clear to whom *die ērsten* 'the first men' refers. The verb is *in drungen* 'forced their way into', although Hartmuot's men do not actually get into the fortress for some time. (781, 4)

3   This is strophe 787, but the order of this and 786, which most editors reverse, is determined by the sense.

Notes

4   Hildeburc is a companion not only of Kudrun, but also of her mother and indeed her grandmother, having been rescued by Hagen from the griffins' island. Here as elsewhere (with Wate, for example) rather more suspension of disbelief is required than usual. (804, 4)

5   The text has *in daz vierde lant* 'in the fourth country', which seems to mean 'four countries away' or 'at a distance'. The proposed emendation to *der viende lant* 'the enemy country' is not accurate, as Herwic is not an enemy. (805, 1)

6   The Wülpensand is a sand-islet or eyot, and has been identified as Wulpen, a now submerged island in the estuary of the Scheldt in the Netherlands. It appears – as the site of the central battle in the story – here and in other Middle High German texts as *Wülpensant* or as *Wülpenwerde*, and I have used the first form to retain the -sand element. (809, 4)

Chapter Sixteen

1   The reference to God here – inappropriate enough in the light of the treatment of the pilgrims which follows – is a corrupt line. Literally 'God forces a way when He wants to', the first part of the line has probably been changed to make for a caesura-rhyme. The Symons/Boesch edition suggests in the notes that the original text might have read something like 'however bad things are, I shall find a way out for us'. However unprovable, that sort of statement on Wate's part makes far more sense than the out-of-place piety of the surviving text. God does not play much of a role in Wate's thinking at the best of times. (838, 2)

Chapter Seventeen

1   A somewhat free adaptation of an unusual mercantile image of battle. (860, 4)

2   It is necessary to expand this strophe a little to make sense of it. Ludewic's silk shirt is worn under his armour, but it must be presumed to have had a hood, providing a thin skin of silk which saves him when Wate's sword cuts through his helmet. We may ignore speculations (see the notes to the Symons/Boesch edition) that the shirt has relics sewn into it: Ludewic is saved simply 'by a hair's breadth'. (864, 4)

3   Literally 'who died without wounds'. Since the battle is taking place in the water and on the shore, drowning is clearly implied here, the

fate wished for Herwic by his enemies a few strophes earlier. (870, 3)

Chapter Eighteen

1   Both parts of this line are unclear. I have followed the Bartsch/
    Stackmann notes, but take the second part of the line to refer to the
    fall of Hetel. (881, 4)

2   The strategy is not entirely clear in the original. It makes sense,
    however, to have the Norman warriors rest first, and *then* create a
    great deal of noise to cover their activities in getting away. (893)

3   The guilt incurred by the Hegelings presumably refers back to the
    taking of the pilgrim ships. Nevertheless, the strophe is unclear.
    Perhaps it means (as in the Simrock translation) that they had no
    time for anything *except* to consider the expiation of the guilt. (914)

4   A hide of land (translating *huobe*) is that which can be maintained
    with one plough, and is reckoned at a hundred acres (though the
    precise size is variable). What is implied is a comfortable endow-
    ment, however, and I have used 'farm' as a translation later. (916, 3)

5   The *spitälære* are possibly Hospitallers, members of the Order of
    the Hospital of St John of Jerusalem, founded probably in the
    eleventh century and known later as Knights of Rhodes or of Malta.
    The term could refer, however, to the Teutonic Order, who were
    also called *hospitalarii*. The arrangement here seems to be for a
    pilgrim hostel attached to the memorial monastery, as indicated at
    the end of Chapter Nineteen. (916, 4)

Chapter Nineteen

1   That is, with the arms of the dead warriors. (923, 3)

2   This is strophe 942, which needs for the sense to be switched with
    strophe 940. The meaning of the corrupt last line is unclear, and the
    editions make a number of different suggestions. (940, 942)

3   Although the Bartsch/Stackmann text now has *Westerwalt*, which
    looks like the forest area in present-day West Germany, the MS
    reads *zu dem vesten wald*, which might be an error for *besten* 'best,
    finest forests'. At all events, and whatever specific forest-land is
    envisaged, the point is the need for timber for a new fleet. (945, 2)

4   Once again the last line of the strophe has had to be emended. A
    church in Caedsant on the Scheldt has been seen as the original

model for the church (*münster*) built by Hilde at the Wülpensand.
(950, 4)

Chapter Twenty

1   The text reads *Ludewīc der frīe* 'Ludewic the free', but the adjective
is simply to provide a caesura-rhyme and is not applied elsewhere.
(956, 1)

2   There is a pun on *genāde* 'contentment, happiness', and *genædic*
'gracious' (as of polite behaviour in this case; also 'merciful').
(957, 2)

3   Middle High German *ellende* – used frequently in this section in
various forms – means 'exile(d), living in a strange country,
banished', and only by extension 'wretched, miserable' (as now,
elend). I have translated in various ways, because 'exile' implies
banishment from within the native country, whereas Kudrun is a
captive against her will. (969, 3 etc.)

4   Hartmuot's sister is actually named a little later, in strophe 973.
(971, 2)

5   These are presumably vassal princes, rather than brothers. (977, 1)

6   This strophe is unclear, and it is not explained why the men disperse
in different moods. (985, 4)

7   The MS reads *Lannde* 'that (part of the) country', but I have adopted
the Symons/Boesch reading of *sande*, since they are encamped on
the shore. (986, 1)

8   The MS attaches to Gerlint at this point the adjective *edel* 'noble',
common enough as a fixed epithet for queens, but unusual and quite
inappropriate for Gerlint. Most emend to *übel* 'wicked'. (993, 1:
note that the Bäuml transcript numbers this in error as 933)

9   Hildeburc is not named until later, in the next chapter, but the
(apparently ageless) companion of Kudrun's mother and grand-
mother is clearly meant, and, as with Wate, to read the story as a
whole requires further suspension of disbelief. This strophe and the
next are reversed in the MS, but the sense demands a reversal of the
order. (1008/9)

10   The two strophes describing the treachery – or at least the disloyalty

– of Heregart appear in Chapter Twenty-Two, where they are plainly misplaced, coming in the middle of a section set in the land of the Hegelings. There is no consensus as to where they should be placed, and it seems sensible to put them with the first reference to the lady, who is not mentioned again until her demise at the hands of Wate in strophes 1514 and 1526–8. (1093–4)

11 Modern editors consider that one or more strophes here are missing in the mother/son conversation in which the (admittedly only apparent) change of heart by Gerlint for her son's benefit would have been motivated. (1017)

12 The strophe is corrupt and has been emended by different editors in various ways. Hartmuot can assume the title of king while his father is still alive, but feels that he needs a queen, just as Hagen did. (1023)

13 Since the text has, of course, no quotation marks, it is not clear whether the final statement comes from Kudrun herself or from the poet-narrator. (1034, 3)

14 The *si* 'they' at the beginning of the strophe is unclear, since only Hartmuot seems to be involved. It might be noted that some earlier editors revised the order of strophes 1029–1049 somewhat radically and this was placed in the next chapter: see Bäuml's notes to the MS transcription. (1037, 1)

Chapter Twenty-One

1 This strophe summarises the action of the whole chapter and points on to the conclusion. It may have been added, with the strophe which follows (also a *Nibelungen*-strophe) somewhat later, and the first part of the chapter is indeed somewhat difficult to follow. Strophes 1044–1047 may also be a later interpolation. As indicated in the final note to Chapter Twenty, attempts have been made to revise the order of the whole section treating of Gerlint's bullying of Kudrun. (1041)

2 The last line of the strophe is unclear, meaning literally 'the poor girl was not so wise'. Bartsch considered (see the Bartsch/Stackmann notes) that the line implied that Kudrun would have been treated less harshly had she been less unfriendly. (1046, 4)

3 Once again the sense is not quite clear and it is not apparent what kind of harm Hartmuot fears. (1050, 4)

4 Hildeburc's father is described as a ruler over lands in Chapter

Three, and in Chapter Twenty as a prince. Honorifics and designa-
tions of rulership are used loosely throughout the work, however.
(1059, 1)

Chapter Twenty-Two

1 This is strophe 1090 in the MS, but modern editors normally
   transpose it with MS strophe 1088 for the sake of the sense. It is also
   assumed that there is a gap with some strophes missing after 1089.
   (1088)

2 *Holzāne* can be identified as Holstein, but it has not been referred to
   so far, and its inhabitants are named even later, which, given the
   more or less identifiable geographical areas of the text, is rather
   strange. (1089, 1)

3 1093 and 1094, which tell of Heregart, and which I have placed in
   Chapter Twenty, follow at this point. (1092)

4 Bell-metal is made from copper and tin, and, like brass, is not
   magnetic. Spain provided metals for making brass. The passage is
   discussed by Gerhard Eis in *Studia Neophilologica* 30 (1958),
   27–30. In spite of the Bartsch/Stackmann note, the second part of
   the strophe seems to mean that the anchors were bound with brass.
   The notion of a magnetic mountain, situated in a still or sticky sea
   (often identified with the Mediterranean), recurs in medieval writ-
   ings where it sometimes draws all the nails out of a ship. (1109)

5 Since Ortwin fought at the Wülpensand (strophe 698) the fact that
   he is now, fourteen years later, only twenty, is part of the confused
   chronology of the text. (1113)

6 Sifrit is referred to here by his title only. The two strophes dealing
   with him are separated in the MS by those describing the ceremonies
   on the Wülpensand, but I follow the order of the Symons/Boesch
   edition, which places MS strophe 1123 after 1120. (1120–1123)

7 *Gyfers*, the name which occurs several times in this episode, is
   plainly not the same place as that in Horant's territory with the same
   name and which is probably Jever in North Germany. Here, of
   course, much depends on whether *Ormanielant* is taken as the
   Norman kingdom of Sicily, or as the Duchy in France. For the sake
   of a coherent story, one of these has to be chosen, although the
   geography remains in any case highly confused. Aetna or Etna, in
   Sicily, appears in medieval sources as *mons Gyber*, and this identi-

fication is adopted here, although it is difficult to fit in other places. Possibly the geography derives from Crusader accounts inaccurate in origin, transmission, understanding or memory. The Sea of Darkness sounds more like the Arctic than the Tyrrhenian, and it is unclear how a fleet might have reached the Mediterranean after leaving the Wülpensand, nor why Sifrit met them before this, unless his kingdom is thought of as lying in Spain or the Algarve. The length of the journey seems to indicate something other than present-day Normandy, however, as does the traditional location of the magnetic mountain, and also the fact that Kudrun would be more likely to wash clothes in a non-tidal sea (in spite of freak weather in Chapter Twenty-Four!). It would be tempting, finally, to see *Gyfers* as referring in fact to Gibraltar (= Jebel Tarik, after an eighth-century Saracen), but the identification is not possible etymologically, even if it fits a fictional geography fairly well. (1126)

Chapter Twenty-Three

1   The Bartsch/Stackmann edition interprets the reference here to 'the king' as meaning Ortwin. He is designated in various ways, but not until strophe 1173 as king, whereas Herwic is referred to by that title in two subsequent strophes. Ortwin does speak next, however, and is clearly present. (1151, 2)

2   Ortwin stresses the point because it would not always be the case, especially in a royal household. (1154, 3)

3   *Gustrāte* is one of the most problematic names in the text. It indicates clearly a place where the sun is setting, and it is distant. The identification with Start Point on the South Devon coast is at best unhelpful (though in spite of Wisniewski, *Kudrun*, p. 52, it is indeed to the West of some parts of Normandy). Several other suggestions have been made, but since none is convincing, the name must remain enigmatic, within a fictional geography that becomes increasingly vague the further away we travel from the Hegeling lands of Northern Europe. (1164, 3)

Chapter Twenty-Four

1   We hear that Palm Sunday is approaching, so that the scene presumably takes place at the end of Lent, perhaps in mid-March, this accounting for the snow and ice referred to in Chapter Twenty-Five. The bird, simply *vogel* in the text, is presumably either a sea-bird or a swan. (1166, 1)

2 Ortwin, while taking his father's subsidiary title as being 'of North-land', is usually called *der degen* 'thane', 'warrior', 'lord', or *der helt* 'warrior'. Here for the first time he is referred to as 'King of Northland'. Both he and Herwic are also described as princes. (1173, 3)

Chapter Twenty-Five

1 The notion of ice breaking up is plainly more suited to a northern situation than to Sicily, but the scene-painting makes a powerful contribution to the story, with the image of the two girls clad only in shifts with their (very long) hair in a poor state. (1219, 2)

2 The reading of the last line is uncertain, and in the MS it is metrically corrupt. The deep-seated objection to wearing men's clothing, even *in extremis*, makes clear that Kudrun has never stopped being a princess. The princesses rescued with Hagen in the third chapter showed a similar reluctance to borrow masculine clothing, this being a quite unthinkable breach of propriety. (1233)

3 Quite apart from the fourteen years spent by Kudrun in the Norman kingdom, Ortwin was brought up away from the Hegeling court, presumably from his seventh year, hence has not seen his sister for a very long time, though his actual age is confused. (1239, 2)

4 The MS contains the phrase *Sy sprach* 'she said', but it is omitted in the editions for metrical reasons. I have reinstated it for clarity. (1241, 1)

5 The MS has the word *mÿnniclich*, which I have rendered 'for the sake of that love', but its precise meaning here remains a problem. The Symons/Boesch edition (though not the others) emends to *gewalticlīche* 'by force', which seems inappropriate, as he is planning to take her away by stealth. (1247, 4)

6 The strophes containing the argument between Ortwin and Herwic, with alternating dialogue, are plainly in the wrong order in the MS, and many editors have rearranged them. I follow the Bartsch/Stackmann order (1257–1261 = MS 1259–1261, 1257–1258) although this, too, is not entirely satisfactory; Herwic's fears in strophe 1260 (MS 1257) might very well merit an earlier position. (1257–1261)

7 Strophe 801, 3 refers to the taking of sixty-two maidens. Numbers are fairly loosely treated in the whole work (see for example the

numbers of men taken on any expedition), but here the difference is a very small one indeed, unless the sixty-three now assembled *include* Kudrun and Hildeburc. (1300, 1)

8   The under-blankets are made, according to the text *von maniger vische hūt* 'of the skin of many fish', meaning, however, anything that swims, especially a fish-*eater* of some sort: the Bartsch/Stackmann (and earlier editors') notes suggest otter-skin or seal-skin, either of which will do. (1327, 1)

Chapter Twenty-Six

1   The sentry cries out *wāfen, herre, wāfen*, which usually means 'alas, my lord, alas' in Middle High German, but here it retains its earlier sense of 'weapons'. (1360, 3)

Chapter Twenty-Seven

1   I have rendered *brūn* as 'tawny' to match the heraldic tenné, a tincture used in continental heraldry sometimes. The device is presumably an heraldic Moor's head. (1368)

2   Heraldically Ortwin's banner is probably barry indented, this providing for a set of canting arms, the pun being on *ort* 'spear-point' and both his name and his place of origin, which appears as *Ortland* as well as *Nortland* etc. H. Rosenfeld, 'Die Kudrun: Nordseedichtung oder Donaudichtung', *Zeitschrift für deutsche Philologie* 81 (1962), 300–305 comments on, and offers putative historical parallels for, the heraldic banners in this section. (1371)

3   Herwic's banner is sky-blue (heraldic *bleu celeste*, a continental variety of azure), with *sēbleter*, literally the leaves of a sea-plant, or perhaps the water-lily. The device again plays on his lands of *Sēlant* or *Sēwen*. Hilde's banner in the preceding strophe is unclear heraldically, and seems to break the rules by having gold on silver (or white). However, French kings once had their golden fleurs-de-lys as badges on a white battle-standard. (1373)

4   It was in fact Ludewic, not Hartmuot, who killed Hetel. (1405, 3)

5   Literally 'he dunged the earth with dead men', an image similar to that in strophe 675. (1415, 4)

6   Unlike the combat between Hartmuot and Ortwin this encounter is taking place at the stage when the warriors are fighting on foot. (1438, 1)

Notes

Chapter Twenty-Eight

1 The MS is confused here, line 3 of the strophe being rather short and the last line too long. The more recent editors remove the phrase 'he did not know why' from the last line and add the word *tumbe*, meaning 'inexperienced, young (men)' after 'many' in the third line. Earlier editors, such as Martin, rearrange the lines to retain the idea. I have retained it, as even though Hartmuot does not yet know (and will not for some time find out) what has happened, the passage contributes to his gradual realisation – beautifully drawn – of the fact that the day is quite lost. (1449)

2 The design of the castle or fortress is not entirely clear. The gates referred to are 'outer', 'second', 'third' and 'fourth' – the last being perhaps the main gate, and the outer gate perhaps meaning either the furthest away or that facing the sea, rather than one in an additional outer wall or a kind of extended barbican. (1462, 3)

3 Herwic's diversion seems to have been sufficient to ensure that Hartmuot is taken rather than killed by Wate, in spite of the anger of the latter. The note in the Bartsch/Stackmann edition that the last part of the strophe means 'in spite of Herwic's efforts' makes no sense and may be disregarded. (1493, 3)

Chapter Twenty-Nine

1 It is not entirely clear to whom the pronouns refer in this strophe and it has been suggested that the sixty-two warriors are in fact a guard, mounted to preserve the women from being cut to pieces. An emendation does not seem necessary here, however, and this interpretation would require the loss of *niht* 'not' in the last line. (1507, 3f.)

2 The MS order here has been changed by recent editors to place the two strophes in which Gerlint comes to Kudrun for shelter *after* Wate has been greeted and has left again. This makes good sense, and 1518 follows quite well after the strophe numbered 1509 in the MS, though some editions consider that there is still a gap after Kudrun's response to Gerlint, and before her agreement to try and save her. (1508–1517)

3 Strophe 1540 in the MS, recording the greeting given to Sifrit, has been misplaced, and it has been shifted by the recent editors to become strophe 1534, with the MS order resuming at 1541. (1534)

4   The suitably Italian-sounding name of Ludewic's capital is here mentioned for the first time (it recurs twice) and is not identifiable with any real place, though Catania is tempting (and was certainly taken by the Normans) as a name-echo. (1535, 2)

5   Ortwin might be expected to be Kudrun's closest relative, since he is her brother and Horant only her cousin, but he appears not to be considered here. (1541, 3)

Chapter Thirty

1   Since the campaign as such seems to have been one battle, the rest of the time is covered by the campaigning within the Norman kingdom and the journey there (with its problems) and back. Within the logic of the narrative, continental Normandy is most unlikely as Ludewic's kingdom. (1571, 2)

2   The MS reads *wie seyn* 'what are' (their names), which refers perhaps to Ortrun's kinsmen. I have, however, followed the change adopted by Martin and by Symons/Boesch (but not in the most recent Bartsch/Stackmann text) to *wie ist* 'what is' (her name), since Kudrun answers by giving Ortrun's name first. (1580, 2)

3   This strophe is incomplete in the MS, three lines being omitted. The text has been reconstructed with reference to a similar strophe in the *Nibelungenlied*, and the reconstruction is adopted here. (1591)

4   There is no reference to Irolt, Wate or Fruote as having *left* Hilde's lands, so that the strophe is somewhat curious. (1611)

5   Fruote appears to be subordinate to Horant, although both are referred to as *von Tenemarke, Tenelant,* etc. and they appear to be related in some degree. Fruote's joke is to claim the lands and war-banners that would be his as overlord. The various court functions, however, are distributed inconsistently in the work. Thus Irolt and Wate act as chamberlains at different times. (1612)

6   The MS has *Normandinen* at this point, but this is one of the more straightforward scribal errors. (1618, 1)

7   The circle is formed by relatives of the couple, with the bride in the centre, as part of the betrothal formalities. (1648, 1)

8   The second line of the strophe is a little unclear, but probably refers to the coming betrothal festival. It is not made explicit that the

clothes and food to be provided by Hilde are for the envoys, but the sense seems to demand this. (1653)

9   It is unclear why Wate should behave in this fashion, and the entirely unmotivated idea serves only to remind us of Wate's generally belligerent nature. (1656, 2–3)

10   Sifrit is described as dark in 583, 3, so that we have a somewhat *ad hoc* change of colour to make him a more suitable husband for Herwic's sister. Products of similar 'mixed marriages' are found elsewhere in medieval German, the most famous being Parzival's half-brother Feïrefîz in Wolfram's *Parzival*, who is literally parti-coloured. (1664, 2)

11   Exchange of vows and then the consummation of the marriages precede the formal celebration of mass or the anointing in public view, as here. There is another possible echo of Wolfram's *Parzival* here, as it also contains a fourfold wedding. (1666)

Chapter Thirty-One

1   Reminders that one should be generous to performers are frequent in medieval German and elsewhere. Here the point is hammered home, close to the end of the telling of the story! (1673, 1 etc.)

2   The sense of these two strophes is not entirely clear in detail, but the point is that Hartmuot is unable to cut such a generous figure as the rest (as he was brought to Hilde's lands as a prisoner). Kudrun gives him goods from her own vast stores so that he can do so after all, and not shame his bride, Hildeburc. (1680–1681)

3   That Fruote is here called *kameraere* is at variance with 1611, in which this task is taken by Irolt (and elsewhere claimed by Wate). Once again, the court functions are not fixed at all. (1686, 3)

4   This final strophe takes us back rather abruptly to Hilde's court, and I have added a clarification of what feast is meant. In fact Sifrit, Ortwin and Herwic are all still in Hilde's land. (1695)

Chapter Thirty-Two

1   The word *ungebunden* means 'without the *gebende*', the head-dress worn by married ladies. (1702, 1)

2   The work closes in the MS with the straightforward sentence *Hie hat Chautrum ein ennde* (*Hie hat Kudrun ein ende*) 'This is the end of *Kudrun*.'

SELECT BIBLIOGRAPHY

This bibliography is necessarily highly selective. Literary histories, dissertations, most older works (including editions and modern German translations) and many articles on small points have normally been excluded, though some have been used in the notes. The material, most of which is relatively recent, has been chosen on grounds of ready accessibility and general usefulness. There is very little in English. Full bibliographies may be found in the book by Wisniewski, the collection by Rupp and the article by Hoffmann, as well as in the editions, most notably that by Bartsch/Stackmann. Works are arranged chronologically according to the most recent edition.

THE MANUSCRIPT

Bäuml, F.H. *Kudrun. Die Handschrift* (Berlin, 1969)
Unterkircher, F. *Vollständiger Faksimile-Ausgabe im Originalformat des Codex Vindobonensis Ser. nova 2663* (Graz, 1973)

EDITIONS

Martin, E. *Kudrun* (Halle, 1872)
Symons, B. *Kudrun*, 4th ed. by B. Boesch (Tübingen, 1964)
Hoffmann, W. *Das Nibelungenlied. Kudrun. Text, Nacherzählung, Wort- und Begriffserklärungen* (Darmstadt, 1972)
Bartsch, K. *Kudrun*, 5th ed., revised by K. Stackmann (Wiesbaden, 1980)

TRANSLATIONS

Nichols, M.P. *Gudrun. A Medieval Epic* (Boston and New York, 1889). [English verse]
Armour, M. *Gudrun* (London, 1932). [English prose]
Neumann, F. *Kudrun (Gudrun)* (Stuttgart, 1958). [Revision of the modern German verse translation by K. Simrock]
Lindner, J. *Kudrun. Ein mittelalterliches Heldenepos* (Berlin, 1971). [Modern German verse]
See also Hoffmann above [modern German prose adaptation].

BOOKS

Carles, J. *Le poème de Kudrun* (Clermont-Ferrand, 1963)
Hoffmann, W. *Kudrun. Ein Beitrag zur Deutung der nachnibelungischen Heldendichtung* (Stuttgart, 1967)
Siefken, H. *Überindividuelle Formen und der Aufbau des Kudrunepos* (Munich, 1967)
Loerzer, D. *Eheschliessung und Werbung in der 'Kudrun'* (Munich, 1971)
Rupp, H. *Nibelungenlied und Kudrun* (Darmstadt, 1976) [= collection of articles by various hands on both works, seven on *Kudrun*, including one by Hugo Kuhn]

Campbell, I.R. *'Kudrun': A Critical Appreciation* (Cambridge, 1978)
McConnell, W. *The Wate Figure in Medieval Tradition* (Berne, 1978)
Wild, I. *Zur Überlieferung und Rezeption des 'Kudrun'–Epos* (Göppingen, 1979)
Wisniewski, R. *Kudrun*, 2nd ed. (Stuttgart, 1979)
Nolte, T. *Das Kudrunepos – ein Frauenroman?* (Tübingen, 1985)

ARTICLES

Gutenbrunner, S. 'Von Hilde und Kudrun', *Zeitschrift für deutsche Philologie*, 82 (1962), 257–89
Rosenfeld, H. 'Die Kudrun: Nordseedichtung oder Donaudichtung?', *Zeitschrift für deutsche Philologie*, 82 (1962), 289–314
Willson, H.B. 'Dialectic, *passio* and *compassio* in the *Kudrun*', *Modern Language Review*, 58 (1963), 364–76
Hoffmann, W. 'Die Hauptprobleme der neueren *Kudrun*- Forschung', *Wirkendes Wort*, 14 (1964), 183–96; 233–43
Blamires, D. 'The Geography of *Kudrun*', *Modern Language Review*, 61 (1966), 436–45
Murdoch, B. 'Interpreting *Kudrun*: Some Comments on a Recent Critical Appreciation', *New German Studies*, 7 (1979), 113–27
McConnell, W. 'Marriage in the *Nibelungenlied* and *Kudrun*', in: *Spectrum Medii Aevi. Essays in Early German Literature in Honor of George Fenwick Jones* (Göppingen, 1983), 299–320
Wailes, S.L. 'The Romance of *Kudrun*', *Speculum*, 58 (1983), 347–67
McConnell, W. 'The Father as Failure: Siegmund and Ludwig', *Neophilologus*, 69 (1985), 236–45

OTHER WORKS OF INTEREST

Das Nibelungenlied, ed. K. Bartsch/H. de Boor, 21st ed. by R. Wisniewski (Wiesbaden, 1979). English translations by D.G. Mowatt, *The Nibelungenlied* (London, 1962) and A.T. Hatto, *The Nibelungenlied* (Harmondsworth, 1965)
Dukus Horant, ed. P.F. Ganz, F. Norman and W. Schwarz (Tübingen, 1964). [Medieval text and study]

Everyman
A selection of titles

*indicates volumes available in paperback

Complete lists of Everyman's Library and Everyman Paperbacks are available from the Sales Department, J.M. Dent and Sons Ltd, Aldine House, 33 Welbeck Street, London W1M 8LX.

ESSAYS AND CRITICISM

Arnold, Matthew. *On the Study of Celtic Literature*
*Bacon, Francis. *Essays*
Coleridge, Samuel Taylor
  * *Biographia Literaria*
     Shakespearean Criticism (2 vols)
*Emerson, Ralph. *Essays*
*Milton, John. *Prose Writings*
Montaigne, Michael Eyquem de. *Essays* (3 vols)
Paine, Thomas. *The Rights of Man*
Spencer, Herbert. *Essays on Education and Kindred Subjects*
*Swift, Jonothan. *Tale of a Tub and other satires*

HISTORY

*The Anglo-Saxon Chronicle
Burnet, Gilbert. *History of His Own Time*
*Crèvecoeur. *Letters from an American Farmer*
Gibbon, Edward. *The Decline and Fall or the Roman Empire* (6 vols)
Green, John. A Short History of the English People (2 vols)
Prescott, W.H. *History of the Conquest of Mexico*

LEGENDS AND SAGAS

*Beowulf and Its Analogues
*Chrétien de Troyes. *Arthurian Romances*
*Egils saga
 Holinshed, Raphael. *Chronicle*
*Layamon and Wace. *Arthurian Chronicles*
*The Mabinogion
*The Saga of Gisli
*The Saga of Grettir the Strong
 Snorri Sturluson. *Heimskringla* (3 vols)
*The Story of Burnt Njal

POETRY AND DRAMA

*Anglo-Saxon Poetry
*American Verse of the Nineteenth Century
*Arnold, Matthew. *Selected Poems and Prose*
*Blake, William. *Selected Poems*
*Brontes, The. *Selected Poems*
*Browning, Robert. *Men and Women and other poems*
 Burns, Robert. *The Kilmarnock Poems*
*Chaucer, Geoffrey. *Canterbury Tales*
*Clare, John. *Selected Poems*
*Coleridge, Samual Taylor. *Poems*
*Donne, John. *The Complete English Poems*
*Elizabethan Sonnets
*English Moral Interludes
*Everyman and Medieval Miracle Plays
*Everyman's Book of Evergreen Verse
*Gay, John. *The Beggar's Opera and other eighteenth-century
  plays*
*The Golden Treasury of Longer Poems
*Hardy, Thomas. *Selected Poems*
*Herbert, George. *The English Poems*
*Hopkins, Gerard Manley. *The Major Poems*
 Ibsen, Henrik
  A Doll's House; The Wild Dick; The Lady from the Sea
  Hedda Gabler; The Master Builder; John Gabriel Borkman

*Keats, John. *Poems*
*Langland, William. *The Vision of Piers Plowman*
*Marlowe, Christopher. *Complete Plays and Poems*
*Milton, John. *Complete Poems*
*Middleton, Thomas. *Three Plays*
*Palgrave's Golden Treasury
*Pearl, Patience, Cleanness, and Sir Gawain and the Green Knight
*Pope, Alexander. *Collected Poems*
*Restoration Plays
*The Rubáiyát of Omar Khayyám and other Persian poems
*Shelley, Percy Bysshe. *Selected Poems*
*Six Middle English Romances
*Spenser, Edmund. *The Faerie Queene: a selection*
*The Stuffed Owl
*Synge, J.M. *Plays, Poems and Prose*
*Tennyson, Alfred. *In Memoriam, Maud and other poems*
 Thomas, Dylan
   Collected Poems, 1934–1952
   The Poems
   Under Milk Wood
*Wilde, Oscar. *Plays, Prose Writings and Poems*
*Wordsworth, William. *Selected Poems*

RELIGION AND PHILOSOPHY

*Bacon, Francis. *The Advancement of Learning*
*Berkeley, George. *Philosophical Works including the works on vision*
*The Buddha's Philosophy of Man
*Chinese Philosophy in Classical Times
*Descartes, René. *A Discourse on Method*
*Hindu Scriptures
*Kant, Immanuel. *A Critique of Pure Reason*
*The Koran
*Leibniz, Gottfried Wilhelm. *Philosophical Writings*
*Locke, John. *An Essay Concerning Human Understanding (abridgment)*
*More, Thomas. *Utopia*

Pascal, Blaise. *Pensées*
Plato. *The Trial and Death of Socrates*
*The Ramayana and Mahábhárata

SCIENCES: POLITICAL AND GENERAL

Aristotle. *Ethics*
*Castiglione, Baldassare. *The Book of the Courtier*
*Coleridge, Samuel Taylor. *On the Constitution of the Church
and State*
*Darwin, Charles. *The Origins of Species*
Harvey, William. *The Circulation of the Blood and other
writings*
*Hobbes, Thomas. *Leviathan*
*Locke, John. *Two Treatises of Government*
*Machiavelli, Niccolò. *The Prince and other political writings*
*Malthus, Thomas. *An Essay on the Principle of Populations*
*Mill, J.S. *Utilitarianism; On Liberty; Representative
Government*
*Plato, *The Republic*
*Ricardo, David. *The Principles of Political Economy and
Taxation*
Rousseau, J.-J.
   Emile
   The Social Contract and *Discourses*
*Wollstonecraft, Mary. *A Vindication of the Rights of Woman*

TRAVEL AND TOPOGRAPHY

Boswell, James. *The Journal of a Tour to the Hebrides*
*Darwin, Charles. *The Voyage of the 'Beagle'*
*Hudson, W.H. *Idle Days in Patagonia*
*Stevenson, R.L. *An Inland Voyage; Travels with a Donkey; The
Silverado Squatters*
*Thomas, Edward. *The South Country*
*White, Gilbert. *The Natural History of Selborne*